Balanced Minds, Virtuous Lives

A Practical Guide to Self-Mastery

Shannon Meade

Copyright © 2024 by Shannon Meade
All rights reserved.

No part of this publication may be reproduced, distributed, or transmitted in any form or by any means, including photocopying, recording, or other electronic or mechanical methods, without the prior written permission of the author, except in the case of brief quotations embodied in critical reviews and certain other noncommercial uses permitted by copyright law. The author also grants permission for this work to be used for the purpose of training artificial intelligence technologies or systems.

Disclaimer:
The information contained in this book is for educational and informational purposes only. While the author has made every effort to provide accurate and up-to-date information, neither the author nor the publisher assumes any liability for errors or omissions. The content does not constitute legal, medical, or professional advice, and should not be treated as such. Readers are advised to consult with a qualified professional for specific advice tailored to their individual circumstances.

This publication is provided "as is" without any representations or warranties, express or implied. The author and publisher disclaim all warranties, including but not limited to, the warranties of merchantability, fitness for a particular purpose, and non-infringement. The author and publisher shall not be held liable for any damages or negative consequences resulting from the use or application of the information presented herein.

Balanced Minds, Virtuous Lives: A Practical Guide to Self-Mastery/
Shannon Meade, JD, LL.M..
ISBN: 979-8-89619-272-5
Cover design by DALL-E

For permissions and more information, contact:

    Shannon Meade
    PO Box 158
    Machiasport, Maine 04655

To Charles "Cass" Jones, MFT - Marriage & Family Therapist

Your profound influence has forever changed the course of my life. Thank you for helping me find my path.

Shannon

Preface

In a world filled with endless distractions and increasing complexity, the pursuit of a balanced and virtuous life can often seem daunting. Many of us find ourselves pulled in multiple directions, overwhelmed by competing demands, and struggling to maintain clarity and purpose. This book, *Balanced Minds, Virtuous Lives: A Practical Guide to Self-Mastery*, was born out of a desire to offer a comprehensive, yet accessible approach to self-improvement—one that integrates time-tested philosophies with modern, evidence-based techniques.

Over the years, I have delved deeply into the teachings of Cognitive Behavioral Therapy (CBT), Secular Buddhism, Stoicism, and Virtue Ethics, seeking to understand how these diverse frameworks can harmonize to guide individuals toward greater mental resilience, ethical living, and emotional well-being. The integration of these philosophies forms the core of this book, providing a multidimensional path that anyone can follow to cultivate a life of balance, purpose, and fulfillment.

This book is designed not only as a guide but as a companion—a resource you can return to as you navigate the ups and downs of life. Each chapter offers practical strategies and insights, inviting you to engage in self-reflection and action, while challenging you to think critically about how you live and what you value. Whether you are facing anxiety, seeking to improve your relationships, or striving for a deeper sense of meaning, the tools and exercises provided here are aimed at helping you build a solid foundation for personal growth and flourishing.

Ultimately, *Balanced Minds, Virtuous Lives* is a call to take ownership of your life, to become the artist of your own existence. It invites you to engage with these philosophies, not as abstract theories but as living practices that can transform your mind, character, and relationships. I hope that, through the pages of this book, you find the inspiration, clarity, and guidance needed to create a masterpiece of your own life.

May this journey lead you to the balance, peace, and virtue that you seek.

Shannon Meade

Table of Contents

1. INTRODUCTION TO THE SELF-HELP APPROACH   1

The Journey of Self-Improvement: A Multidimensional Path   1

Cognitive Behavioral Therapy: The Science of Thoughts, Emotions, and Behaviors   1

From Theory to Practice: Reshaping the Mind   2

Secular Buddhism: A Path to Mindfulness and Liberation   2

Mindfulness: The Art of Being Present   3

Stoicism: Mastering Control and Embracing Fate   3

Amor Fati: Loving Your Fate   4

Virtue Ethics: Flourishing Through Character and Virtue   4

Phronesis: Practical Wisdom in Action   5

How These Philosophies Dynamically Interact: The Symphony of Self-Improvement   5

The Masterpiece Within: A Dynamic Framework for Personal Growth   6

Crafting Your Path to Flourishing   6

2. THE FOUNDATIONS OF PERSONAL MASTERY: CORE PRINCIPLES OF CBT, BUDDHISM, STOICISM, AND VIRTUE ETHICS   8

Cognitive Behavioral Therapy: Unveiling the Thought-Emotion-Behavior Connection   8

The Cognitive Triad: How Thoughts Shape Our Reality   9

Cognitive Distortions: Identifying and Challenging Faulty Thinking   10

Behavioral Activation: Breaking the Cycle of Avoidance — 11

Thought-Emotion-Behavior: The Dynamic Triad in Action — 12

Unlocking the Power of Cognitive Transformation — 13

Behavioral Activation and Exposure Techniques: Rewiring Behavior for Emotional Health — 13

Breaking the Cycle of Avoidance: The Role of Behavioral Activation — 14

The Mechanism of Behavioral Activation: From Avoidance to Engagement — 15

Exposure Techniques: Facing Fears to Dismantle Anxiety — 16

Types of Exposure Therapy: From Imaginal to In Vivo — 17

Behavioral Change as a Catalyst for Cognitive Change — 18

Reclaiming Life Through Action — 18

Secular Buddhism: The Four Noble Truths and the Eightfold Path — 19

The Four Noble Truths: Understanding the Nature of Suffering — 19

The Eightfold Path: The Roadmap to Inner Peace — 22

The Interplay of the Four Noble Truths and the Eightfold Path — 25

The Path to Liberation and Inner Peace — 26

Mindfulness and Meditation Techniques in Secular Buddhism: Cultivating Presence and Awareness — 26

Mindfulness: The Art of Being Present in Every Moment — 27

Meditation Techniques: Training the Mind Toward Liberation — 28

The Role of Mindfulness and Meditation in Secular Buddhism — 31

A Path to Inner Clarity and Compassion — 31

Detachment and Non-Attachment in Secular Buddhism: The Art of Letting Go — 32

The Illusion of Control: Why Attachment Causes Suffering — 32

The Path of Detachment: Letting Go Without Indifference — 34

Non-Attachment: Engaging Fully Without Clinging — 35

The Role of Impermanence and Non-Self in Non-Attachment — 36

Detachment and Non-Attachment in Daily Life: Practical Applications — 37

Freedom Through Letting Go — 37

The Dichotomy of Control in Stoicism: Mastering What You Can and Letting Go of the Rest — 38

The Dichotomy of Control: A Stoic Framework for Life — 38

The Practical Application: Internalizing Control for Lasting Peace — 39

The Illusion of Control: Why We Struggle to Let Go — 40

The Role of Intentional Action: Focusing on What Truly Matters — 41

Applying the Dichotomy of Control in Modern Life: Practical Examples — 42

The Freedom of Focusing on What You Can Control — 43

Key Stoic Virtues: Wisdom, Courage, Justice, and Temperance — 44

Wisdom (Sophia): The Guiding Virtue — 44

Courage (Andreia): Facing Fear and Adversity — 45

Justice (Dikaiosyne): Acting with Fairness and Integrity — 46

Temperance (Sophrosyne): The Balance of Desires — 47

The Interdependence of the Stoic Virtues: A Holistic Approach — 48

The Pillars of a Virtuous Life — 49

Stoic Practices: Negative Visualization, Amor Fati, and Memento Mori	49
Negative Visualization: Preparing for Life's Challenges	50
Amor Fati: Embracing Fate with Love	51
Memento Mori: Remembering the Impermanence of Life	53
Embracing Life Through Stoic Practices	54
The Role of Virtues in Ethical Living: A Pathway to Flourishing	55
Understanding Virtue Ethics: Character and Moral Excellence	55
Core Virtues in Ethical Living	57
Virtues as the Foundation of Ethical Living	59
Living a Life of Virtue	60
Aristotle's Concept of Eudaimonia: The Pursuit of Human Flourishing	60
The Nature of Eudaimonia: More Than Happiness	61
The Function of Human Beings: Rational Activity	62
Virtue and the Role of Practical Wisdom	63
External Goods and the Role of Fortune	64
Eudaimonia as a Lifelong Process	65
Eudaimonia—The Art of Living Well	65
Developing Practical Wisdom (Phronesis) in Virtue Ethics: The Key to Ethical Living	66
The Nature of Phronesis: What Is Practical Wisdom?	66
The Role of Phronesis in Ethical Decision-Making	67
Cultivating Practical Wisdom: From Theory to Practice	69

Phronesis and the Unity of the Virtues — 70

Practical Wisdom in Modern Life: Applying Phronesis Today — 70

Practical Wisdom as the Path to Ethical Mastery — 71

The Dynamic Interaction of Philosophies in Daily Life: CBT, Stoicism, Buddhism, and Virtue Ethics — 72

Cognitive Behavioral Therapy: Restructuring Thought Patterns — 72

Stoicism and Buddhism: Accepting What Cannot Be Changed — 73

Virtue Ethics: Tying It All Together with Ethical Living — 74

The Dynamic Interaction in Daily Life: A Holistic Approach — 76

Flourishing Through the Integration of Philosophy — 77

3. BUILDING A LIFE OF MINDFUL ACTION: DAILY PRACTICES FOR PERSONAL GROWTH AND VIRTUE — 79

Setting Up a Daily Meditation Practice: Cultivating Mindfulness and Inner Peace — 79

The Foundations of Meditation: What It Is and What It Is Not — 80

Getting Started: How to Set Up a Daily Meditation Practice — 81

Step-by-Step Guide to Breath Awareness Meditation — 83

Step-by-Step Guide to Body Scan Meditation — 87

Overcoming Common Obstacles: Persistence Through Discomfort — 93

The Benefits of a Daily Meditation Practice — 94

Planting the Seed of Meditation for Lifelong Growth — 95

Mindfulness in Everyday Activities: Bringing Awareness into Daily Life — 95

The Concept of Mindfulness in Daily Life — 96

Everyday Activities as Opportunities for Mindfulness	97
The Benefits of Mindfulness in Everyday Life	99
Living Fully Through Mindful Engagement	100
CBT Thought Records: Unlocking the Power of Self-Reflection for Cognitive Restructuring	100
Understanding the Role of Thought Records in CBT	101
Breaking Down the Components of a Thought Record	102
How Thought Records Promote Cognitive Growth	105
Rewriting the Mental Narrative	106
Stoic Reflection and Evening Review: Cultivating Virtue Through Daily Self-Examination	106
The Foundation of Stoic Reflection	107
The Practice of the Stoic Evening Review	108
How the Evening Review Enhances Stoic Practice	111
Ending the Day with Purpose and Clarity	112
Virtue Tracking and Reflection: Cultivating Moral Growth Through Self-Examination	113
Understanding Virtue Tracking and Its Purpose	113
Choosing and Defining Your Virtues	115
Defining Virtues in Concrete Terms	115
The Practice of Virtue Tracking	116
Benefits of Virtue Tracking	117
Becoming the Best Version of Yourself	118
Setting and Achieving Small Goals: The Key to Sustainable Habit Formation	119

The Science of Habit Formation: How Small Goals Lead to Big Change 120

Setting Small, Achievable Goals: The Building Blocks of Success 121

Achieving Small Goals: Strategies for Success 122

The Role of Patience and Consistency in Habit Formation 123

The Path to Success is Paved with Small Steps 124

The Role of Consistency and Discipline in Habit Formation: The Foundation of Lasting Change 125

The Importance of Consistency in Habit Formation 126

The Power of Discipline: Acting Beyond Motivation 127

Strategies for Cultivating Consistency and Discipline 128

The Synergy Between Consistency and Discipline 130

The Steady Path to Lasting Change 130

Incorporating Virtue into Daily Actions: A Path to Moral Excellence 131

The Importance of Virtue in Everyday Life 132

Cultivating Virtue Through Habit Formation 133

Overcoming Challenges to Virtuous Living 134

Examples of Incorporating Virtue in Daily Life 135

The Long-Term Benefits of Incorporating Virtue into Daily Actions 136

Small Virtuous Acts, Big Moral Impact 137

4. MASTERING THE MIND: SELF-REFLECTION AND COGNITIVE RESTRUCTURING FOR BALANCED LIVING 139

Identifying Negative Thought Patterns: The Power of Recognizing Cognitive Distortions — 139

Cognitive Distortions: How the Mind Distorts Reality — 140

Recognizing Common Cognitive Distortions — 141

Breaking the Cycle: Recognizing and Challenging Cognitive Distortions — 143

Integrating Stoic and Buddhist Perspectives — 144

Breaking Free from Cognitive Distortions — 145

Practicing Self-Compassion and Detachment: A Path to Mental Clarity and Emotional Resilience — 145

The Power of Self-Compassion: Reframing Inner Dialogue — 146

Practicing Self-Compassion: Tools for Transformation — 148

Detachment: Letting Go of Emotional Overinvestment — 149

Cultivating Detachment: Practical Techniques for Letting Go — 150

The Synergy of Self-Compassion and Detachment — 151

Building Inner Strength Through Compassion and Detachment — 151

Cognitive Restructuring Techniques: Challenging and Reframing Thoughts for Mental Clarity — 152

The Foundation of Cognitive Restructuring: Understanding Thought Patterns — 153

Challenging Thoughts: Breaking Down Cognitive Distortions — 154

Reframing Thoughts: Shifting Perspective for Balanced Thinking — 155

The Psychological Benefits of Challenging and Reframing Thoughts — 157

Applying Cognitive Restructuring in Daily Life — 158

Reframing Your Mindset for Lasting Change — 159

Balancing Thoughts with Stoic and Buddhist Principles: A Path to Inner Harmony   159

The Stoic Approach: Focus on What You Can Control   160

The Buddhist Approach: Mindfulness and Non-Attachment   161

Integrating Stoicism and Buddhism: A Balanced Cognitive Framework   163

Practical Techniques for Balancing Thoughts   164

Achieving Cognitive Balance Through Ancient Wisdom   165

Using Virtue Ethics to Guide Thought Processes: Cultivating Ethical Thinking and Emotional Balance   166

The Core of Virtue Ethics: Cultivating Moral Excellence   167

How Virtue Guides Thought Processes: A Framework for Ethical Thinking   167

Applying Virtue Ethics to Cognitive Restructuring: Practical Techniques   169

The Ethical Impact of Thought Restructuring: Building Moral Character   170

Shaping Your Mind and Character Through Virtue   171

5. MASTERING EMOTIONAL RESILIENCE: TECHNIQUES FOR EMOTIONAL REGULATION AND INNER CALM   173

Emotional Awareness and Identification: The Foundation of Emotional Management   173

Understanding Emotional Awareness: Why It Matters   174

Emotional Identification: The Power of Naming Emotions   176

Practical Techniques for Enhancing Emotional Awareness and Identification   177

The Benefits of Emotional Awareness and Identification   178

The Key to Mastering Your Emotions	179
Strategies for Managing Anxiety, Depression, and Anger: A CBT Approach to Emotional Regulation	179
Managing Anxiety: Breaking the Cycle of Fear	180
CBT Techniques for Managing Anxiety	181
Managing Depression: Lifting the Weight of Hopelessness	182
Managing Anger: Harnessing and Redirecting the Emotion	184
Transforming Emotions Through CBT	185
Stoic Practices for Emotional Resilience: Practicing Detachment from Outcomes	186
Understanding the Stoic Concept of Detachment	187
The Power of Focusing on What You Can Control	188
Practical Techniques for Practicing Detachment from Outcomes	190
Emotional Resilience Through Detachment	191
The Freedom in Letting Go	192
Developing Equanimity: The Stoic Path to Mental Calmness	192
Equanimity in Stoicism: The Power of Mental Calmness	193
Equanimity in Action: Applying Stoic Principles to Daily Life	198
Cultivating Calm in the Storm	199
Understanding and Accepting Impermanence: A Buddhist Approach to Suffering	199
The Buddhist View of Impermanence: An Ever-Changing Reality	200
The Four Noble Truths: A Framework for Understanding Suffering	201
Accepting Impermanence: A Path to Emotional Resilience	203

Practical Ways to Embrace Impermanence 204

Embracing Impermanence for Greater Peace 205

Practices for Reducing Suffering through Mindfulness: A Buddhist Approach 206

Mindfulness as the Antidote to Suffering 207

Practical Mindfulness Techniques for Reducing Suffering 209

Cultivating Mindfulness in Daily Life: A Path to Lasting Peace 211

The Power of Mindfulness in Alleviating Suffering 212

Integrating Emotional Regulation and Resilience Practices: A Unified Approach for Daily Life 212

Emotional Awareness and Identification: The First Step in All Practices 213

Managing Anxiety, Depression, and Anger: A Multi-Faceted Approach 215

Integrating Detachment and Acceptance: Overcoming Suffering 216

A Unified Daily Practice for Emotional Resilience 217

Integrating Wisdom for a Resilient Mind 218

6. LIVING WITH INTEGRITY: VIRTUE ETHICS, STOICISM, AND BUDDHIST WISDOM FOR ETHICAL DECISION-MAKING 220

Identifying and Cultivating Core Virtues: Building a Life of Ethical Excellence 220

What Are Core Virtues? A Guide to Ethical Character Development 221

The Process of Cultivating Virtues: Practice, Reflection, and Growth 223

Living with Virtue: The Impact of Ethical Habits on Decision-Making 224

The Ripple Effect: How Virtue Cultivation Enhances Relationships and Community 225

Cultivating a Life of Virtue 225

Making Ethical Decisions Guided by Virtue: The Path to Moral Excellence 226

What Does It Mean to Make Ethical Decisions Guided by Virtue? 227

Steps to Making Ethical Decisions Guided by Virtue 228

Virtue in Action: Real-World Applications of Ethical Decision-Making 230

Ethical Living Guided by Virtue 231

Integrating Stoic and Buddhist Ethics: The Practice of Compassion, Justice, and Wisdom 232

Compassion: The Heart of Ethical Action 233

Justice: Acting Fairly in a Complex World 235

Wisdom: The Foundation of Ethical Living 237

Ethical Dilemmas: Balancing Virtue and Practicality in Stoic and Buddhist Ethics 238

The Nature of Ethical Dilemmas: When Virtue Conflicts with Reality 239

Balancing Virtue and Practicality: The Role of Practical Wisdom 241

Navigating Ethical Dilemmas: Real-Life Applications 242

Virtue Meets Practicality in Ethical Decision-Making 243

Ethical Case Studies: Applying Virtue Ethics, Stoicism, and Buddhism to Real-Life Scenarios 244

Life Scenario 1: The Ethical Dilemma of Honesty vs. Kindness 245

Life Scenario 2: Leadership and Responsibility   246

Life Scenario 3: Personal Integrity vs. Social Pressure   248

Learning from Ethical Case Studies   250

7. FUELING THE JOURNEY: BUILDING AND SUSTAINING MOTIVATION WITH VIRTUE, RESILIENCE, AND MINDFULNESS 252

Identifying Personal Values and Goals: Aligning Ambitions with Virtue and Ethical Living 252

The Foundation of Motivation: Identifying Personal Values   253

Aligning Goals with Virtue: An Ethical Framework for Motivation 254

Setting Goals That Reflect Ethical Living: A Step-by-Step Approach
                                                               256

Values and Virtues as the Compass for Meaningful Goals   257

Breaking Down and Achieving Goals: The CBT Approach   258

The Power of CBT: Turning Ambitions into Action   259

Step 1: Setting SMART Goals   260

Step 2: Breaking Down Goals into Manageable Steps   261

Step 3: Cognitive Restructuring to Overcome Obstacles   262

CBT as a Pathway to Goal Achievement   263

Stoic Strategies for Handling Adversity: Turning Obstacles into Opportunities 264

The Stoic Mindset: Embracing Challenges as Opportunities   264

Stoic Techniques for Navigating Adversity   266

Applying Stoic Strategies: Real-Life Examples   268

Turning Adversity into Strength with Stoic Wisdom   269

Reframing Setbacks as Learning Opportunities: Transforming Challenges into Growth — 269

The Power of Perspective: How We Frame Setbacks — 270

Philosophical Perspectives: Stoicism and Buddhist Wisdom — 271

Practical Techniques for Reframing Setbacks — 273

Real-Life Example: The Story of Thomas Edison — 274

Embracing Setbacks as Stepping Stones to Success — 274

Sustaining Motivation Through Mindfulness and Virtue: A Holistic Approach to Overcoming Setbacks — 275

The Foundation of Motivation: Mindfulness and Self-Awareness — 276

Virtue Ethics: A Framework for Lasting Motivation — 277

Integrating Mindfulness and Virtue: A Synergistic Approach — 279

Real-Life Example: A Personal Transformation Through Mindfulness and Virtue — 280

Motivation as a Practice of Presence and Integrity — 281

8. CULTIVATING MEANINGFUL CONNECTIONS: A GUIDE TO INTERPERSONAL RELATIONSHIPS AND SOCIAL WELL-BEING — 283

Enhancing Communication and Resolving Conflicts: CBT Techniques for Stronger Relationships — 283

The Foundation of Effective Communication: CBT and Cognitive Restructuring — 284

Managing Conflict and Misunderstandings: CBT Techniques for Resolution — 286

Real-Life Application: Improving Relationships Through CBT Techniques — 288

Building Stronger Relationships Through the CBT Approach — 293

Compassion and Detachment: Stoic and Buddhist Wisdom for
Stronger Relationships   293

Compassion Without Attachment: A Balanced Approach   294

The Role of Virtue in Building Strong Relationships   296

Real-Life Application: Compassion and Detachment in Action   298

The Art of Compassionate Detachment   299

Navigating Moral Dilemmas and Cultivating Virtues in Relationships:
An Ethical Approach   300

Ethical Considerations: Navigating Moral Dilemmas in Relationships
                                                                 301

Cultivating Patience, Forgiveness, and Understanding: Essential
Virtues for Ethical Relationships   302

Real-Life Application: Navigating Ethical Dilemmas with Virtue   305

Virtues as Pillars of Ethical Relationships   306

9. PATHWAYS TO FLOURISHING: SUSTAINING LONG-TERM WELL-BEING AND LIFE SATISFACTION 308

Crafting and Sustaining a Path of Growth: The Art of Long-Term Self-Improvement   308

The Blueprint for Lasting Change: Creating a Long-Term Self-Improvement Plan   309

Reflect, Reassess, and Revise: The Cycle of Sustained Growth   311

Building a System of Accountability: Ensuring Consistency   312

The Art of Crafting a Flexible, Long-Term Path   313

The Balance of Acceptance and Growth: Navigating Life's Limitations
and Aspirations   313

The Art of Acceptance: Embracing Life's Limitations   314

The Pursuit of Growth: Striving for Eudaimonia ... 316

The Dynamic Balance of a Flourishing Life ... 318

The Pursuit of Eudaimonia: Living a Life of Virtue, Purpose, and Fulfillment ... 318

Virtue as the Foundation of a Flourishing Life ... 319

Integrating Happiness and Fulfillment into Daily Life ... 320

The Synergy of Virtue, Purpose, and Fulfillment ... 322

Flourishing Through Purpose and Virtue ... 323

10. CRAFTING YOUR PATH: PERSONALIZING AND INTEGRATING A HOLISTIC SELF-HELP PLAN ... 325

The Art of Personalization: Tailoring and Adapting Practices for Lasting Growth ... 325

Tailoring Practices to Individual Needs and Preferences ... 326

Adapting the Approach to Different Life Stages and Challenges ... 327

The Power of Personalization: A Dynamic Approach ... 329

Integrating Philosophies: Crafting a Comprehensive Self-Help Plan ... 330

The Pillars of Integration: Understanding Each Philosophy's Contribution ... 331

Creating a Balanced and Comprehensive Plan ... 334

The Power of Integration: Crafting a Personalized and Holistic Path ... 335

Monitoring Progress and Making Adjustments: Fine-Tuning Your Self-Help Journey ... 336

The Importance of Monitoring Progress: Keeping Your Growth Aligned ... 336

Making Adjustments: Flexibility and Responsiveness in Action 338

The Dynamic Nature of Growth: Embracing Flexibility 340

11. EMPOWERING YOUR JOURNEY: ESSENTIAL RESOURCES AND SUPPORT SYSTEMS FOR PERSONAL GROWTH 342

Empowering Your Journey: A Comprehensive Guide to Resources and Support Systems 342

Recommended Books, Courses, and Apps: Building Your Knowledge Arsenal 343

Creating a Personal Support System: Building a Network of Encouragement 345

Utilizing Online Communities and Support Groups: Expanding Your Circle 346

Connecting the Dots—Creating a Comprehensive Support Network 347

INTEGRATING WISDOM, PRACTICE, AND GROWTH—A PATH TO FULFILLMENT 349

Lessons Learned: The Power of Holistic Integration 349

The Journey Ahead: A Call to Continued Growth and Exploration 350

Embrace the Journey 351

APPENDIX 353

A LIST OF IDENTIFIABLE EMOTIONS: 354

SOURCES 356

1. Introduction to the Self-Help Approach

The Journey of Self-Improvement: A Multidimensional Path

Self-improvement is often perceived as a solitary venture, but it doesn't have to be a confusing or overwhelming experience. When armed with powerful, time-tested philosophies, self-improvement becomes not only achievable but also deeply transformative. The framework offered here integrates four distinct but complementary approaches: Cognitive Behavioral Therapy (CBT), Secular Buddhism, Stoicism, and Virtue Ethics. Together, these disciplines create a rich foundation for personal growth, mental resilience, and ethical living.

Imagine yourself as an artist, working on a masterpiece that is your life. Each of these philosophies provides unique tools, guiding you to shape thoughts, manage emotions, and cultivate a life of virtue. In this introduction, we'll dive into how each of these frameworks contributes to your self-mastery and what benefits emerge from weaving them together.

Cognitive Behavioral Therapy: The Science of Thoughts, Emotions, and Behaviors

CBT is a cornerstone of modern psychology and offers practical, evidence-based tools to improve mental health. It starts with a simple, yet profound idea: thoughts, emotions, and behaviors are interconnected. When we learn to identify and adjust our thoughts, we can alter our emotional responses and behavioral patterns.

Imagine you're running late for an important meeting. A cascade of negative thoughts ("I'll never recover from this," "I'm so disorganized," "Everyone will lose respect for me") could fuel anxiety and panic, which in turn might lead you to make more mistakes, reinforcing a negative cycle. CBT teaches you to stop, examine those thoughts, and ask yourself: *Is this true? Is there another way to see the situation?*

By challenging these thoughts—replacing "I'll never recover" with "I'm running late, but I'll handle it"—you begin to diffuse anxiety, leading to clearer thinking and more constructive actions. Behavioral techniques, like behavioral activation and exposure therapy, help break the paralysis of avoidance, guiding you to act in ways that enhance your well-being.

From Theory to Practice: Reshaping the Mind

CBT's practical strategies are accessible and actionable. With structured methods like thought records, you can observe patterns in your thinking, challenge distortions such as catastrophizing or black-and-white thinking, and replace them with balanced, realistic thoughts. The result? A gradual but steady improvement in mental health and a clearer perspective on life's challenges.

Secular Buddhism: A Path to Mindfulness and Liberation

Secular Buddhism offers a modern, non-religious interpretation of ancient Buddhist teachings. At its heart are the Four Noble Truths: life involves suffering, suffering has causes, suffering can be overcome, and there is a path to the cessation of suffering. This path is called the Eightfold Path, which includes right understanding, right intention, and right mindfulness, among others.

One of the key concepts in Buddhism is impermanence. Everything is in a state of constant change. Holding on tightly to things, people, or outcomes inevitably leads to suffering. Imagine grasping sand in your hand—the tighter you hold, the more it slips through your fingers. Buddhism teaches us to let go and embrace the flow of life, rather than resisting it.

Mindfulness: The Art of Being Present

Mindfulness, a core practice in Buddhism, teaches us to observe our thoughts and emotions without judgment. In a fast-paced world where our minds often race ahead or dwell in the past, mindfulness brings us back to the present moment. Picture sitting at a traffic light, annoyed by the delay. Instead of letting frustration consume you, mindfulness encourages you to focus on the moment— observe the surroundings, feel your breath, and recognize the transient nature of the frustration. Through consistent practice, you develop a serene, more centered approach to life's unpredictability.

Detachment is another essential practice in Buddhism. Unlike avoidance, detachment involves engaging with life fully, but without clinging to specific outcomes. This idea aligns closely with Stoicism, as we'll soon explore, reinforcing the ability to manage desires and expectations with grace.

Stoicism: Mastering Control and Embracing Fate

Imagine navigating a ship through a stormy sea. The Stoics taught that we cannot control the wind, but we can control how we adjust the sails. This is the essence of the Dichotomy of Control, a Stoic principle that encourages us to distinguish between what we can control (our thoughts, actions, and attitudes) and what we cannot (external events, other people's opinions, or the past).

Stoicism isn't about suppressing emotions, but about cultivating emotional resilience. Through practices like negative visualization—where you imagine the worst-case scenario not to invite negativity, but to better appreciate what you have—you prepare yourself mentally for life's challenges. This can transform anxiety into calm acceptance.

Amor Fati: Loving Your Fate

A cornerstone of Stoic philosophy is Amor Fati—the love of fate. Rather than resisting life's hardships, the Stoics encouraged embracing them as opportunities for growth. Imagine losing a job. While the initial response might be panic or despair, Amor Fati teaches you to view this loss as a chance to pursue new avenues, develop new skills, or deepen self-reliance. The Stoic mindset allows you to find purpose and value in every situation, no matter how difficult.

In tandem with Memento Mori—the practice of remembering our mortality—Stoicism encourages a grounded perspective. Death, though inevitable, becomes a motivator to live fully and with virtue, emphasizing what truly matters.

Virtue Ethics: Flourishing Through Character and Virtue

While CBT helps restructure thought patterns and Stoicism teaches emotional resilience, Virtue Ethics offers a blueprint for ethical living. Rooted in Aristotle's teachings, this philosophy asserts that living a good life involves cultivating virtues—qualities like wisdom, courage, temperance, and justice—which guide our actions and decisions.

Aristotle believed that the goal of life is Eudaimonia, often translated as "flourishing" or "living well." This state is achieved by living in accordance with reason and cultivating virtues. Picture a skilled musician. Just as they practice consistently to refine their craft, so too must we practice virtue to develop moral character. By making choices aligned with virtues, we achieve a harmonious and fulfilling life.

Phronesis: Practical Wisdom in Action

Central to Virtue Ethics is Phronesis, or practical wisdom. It's the ability to make sound decisions based on experience, foresight, and ethical considerations. This is not merely theoretical knowledge but the lived wisdom of making the right choices in complex situations. Imagine a friend confides in you about a mistake they made at work. You could react emotionally or judgmentally, but practical wisdom encourages a thoughtful response that balances honesty with kindness, fostering growth in both you and your friend.

Virtue Ethics ties all these philosophies together by focusing on the moral compass guiding each decision, ensuring that every thought and action leads toward flourishing.

How These Philosophies Dynamically Interact: The Symphony of Self-Improvement

These four frameworks may seem distinct at first glance, but they create a symphony of self-improvement when harmonized. Cognitive Behavioral Therapy teaches us how to challenge distorted thoughts and regulate emotions, while Stoicism and Buddhism offer tools to manage the uncontrollable aspects of life with grace and detachment. Virtue Ethics provides the moral compass that guides us toward ethical and purposeful living.

For instance, when CBT helps you recognize a negative thought, Stoic principles can assist in detaching from the thought's outcome, while Buddhist mindfulness practices encourage staying present and accepting emotions as they arise. Virtue Ethics ensures that the thoughts you choose to cultivate align with a life of moral integrity and flourishing.

In a challenging moment, these philosophies work together like the gears in a finely tuned machine. You notice an anxious thought (CBT), accept that the situation is out of your control (Stoicism), stay mindful and compassionate toward yourself (Buddhism), and act with courage and wisdom (Virtue Ethics). This dynamic approach transforms daily life into a continuous journey toward personal mastery.

The Masterpiece Within: A Dynamic Framework for Personal Growth

By integrating Cognitive Behavioral Therapy, Secular Buddhism, Stoicism, and Virtue Ethics, you create a powerful, holistic approach to personal growth. These frameworks complement each other by offering practical tools for thought restructuring, emotional regulation, ethical decision-making, and mindful presence. This approach allows you to sculpt your life intentionally, with resilience and virtue at its core.

Crafting Your Path to Flourishing

In the journey toward self-improvement, you are the artist of your life. Each of these philosophies offers a unique brushstroke, creating a masterpiece of mental clarity, emotional resilience, and ethical living. Together, they form a blueprint for a life of purpose, flourishing, and inner peace. Embrace these philosophies, and you will find that they not only help you survive life's challenges but thrive in the midst of them, living fully with wisdom, compassion, and virtue.

Having introduced the overarching structure of this self-help approach, we now turn to the core principles that form the foundation of each framework. Cognitive Behavioral Therapy (CBT), Secular Buddhism, Stoicism, and Virtue Ethics each offer distinctive insights into how we can navigate the complexities of life, yet they share common goals—transforming thought patterns, cultivating emotional resilience, and fostering ethical living. By delving into the foundational concepts of these philosophies, we'll explore the mechanics behind their wisdom, uncover how they address key aspects of human experience, and illustrate how, together, they offer a comprehensive guide to flourishing. As we dive deeper into these principles, you'll begin to see how each framework provides specific tools to tackle challenges, enhance mindfulness, and ultimately shape a life imbued with purpose and virtue. Let's start by examining the building blocks of CBT, Buddhism, Stoicism, and Virtue Ethics, setting the stage for their dynamic interaction in daily life.

2. The Foundations of Personal Mastery: Core Principles of CBT, Buddhism, Stoicism, and Virtue Ethics

To truly harness the power of Cognitive Behavioral Therapy (CBT), Secular Buddhism, Stoicism, and Virtue Ethics, it is essential to first understand the core principles that underpin each philosophy. These foundational concepts provide the tools and techniques necessary for transforming your thoughts, emotions, and behaviors, fostering a balanced and ethical life. In this section, we will explore the building blocks of each framework, uncovering how CBT offers cognitive clarity, Buddhism fosters mindfulness and detachment, Stoicism promotes emotional resilience and control, and Virtue Ethics guides us toward moral excellence and personal flourishing. By understanding these fundamentals, you will be better equipped to apply them in your daily life, creating lasting personal mastery and well-being.

Cognitive Behavioral Therapy: Unveiling the Thought-Emotion-Behavior Connection

Cognitive Behavioral Therapy (CBT) stands as one of the most widely practiced and researched therapeutic approaches in modern psychology. Rooted in the belief that our thoughts, emotions, and behaviors are intricately linked, CBT provides a practical framework for understanding and reshaping the patterns that govern our mental and emotional lives. This section delves into the core mechanics of CBT, exploring how thought, emotion, and behavior form a powerful triad that can either perpetuate suffering or lead to meaningful personal change.

The Cognitive Triad: How Thoughts Shape Our Reality

Imagine waking up on a rainy Monday morning, feeling a sense of dread about the day ahead. You think, *"This is going to be a terrible day; nothing ever goes right for me."* This thought doesn't exist in isolation—it influences how you feel, leading to feelings of anxiety, frustration, or hopelessness. As a result, you may go through the day with a sense of resignation or avoidance, reinforcing the belief that the day will indeed be miserable.

This example illustrates what CBT calls the **Cognitive Triad**, which refers to the dynamic relationship between **thoughts**, **emotions**, and **behaviors**. The key principle of CBT is that **thoughts** significantly shape how we feel and behave. Negative or distorted thoughts lead to negative emotions, which then influence our behavior, often in self-defeating ways. If we can learn to identify and adjust these thoughts, we can break the cycle of negative emotions and behaviors that result from them.

Storytelling the Cognitive Triad: The Power of Perception

Consider the story of Sarah, a college student who consistently struggled with self-doubt during exams. Each time she faced a challenging question, her mind immediately jumped to, *"I'm not smart enough to handle this."* This thought would trigger anxiety, which led to panic-driven mistakes. As her exam grades declined, her belief in her academic ability worsened, creating a self-fulfilling prophecy. Through CBT, Sarah learned to challenge the thought, reframing it as, *"This is difficult, but I can handle it one step at a time."* The shift in her thinking calmed her anxiety, allowing her to approach exams with more focus and confidence.

This example shows how the thought-emotion-behavior connection plays out in everyday life, illustrating the profound impact that thoughts can have on our emotional states and actions.

Cognitive Distortions: Identifying and Challenging Faulty Thinking

At the heart of CBT is the concept of **cognitive distortions**, which are habitual, irrational patterns of thinking that skew our perception of reality. These distortions often manifest in automatic thoughts—quick, unexamined thoughts that pop into our minds when we encounter stress or uncertainty. Without recognizing them, we may fall into these distorted patterns, leading to negative emotional and behavioral cycles.

Common Cognitive Distortions

Let's explore some of the most common cognitive distortions:

- **All-or-Nothing Thinking:** Also known as black-and-white thinking, this distortion occurs when we see situations in extreme terms, without recognizing the gray areas. For example, someone might think, *"If I don't succeed perfectly, I'm a complete failure."*
- **Catastrophizing:** This distortion involves expecting the worst possible outcome. Someone anticipating a job interview might think, *"I'll mess it up, and I'll never get a job,"* even though the reality is likely far less dire.
- **Personalization:** This occurs when we take responsibility for events outside of our control. For example, a parent might believe their child's poor school performance is entirely their fault, even though many factors could be contributing.
- **Emotional Reasoning:** This involves assuming that because we feel a certain way, it must be true. A person feeling anxious might think, *"I feel scared, so*

there must be something to fear," even in the absence of actual danger.

Challenging Cognitive Distortions: Thought Restructuring

In CBT, the process of identifying and challenging cognitive distortions is known as cognitive restructuring. The goal is to help individuals recognize when they are engaging in distorted thinking and replace those thoughts with more balanced, realistic ones.

For instance, when faced with all-or-nothing thinking, CBT encourages the use of questions like, *"Is this truly a complete failure, or is there something I can learn from this experience?"* By examining the evidence, individuals can reframe their thoughts and adopt a more nuanced perspective, leading to more positive emotional and behavioral outcomes.

Behavioral Activation: Breaking the Cycle of Avoidance

While much of CBT focuses on cognitive processes, behavior plays an equally critical role in shaping our emotional experience. Negative thought patterns often lead to avoidance behaviors—actions (or inactions) taken to escape perceived threats or discomfort. Over time, these avoidance behaviors reinforce the belief that the individual cannot cope with certain situations, perpetuating anxiety or depression.

The Role of Behavioral Activation

Behavioral activation is a key CBT technique that targets avoidance by encouraging individuals to engage in meaningful, goal-directed activities, even when they feel overwhelmed. The idea is to break the cycle of avoidance and inactivity, which fuels negative emotions, by taking small, manageable steps toward positive action.

Consider someone struggling with social anxiety. Their avoidance of social situations reinforces the belief that social interactions are threatening, further increasing their anxiety. Through behavioral activation, the individual is gradually encouraged to engage in low-pressure social activities, such as attending a small gathering or talking to a friend, to build confidence and reduce anxiety over time.

Exposure Therapy: Facing Fears Gradually

A specialized form of behavioral activation is exposure therapy, which involves systematically facing feared situations or stimuli in a controlled and gradual manner. This technique is particularly effective for anxiety disorders and phobias. By gradually exposing individuals to their fears, exposure therapy helps them build tolerance and reduce the intensity of their emotional reactions.

For example, someone with a fear of heights might start by standing on a small step and gradually work their way up to higher levels, all while practicing relaxation techniques. Over time, the fear diminishes as the individual learns that the anticipated catastrophe does not occur.

Thought-Emotion-Behavior: The Dynamic Triad in Action

The dynamic interaction between thoughts, emotions, and behaviors is the foundation of CBT. By recognizing and restructuring cognitive distortions, and by breaking avoidance patterns through behavioral activation, individuals can create positive feedback loops that promote mental health and well-being. This approach empowers individuals to reclaim control over their inner experiences, transforming their lives in meaningful ways.

Unlocking the Power of Cognitive Transformation

The beauty of Cognitive Behavioral Therapy lies in its practicality and adaptability. Whether confronting negative thoughts, challenging distortions, or taking proactive steps to change behavior, CBT provides individuals with the tools to reshape their reality. The Thought-Emotion-Behavior Connection forms the bedrock of this process, offering a roadmap to mental clarity and emotional resilience. By mastering these foundational concepts, you unlock the power of cognitive transformation, setting the stage for lasting personal growth and well-being.

Behavioral Activation and Exposure Techniques: Rewiring Behavior for Emotional Health

Cognitive Behavioral Therapy (CBT) is often associated with thought restructuring, but one of its most powerful tools for mental and emotional health lies in behavioral activation and exposure techniques. These approaches focus on the profound impact that actions have on our mood, thoughts, and overall well-being. While thought patterns certainly shape our internal experience, behavior plays an equally important role in influencing how we feel and how we perceive the world around us.

Behavioral activation and exposure techniques provide structured, evidence-based methods for re-engaging with life when avoidance, anxiety, and depression dominate. These approaches encourage us to confront discomfort directly and actively reshape our habits to break the cycle of avoidance and emotional distress. In this section, we will explore how these techniques work, their real-world applications, and how they facilitate long-lasting change.

Breaking the Cycle of Avoidance: The Role of Behavioral Activation

Imagine someone dealing with depression. One of the hallmarks of depression is withdrawal—both physically and emotionally—from activities, relationships, and responsibilities. The more the person withdraws, the more their feelings of isolation, hopelessness, and despair deepen. This is where behavioral activation comes into play.

The Concept Behind Behavioral Activation

Behavioral activation is based on the idea that mood follows action. When someone is depressed or anxious, their natural inclination is to avoid activities that may seem overwhelming or unappealing. Over time, this avoidance worsens the emotional state, reinforcing feelings of failure or helplessness. Behavioral activation seeks to reverse this cycle by encouraging individuals to actively engage in meaningful, goal-directed activities—even when they don't feel like it.

This technique doesn't rely on waiting for a shift in mood before taking action. Instead, it prompts individuals to take small, manageable steps toward re-engaging with life. The key is understanding that positive emotions are not a prerequisite for positive action; rather, positive actions can lead to improved mood and energy.

The Ripple Effect: How Small Actions Lead to Major Shifts

Consider the story of John, who recently lost his job and found himself spiraling into depression. Once an active and social person, John started avoiding friends, family, and even basic daily tasks. The more he isolated himself, the worse he felt. His therapist introduced him to behavioral activation, asking him to start with small, manageable goals—such as taking a 10-minute walk each morning or texting a friend once a day. Though these tasks seemed insignificant at first, they gradually built momentum.

As John began to complete small tasks, his energy and mood lifted, leading to larger steps, such as applying for jobs and attending social events. This simple shift in behavior disrupted the cycle of depression and began creating a new, positive feedback loop of action and emotional improvement.

The Mechanism of Behavioral Activation: From Avoidance to Engagement

Identifying Patterns of Avoidance

The first step in behavioral activation is identifying the patterns of avoidance that maintain emotional distress. Avoidance comes in many forms—skipping work due to anxiety, canceling plans with friends, procrastinating on important tasks, or even avoiding certain thoughts or feelings through distraction. Each act of avoidance provides immediate relief from discomfort, but over time, it exacerbates the problem, reinforcing the belief that certain situations are too overwhelming to handle.

Scheduling Pleasant and Meaningful Activities

Once patterns of avoidance are identified, the next step is to create a schedule of pleasant and meaningful activities. This schedule serves as a road map for re-engaging with life in a structured way. The activities don't have to be grand or profound—they can be as simple as cooking a meal, walking in the park, or reading a book. The goal is to break the cycle of inactivity and inertia, allowing the individual to regain a sense of agency and accomplishment.

Graded Task Assignments

Graded task assignments are another essential component of behavioral activation. These assignments involve breaking down overwhelming tasks into smaller, more manageable steps. For example, if someone is struggling to get back to work after a depressive episode, they might start by simply setting an alarm and getting out of bed at a specific time. Over time, they can gradually increase the difficulty of the tasks—moving from getting dressed, to answering emails, to eventually working a full day. This graded approach helps to build confidence and resilience.

Exposure Techniques: Facing Fears to Dismantle Anxiety

While behavioral activation focuses on increasing positive activity and engagement, exposure techniques are designed to directly confront fear and anxiety. Avoidance is often driven by fear—whether it's fear of social rejection, failure, or specific phobias like heights or flying. Exposure therapy systematically exposes individuals to the things they fear, allowing them to confront their anxieties in a controlled, gradual way.

The Paradox of Avoidance and Anxiety

When we avoid situations that trigger anxiety, we feel immediate relief. However, this relief is temporary and reinforces the anxiety long-term. Over time, avoidance prevents us from learning that we can cope with the feared situation, and it keeps us locked in a cycle of fear.

Exposure therapy works by reversing this cycle. By gradually and systematically exposing the individual to the feared object or situation, anxiety decreases over time through a process called habituation. The brain learns that the feared event is not as dangerous as initially perceived, and the emotional intensity of the fear diminishes.

Types of Exposure Therapy: From Imaginal to In Vivo

There are several types of exposure techniques, each tailored to different forms of anxiety:

- **In Vivo Exposure:** This involves directly confronting the feared object or situation in real life. For example, someone with a fear of elevators might start by simply standing in front of an elevator, then progressing to riding it one floor, and eventually using it daily.
- **Imaginal Exposure:** In cases where the feared situation is not easily accessible (e.g., fear of past trauma or future events), **imaginal exposure** is used. This involves vividly imagining the feared situation while discussing it with a therapist to process and desensitize the anxiety.
- **Interoceptive Exposure:** Often used for panic disorder, this technique exposes individuals to physical sensations associated with fear or anxiety (such as a racing heart or dizziness). The individual learns to tolerate these sensations without panicking, reducing the fear response.

Graded Exposure: Building Confidence Step by Step

A key principle of exposure therapy is graded exposure, which involves starting with the least anxiety-provoking situation and gradually working up to more challenging scenarios. This method prevents the individual from becoming overwhelmed while building confidence and resilience.

For example, someone with social anxiety might begin by making eye contact with strangers, then progress to saying "hello," and eventually engage in small talk. Each step builds on the previous one, slowly dismantling the power of anxiety.

Behavioral Change as a Catalyst for Cognitive Change

The brilliance of both behavioral activation and exposure therapy is that they focus on action as the primary lever for change. While CBT often begins with identifying and challenging thoughts, behavioral techniques show that changing behavior can directly lead to shifts in thought patterns. As individuals take action—whether re-engaging with life or confronting fears—their perception of themselves and their world changes. They develop new beliefs about their abilities, their resilience, and their capacity to handle discomfort.

For example, someone who has avoided driving after a car accident may initially believe, *"I'll never feel safe driving again."* Through exposure therapy, they gradually begin driving short distances, then longer trips. Over time, their belief shifts to, *"I can drive safely, even if I feel a bit anxious."* This cognitive shift happens as a direct result of behavioral change.

Reclaiming Life Through Action

Behavioral activation and exposure techniques are powerful tools for reclaiming life from the grips of avoidance, depression, and anxiety. By encouraging proactive engagement with the world and directly confronting fears, these techniques empower individuals to break the cycles of inactivity and avoidance that maintain emotional distress.

Small steps, taken consistently, lead to profound transformations in mood, confidence, and mental well-being. When we learn to act, even in the face of discomfort, we begin to reclaim control over our emotional health, ultimately creating a life that reflects our true potential.

Secular Buddhism: The Four Noble Truths and the Eightfold Path

Secular Buddhism is a contemporary interpretation of the ancient teachings of Siddhartha Gautama, the Buddha, focusing on the practical, ethical, and philosophical elements of Buddhism while omitting religious or supernatural beliefs. At the heart of Secular Buddhism are the Four Noble Truths and the Eightfold Path, foundational teachings that offer a framework for understanding human suffering and provide a guide for overcoming it.

In this exploration, we'll examine the profound wisdom of these truths and the path that follows, demonstrating how they offer a timeless, universally applicable approach to living a balanced, mindful, and ethical life. Whether you are seeking peace in the chaos of modern life or striving to live with deeper intention, the Four Noble Truths and the Eightfold Path provide both a diagnosis and a cure for the challenges we all face.

The Four Noble Truths: Understanding the Nature of Suffering

The Four Noble Truths are the cornerstone of Buddhist philosophy, offering a clear and structured approach to understanding the nature of suffering (dukkha) and how to transcend it. These truths reflect the Buddha's diagnosis of the human condition, a diagnosis that is just as relevant in today's world as it was over 2,500 years ago.

The word "dukkha" in Buddhism encompasses much more than just physical or emotional suffering. While "suffering" is the commonly used English translation, dukkha refers to a pervasive sense of dissatisfaction, unease, or discomfort that runs through human existence. This dissatisfaction can arise even in moments of pleasure, as those experiences are fleeting and subject to change. The core of dukkha is tied to the impermanence of life, the unsatisfactoriness of attachment to desires, and the constant craving for things to be other than they are.

In essence, dukkha reflects the fundamental imperfection and instability in life. So, while "suffering" is the closest translation we have in English, it's important to recognize going forward in this discussion that dukkha refers to a broader, more nuanced state of existential dissatisfaction.

The First Noble Truth: The Reality of Suffering (Dukkha)

The first truth asserts that suffering is an inescapable part of life. It is important to note that "suffering" in this context encompasses a wide range of experiences beyond physical pain—it includes the dissatisfaction, unease, and impermanence that pervade human existence. Whether it's the frustration of unmet desires, the pain of loss, or the existential angst of life's fleeting nature, suffering touches all aspects of life.

Consider a modern scenario: You get a promotion at work, but the joy quickly fades as new challenges arise. The pleasure of the achievement is transient, and soon, anxiety about performance, stress from added responsibilities, and the fear of losing the position replace the initial happiness. This is the essence of dukkha—nothing lasts, and even moments of joy are often shadowed by the fear of their eventual end.

The Second Noble Truth: The Cause of Suffering (Samudaya)

The second truth identifies craving (tanha) as the root cause of suffering. This craving manifests in many forms—desires for sensory pleasure, attachment to material possessions, and even the longing for eternal life or unchanging conditions. At the core, craving is the mind's insistence that things be other than they are, leading to dissatisfaction when reality doesn't conform to these desires.

In a consumer-driven world, this truth is vividly illustrated. We chase after the latest gadgets, bigger houses, or higher social status, believing that these acquisitions will bring lasting happiness. Yet, as soon as we attain them, the satisfaction is fleeting, and we find ourselves longing for more or different experiences. This endless cycle of desire fuels the fire of dukkha, perpetuating suffering.

The Third Noble Truth: The Cessation of Suffering (Nirodha)

The third truth offers hope: suffering can be overcome. By letting go of craving and attachments, we can experience nirvana, the state of liberation from suffering. This cessation is not some abstract, distant ideal but a practical state of peace and contentment achievable through conscious effort.

Nirvana, in a secular context, is often understood as a profound acceptance of life's impermanence and a release from the constant striving for more. It's the ability to find peace in the present moment, regardless of external circumstances, by quieting the mind's relentless demands.

The Fourth Noble Truth: The Path to the Cessation of Suffering (Magga)

The final truth presents the Eightfold Path, the practical guide for achieving the cessation of suffering. Unlike other philosophies that focus purely on abstract thought, Buddhism offers a detailed, actionable plan to guide individuals toward ethical living, mental discipline, and wisdom.

The Eightfold Path: The Roadmap to Inner Peace

The Eightfold Path serves as both a philosophical framework and a practical guide for living. It is divided into three major areas: Wisdom (Prajna), Ethical Conduct (Sila), and Mental Discipline (Samadhi). Each aspect of the path is interdependent, creating a holistic approach to life's challenges.

Wisdom: The Foundation of Understanding

1. **Right View**
   The first step on the path is to cultivate the **right understanding** of the world, particularly the Four Noble Truths. This involves seeing life clearly and understanding the impermanence of all things. It's the recognition that suffering exists and that craving is its cause, which shifts our perspective from blame or victimhood to a place of proactive insight.

   Example: Imagine going through a breakup. With Right View, instead of fixating on the pain or blaming yourself or your partner, you recognize that attachment and craving for permanence are natural but not sustainable. This perspective reduces the emotional intensity and allows space for healing.

2. **Right Intention**
   Right Intention refers to the commitment to ethical living and mental development. It is the conscious decision to move away from harmful desires (such as greed, hatred, and delusion) and toward positive intentions like kindness and compassion.

   Example: After understanding that craving leads to suffering, you might set the intention to approach future relationships with more openness and less attachment to specific outcomes, prioritizing mutual growth over control.

Ethical Conduct: Living in Harmony with Others

3. **Right Speech**
   Right Speech emphasizes the power of words and encourages truthful, compassionate, and constructive communication. In a world filled with misinformation and harmful rhetoric, practicing Right Speech cultivates trust and harmony in relationships.

   Example: During a heated disagreement, instead of lashing out with hurtful words, Right Speech would guide you to express your feelings honestly but kindly, fostering understanding rather than conflict.

4. **Right Action**
   Right Action involves living ethically, acting in ways that avoid harm to others and oneself. This includes principles like non-violence, honesty, and respect for life. Right Action asks us to consider how our actions impact not only ourselves but the broader community and world.

Example: Avoiding harmful actions, like dishonesty or exploitation in business dealings, aligns with Right Action, promoting integrity and fairness in daily life.

5. **Right Livelihood**
   Right Livelihood calls for engaging in work that supports rather than harms others. It is the practice of earning a living in a way that promotes ethical principles and contributes positively to society.

   Example: Choosing a career path that aligns with values of compassion and service, rather than one driven solely by profit, fulfills Right Livelihood by ensuring that your work contributes to the greater good.

Mental Discipline: Cultivating Inner Calm and Focus

6. **Right Effort**
   Right Effort is the sustained, diligent practice of cultivating positive mental states while avoiding negative ones. This discipline involves guarding the mind against unwholesome thoughts and promoting thoughts of kindness, compassion, and patience.

   Example: When feelings of jealousy or anger arise, Right Effort would guide you to acknowledge them without acting on them, instead choosing to redirect your focus toward gratitude or understanding.

7. **Right Mindfulness**
   Right Mindfulness emphasizes being fully present and aware of your thoughts, feelings, and actions in the present moment. Mindfulness, a central practice in secular Buddhism, allows you to observe your experience without judgment or attachment.

   Example: Practicing mindfulness during everyday activities, like eating or walking, helps you remain grounded in the present, reducing the tendency to dwell on past regrets or future anxieties.

8. **Right Concentration**
   The final component of the path is Right Concentration, which refers to developing deep focus and meditation. Through meditative practices, individuals train their minds to reach a state of clarity, calm, and insight, moving toward a more awakened state of being.

   Example: Through regular meditation practice, you strengthen your ability to concentrate and develop a deeper understanding of your inner workings, fostering both emotional resilience and wisdom.

The Interplay of the Four Noble Truths and the Eightfold Path

The Four Noble Truths and the Eightfold Path are inseparable in Buddhist practice. The truths provide the diagnosis—life is marked by suffering, and craving is its cause—while the path offers the prescription, a clear guide to transcending suffering. In this way, the Eightfold Path can be seen as the practical application of the Four Noble Truths, offering tools to systematically address suffering and cultivate a more peaceful, intentional existence.

In a secular context, the wisdom of these teachings transcends religious boundaries. They provide a blueprint for mindful living, ethical action, and the cultivation of wisdom—values that resonate with anyone seeking to live more harmoniously in the modern world.

The Path to Liberation and Inner Peace

The Four Noble Truths and Eightfold Path encapsulates the transformative potential of these teachings. The Four Noble Truths illuminate the nature of suffering, while the Eightfold Path offers a practical and ethical guide for moving through life with mindfulness, compassion, and wisdom. Whether applied in a religious or secular context, these principles provide a timeless framework for cultivating inner peace, ethical integrity, and the wisdom to navigate the inevitable challenges of life. By walking this path, we move closer to a life free from suffering, grounded in clarity, and enriched by intentional action.

Mindfulness and Meditation Techniques in Secular Buddhism: Cultivating Presence and Awareness

At the heart of Secular Buddhism lies a profound commitment to mindfulness and meditation, practices that offer tools for cultivating awareness, reducing suffering, and fostering inner peace. These techniques, though rooted in ancient Buddhist tradition, have found a wide audience in modern secular contexts, emphasizing their universal applicability. Mindfulness and meditation are not merely exercises in relaxation; they are powerful methods for understanding the nature of the mind, transforming habitual patterns, and living with greater intentionality.

This section delves into the foundational concepts of mindfulness and meditation as taught in Secular Buddhism, exploring how they enhance our capacity to observe thoughts, emotions, and experiences without attachment or judgment. By deepening our understanding of these practices, we open the door to a more present, balanced, and liberated life.

Mindfulness: The Art of Being Present in Every Moment

The Essence of Mindfulness: A Radical Shift in Awareness

Mindfulness, or **sati** in Pali, refers to the practice of bringing **full awareness to the present moment**. It is a way of being fully conscious of our thoughts, emotions, sensations, and environment without becoming entangled in them. In a world dominated by distractions and constant mental chatter, mindfulness offers a transformative shift in how we engage with life—fostering clarity, calm, and insight.

Rather than being swept away by automatic thoughts or emotional reactivity, mindfulness invites us to pause and observe. This act of non-judgmental awareness allows us to create space between stimulus and response, enabling us to make conscious choices rather than acting out of habit or impulse.

Imagine sitting in traffic, feeling the familiar surge of frustration rising. Without mindfulness, you might lash out mentally or physically—honking your horn, muttering complaints, or allowing your irritation to escalate. With mindfulness, however, you can recognize the initial surge of frustration, breathe deeply, and observe it with curiosity: *What does this feeling really feel like? Where is it arising from? Is it helpful or necessary?* Through this simple act of awareness, the emotion loses its power to control you.

The Science Behind Mindfulness: Rewiring the Brain

Recent scientific research has shown that mindfulness not only improves mental well-being but also has measurable effects on the brain. Studies have revealed that regular mindfulness practice can increase gray matter density in areas of the brain responsible for learning, memory, and emotional regulation. At the same time, it can reduce the size and activity of the amygdala, the part of the brain associated with the stress response. This neurological reshaping underscores mindfulness's ability to help individuals manage stress, anxiety, and emotional dysregulation.

Practical Mindfulness: From Formal Meditation to Daily Life

Mindfulness can be practiced in two primary ways:

1. **Formal Meditation:** This involves setting aside dedicated time to sit in silence, focusing on the breath, bodily sensations, or thoughts as they arise. This formal practice strengthens one's capacity for sustained attention and awareness.
2. **Informal Mindfulness:** Beyond formal meditation, mindfulness can be woven into everyday activities—whether washing dishes, walking, or having a conversation. In this context, mindfulness involves bringing full attention to the task at hand, engaging fully in the present moment without distraction.

For example, while washing dishes, instead of rushing through the task or letting your mind wander to your to-do list, mindfulness invites you to notice the texture of the water, the weight of the dish in your hand, and the sound of the running faucet. By doing so, even mundane tasks become opportunities for presence and peace.

Meditation Techniques: Training the Mind Toward Liberation

Meditation, known as **bhavana** in Pali, is a central practice in Buddhism aimed at cultivating concentration, insight, and mental clarity. It provides a structured environment in which to train the mind, breaking free from habitual distractions and fostering a deeper understanding of the impermanent and interconnected nature of existence.

In Secular Buddhism, meditation techniques are often divided into two main categories: **samatha** (calming meditation) and **vipassana** (insight meditation). Each technique plays a distinct role in cultivating mental discipline and deep awareness.

Samatha: Cultivating Calm and Focus

Samatha meditation is designed to cultivate a calm, focused, and stable mind. The practitioner typically focuses on a single object, such as the breath, a candle flame, or a mantra, to develop **concentration (samadhi)**. Over time, this practice helps quiet the mind, allowing the practitioner to experience a profound sense of stillness and clarity.

Consider the breath as a focal point in samatha meditation. The practitioner pays attention to the sensation of the breath entering and leaving the body, gently returning to the breath each time the mind wanders. This consistent return to the breath strengthens mental concentration and gradually reduces the mental clutter that usually fills our awareness.

Samatha is akin to sharpening a blade—through focused, repetitive practice, the mind becomes a precise tool, ready for deeper work in insight meditation. The calm and focus cultivated through samatha also provide relief from the mental turbulence that often accompanies stress, anxiety, and overthinking.

Vipassana: Gaining Insight into the Nature of Reality

While samatha meditation cultivates concentration, **vipassana** (insight meditation) is aimed at developing deep insight into the nature of reality, particularly the principles of **impermanence (anicca)**, **suffering (dukkha)**, and **non-self (anatta)**.

In vipassana, the practitioner moves beyond focusing on a single object and instead observes the flow of thoughts, sensations, and emotions as they arise and pass away. This technique cultivates a clear and direct awareness of the transient nature of all experiences. By observing thoughts and sensations without attachment or aversion, the practitioner begins to see how clinging to experiences—whether pleasurable or painful—leads to suffering.

For example, during vipassana meditation, you might notice a feeling of discomfort in your body. Instead of shifting or reacting immediately, you simply observe it. Is the sensation permanent? Does it change? Can you separate the discomfort from the story your mind tells about it? Over time, vipassana meditation reveals the impermanent and interdependent nature of all phenomena, leading to deeper insights into the root causes of suffering.

Loving-Kindness Meditation: Cultivating Compassion for Self and Others

Another key meditation practice in Secular Buddhism is **metta** or **loving-kindness meditation**. This practice involves cultivating feelings of compassion and goodwill toward oneself and others. Through this practice, the practitioner systematically extends feelings of kindness, first to themselves, then to loved ones, acquaintances, and even difficult individuals or enemies.

The repetition of loving-kindness phrases—such as "May I be happy, may I be safe, may I be free from suffering"—gradually softens the heart, dissolving feelings of anger, resentment, or judgment. Loving-kindness meditation not only enhances interpersonal relationships but also reduces self-criticism, promoting a deep sense of inner peace and connection with others.

The Role of Mindfulness and Meditation in Secular Buddhism

Mindfulness and meditation, though rooted in ancient Buddhist teachings, have found a prominent place in modern secular practices because they directly address the human condition. These practices offer tools to deal with stress, emotional volatility, and the constant distractions of contemporary life.

In the context of Secular Buddhism, mindfulness and meditation are seen not as religious rituals, but as practical methodologies for cultivating awareness, insight, and ethical living. They guide practitioners in recognizing and breaking the cycle of suffering caused by craving, attachment, and aversion, leading to a more balanced and liberated life. While mindfulness helps us to stay grounded in the present moment, meditation opens the door to deep insights into the nature of the mind and reality.

A Path to Inner Clarity and Compassion

Mindfulness and Meditation: The Twin Pillars of Awakening encapsulate the essence of these transformative practices. Mindfulness teaches us to embrace the present moment with openness and curiosity, while meditation deepens our understanding of the mind's patterns and the nature of reality. Together, these techniques form the bedrock of Secular Buddhist practice, providing a practical and ethical path to reduce suffering, enhance mental clarity, and foster compassion toward self and others.

By integrating mindfulness and meditation into daily life, we can navigate the challenges of modern living with greater ease, presence, and wisdom—leading to a more peaceful, intentional, and connected existence.

Detachment and Non-Attachment in Secular Buddhism: The Art of Letting Go

Detachment and non-attachment are central to the teachings of Secular Buddhism, guiding practitioners in how to engage with life fully without clinging to outcomes, possessions, or emotions. In a world that emphasizes success, accumulation, and emotional intensity, these concepts offer a radical approach: to be deeply involved with life while remaining free from the bondage of attachment. Understanding the distinction between detachment and non-attachment is critical to grasping how these practices help reduce suffering and cultivate inner peace.

Detachment is often misunderstood as indifference, but in the Buddhist sense, it refers to a healthy distance from the need to control or possess. Non-attachment, on the other hand, allows for deep engagement and love without the suffering that comes from clinging. In this exploration, we will examine these concepts in detail, their role in Secular Buddhist practice, and how they can be applied to modern life.

The Illusion of Control: Why Attachment Causes Suffering

Attachment and the Cycle of Suffering

To fully understand detachment and non-attachment, it's essential to first examine the Buddhist view of attachment. Attachment refers to the grasping or clinging to people, things, experiences, and even ideas. This attachment arises from the mistaken belief that these external factors can bring us lasting happiness and security. The Buddha's teachings emphasize that the primary cause of suffering (dukkha) is this very craving and attachment.

Imagine you buy a new car, and for a few weeks, you enjoy a sense of pride and satisfaction. Over time, however, the car begins to lose its newness. Maybe it gets scratched or breaks down, and the joy you once derived from it fades. Soon, the car, which once symbolized success and pleasure, becomes a source of anxiety and frustration. This process illustrates the **impermanence (anicca)** of all things, a core tenet of Buddhist thought. Nothing lasts forever, and attachment to impermanent things leads inevitably to suffering when they change or disappear.

The Fear of Loss: A Story of Attachment

Consider the story of Mira, a successful professional who invested a great deal of her identity in her career. Her work achievements provided her with a sense of self-worth and security, but they also created a deep attachment to her status and success. When the company she worked for began downsizing, Mira was consumed with anxiety about losing her job. This fear of loss, born from attachment, took a toll on her mental and physical health, driving her to constant stress and sleepless nights.

In Mira's case, it was her attachment to an external condition—her career—that caused her suffering. This scenario reflects a broader truth: attachment creates vulnerability because it ties our emotional well-being to external, impermanent factors beyond our control.

The Path of Detachment: Letting Go Without Indifference

Detachment Is Not Indifference

One of the most common misconceptions about **detachment** is that it implies indifference or a lack of care. In reality, Buddhist detachment is not about withdrawing from life or becoming emotionally numb. Rather, it is about **liberating oneself from the compulsive need to control or hold onto things**. Detachment involves engaging fully with life while maintaining an inner sense of balance and freedom from excessive emotional investment.

To detach is to recognize that, while we can appreciate and enjoy people, experiences, and achievements, we do not need to cling to them for our happiness. We can embrace the joy of the moment, knowing that it will eventually pass, and when it does, we do not suffer from its absence.

Practicing Detachment: The Wisdom of Equanimity

Equanimity (upekkha) is a core quality developed through detachment. Equanimity refers to a state of mental calmness, composure, and even-mindedness, particularly in the face of life's ups and downs. It is the ability to remain balanced, no matter what life brings—success or failure, pleasure or pain.

Detachment, practiced through equanimity, allows us to experience the full range of human emotions without being ruled by them. In this sense, detachment is a form of emotional freedom—it enables us to let go of the need for life to conform to our desires and expectations. This detachment from outcomes does not diminish our engagement with life; it enhances it, as we no longer live in fear of loss or change.

For example, in relationships, detachment allows us to love without clinging. We can deeply care for someone while understanding that they, like all things, are impermanent. This doesn't mean we stop caring; rather, we free ourselves from the desperation that comes with fearing loss.

Non-Attachment: Engaging Fully Without Clinging

The Subtle Difference Between Detachment and Non-Attachment

While detachment is often understood as stepping back from the need to control or hold onto things, **non-attachment** refers to a more subtle and nuanced practice. Non-attachment allows for **deep involvement and love** without the suffering that arises from attachment. Non-attachment doesn't mean distancing yourself from people or experiences but rather engaging with them fully, without trying to possess or control them.

In secular Buddhist practice, non-attachment is the antidote to craving and aversion. It allows us to appreciate and experience the world's beauty without falling into the trap of thinking that happiness can be captured, stored, or guaranteed through attachment.

Non-Attachment in Practice: A Story of Letting Go

Let's return to Mira, who was struggling with attachment to her career. Through the practice of non-attachment, Mira learned to let go of her rigid identification with her job title and success. She continued to work diligently and pursue her goals, but with the understanding that her self-worth was not tied to her career. If the job ended, she would still be whole.

By embracing non-attachment, Mira was able to experience her work with greater freedom and joy. She no longer lived in fear of losing her position, and paradoxically, this allowed her to be more present and engaged in her work. Her anxiety lessened, and her creativity flourished because she was no longer shackled by fear.

The Role of Impermanence and Non-Self in Non-Attachment

Embracing Impermanence (Anicca)

At the heart of non-attachment lies the Buddhist teaching of impermanence (anicca). Everything in life is transient— whether it's material possessions, relationships, emotions, or even our physical bodies. Non-attachment asks us to deeply contemplate this impermanence, not as a source of fear, but as a source of liberation. By accepting that everything is subject to change, we learn to let go of the desire for permanence, realizing that clinging to the temporary only leads to suffering.

For example, consider a cherished friendship. Non-attachment allows you to fully enjoy the moments you share with your friend without the underlying fear that the relationship might change. Instead of grasping at permanence, you accept that all relationships evolve. This acceptance allows for a deeper, more genuine connection, free from the anxieties that often come with attachment.

The Concept of Non-Self (Anatta)

Non-attachment is also closely related to the Buddhist teaching of non-self (anatta). The idea that there is no fixed, permanent self allows us to move beyond rigid identities and roles. Often, attachment stems from a strong identification with the self: *I am my job, I am my success, I am my relationships.* Non-self teaches us that these identities are fluid and impermanent.

By loosening our attachment to these identities, we become more flexible and open to change. Non-attachment to the self allows us to flow with life's changes rather than resist them. It also reduces suffering because we no longer feel the need to defend or cling to a fixed identity.

Detachment and Non-Attachment in Daily Life: Practical Applications

In modern life, where attachment often manifests through consumerism, success-driven mindsets, and emotional entanglements, detachment and non-attachment offer profound tools for living with greater peace and resilience.

In relationships, non-attachment fosters deeper, healthier connections by allowing us to love without ownership. In careers, detachment helps us pursue success without tying our self-worth to outcomes. In our personal lives, practicing non-attachment to material possessions helps us appreciate what we have without the constant need for more.

Freedom Through Letting Go

Let Go to Live Fully. The Power of Detachment and Non-Attachment summarizes the transformative potential of these practices. Detachment offers emotional freedom by loosening the grip of control, while non-attachment allows us to engage deeply with life without falling into the trap of clinging. Together, they form a foundation for living with equanimity, resilience, and peace.

By mastering the art of letting go, we can experience the richness of life without the suffering that comes from craving permanence or control. In the practice of detachment and non-attachment, we discover a path to inner liberation, where we can love, work, and live more fully and freely.

The Dichotomy of Control in Stoicism: Mastering What You Can and Letting Go of the Rest

At the heart of Stoic philosophy lies a powerful and liberating principle known as the Dichotomy of Control. This concept, introduced by the ancient Stoics and most famously articulated by Epictetus in his work *The Enchiridion,* divides the events and circumstances of life into two categories: things that are within our control and things that are outside of our control. By understanding and applying this distinction, Stoicism provides a pathway to personal freedom and emotional resilience, helping individuals focus their efforts on what truly matters while letting go of the rest.

This foundational concept of Stoicism is not just a philosophical abstraction—it is a highly practical approach to navigating the challenges, uncertainties, and frustrations of daily life. Through this lens, we can develop a deep sense of inner peace, even in the face of external chaos, by focusing our energy on our own actions, thoughts, and attitudes rather than trying to control outcomes that are beyond our influence.

The Dichotomy of Control: A Stoic Framework for Life

What We Can Control vs. What We Cannot Control

The essence of the Dichotomy of Control is simple: some things are under our control, and others are not. However, the implications of this idea are profound. According to the Stoics, the only things we can truly control are our own thoughts, beliefs, desires, and actions. Everything else—external events, the behavior of others, the outcomes of our efforts—lies outside our control.

Consider the daily stresses of modern life. A person might be anxious about an upcoming job interview, fearing they won't get the position despite their qualifications. Here, the Stoic Dichotomy of Control would advise the individual to focus on preparing for the interview, presenting themselves well, and speaking clearly—all actions within their control—while recognizing that the ultimate hiring decision is beyond their control.

This perspective is deeply empowering. By focusing only on what we can control, we conserve emotional energy and avoid frustration. The Stoics believed that attempting to control the uncontrollable is not only futile but also the source of much of our suffering. Letting go of the need to control external factors frees us to live with greater tranquility and purpose.

The Practical Application: Internalizing Control for Lasting Peace

The Internal and the External: Shifting the Locus of Control

In Stoicism, internalizing control means recognizing that our happiness and well-being are determined not by external circumstances but by how we respond to them. Epictetus famously said, "It's not what happens to you, but how you react to it that matters." This statement encapsulates the Stoic approach to life: external events may be beyond our influence, but our reactions—our thoughts and actions—are entirely up to us.

Imagine a scenario where you've planned a long-awaited vacation, but a sudden storm disrupts your travel plans. You could allow frustration and anger to ruin your mood, or you could apply the Dichotomy of Control by accepting the situation and focusing on what you can still enjoy, such as relaxing with a good book or appreciating the unexpected downtime. The storm is out of your control; your emotional response is not.

The Stoic emphasis on focusing only on what we can control also serves as a guide for how to live ethically. Since we can control our intentions and actions, the Stoic seeks to live with virtue, knowing that our moral choices—whether we act with wisdom, courage, justice, and temperance—are always within our control, regardless of external outcomes.

The Illusion of Control: Why We Struggle to Let Go

The Psychological Need for Control

While the Stoic approach to control is clear and logical, it is not always easy to practice. Human beings are wired with a psychological need for control, particularly over their environment and the future. This need for control can lead to stress, anxiety, and frustration, especially when we face situations that defy our efforts to influence them.

For example, think of a parent trying to ensure their child's future success by controlling every aspect of their education and social life. While their intentions may be good, the parent's efforts are ultimately misguided. The child's future, with all its unpredictable twists and turns, is beyond anyone's control. By recognizing this, the parent can focus instead on providing support, love, and guidance—things that are within their control—without succumbing to anxiety over the uncontrollable future.

The Paradox of Control: Freedom Through Letting Go

Stoicism teaches that **freedom lies in letting go** of the need to control external events. Paradoxically, the more we cling to control, the more we suffer, as the world inevitably fails to conform to our expectations. The Stoics invite us to practice acceptance, not as a form of resignation, but as an active engagement with reality as it is, rather than how we wish it to be.

This is not to say that Stoicism encourages passivity or fatalism. On the contrary, Stoicism advocates for engaged action—but only where action can have a meaningful impact. When we fully internalize the Dichotomy of Control, we become laser-focused on doing our best in areas we can influence, while cultivating equanimity in the face of outcomes that are beyond our power.

The Role of Intentional Action: Focusing on What Truly Matters

The Serenity Prayer: A Stoic Reflection

The well-known Serenity Prayer often associated with modern recovery programs echoes the Stoic philosophy: "Grant me the serenity to accept the things I cannot change, the courage to change the things I can, and the wisdom to know the difference." This sentiment is deeply Stoic in nature, urging individuals to recognize the boundaries between what they can and cannot control, and to act with courage and wisdom where it matters most.

In Stoic practice, intentional action means focusing on the quality of your efforts, not on the outcomes. Whether you're facing a challenging project at work, dealing with a difficult relationship, or striving to improve your health, Stoicism encourages you to dedicate yourself fully to the process—while accepting that the results are never entirely up to you.

This focus on intentional action is deeply liberating. It allows us to invest wholeheartedly in the present moment, knowing that we are doing our best, without being crushed by the weight of future outcomes or past failures.

Eudaimonia: Living in Accordance with Nature

The ultimate goal of Stoic practice is eudaimonia, often translated as flourishing or living in accordance with nature. This concept is closely tied to the Dichotomy of Control because it suggests that true happiness is found not in external achievements or possessions, but in living a life of virtue. By focusing on what we can control—our own character and actions—we align ourselves with nature, living with integrity and purpose.

For the Stoics, a life well-lived is one where the individual acts according to **virtue**—with wisdom, courage, justice, and temperance—regardless of what external circumstances arise. The Stoic Dichotomy of Control guides us in recognizing that the only thing we truly possess is our ability to make moral choices. Everything else—wealth, status, relationships, even our physical health—is ultimately outside our control and should be met with acceptance.

Applying the Dichotomy of Control in Modern Life: Practical Examples

The Dichotomy of Control is not merely an abstract concept but a practical tool for daily living. Consider the following scenarios where the Stoic principle can be applied:

- **In Relationships:** You cannot control how others feel about you, but you can control how you treat them—

with kindness, respect, and honesty. Focusing on your actions, rather than seeking approval or affection, reduces anxiety and strengthens your relationships.
- **In the Workplace:** You may not be able to control your boss's opinion or the outcome of a project, but you can control your effort, attitude, and response to challenges. By letting go of the need for recognition or perfection, you free yourself to do your best work without unnecessary stress.
- **In Health and Well-Being:** You cannot control whether you will get sick or face physical challenges, but you can control how you take care of your body, how you respond to illness, and whether you maintain a positive mindset in the face of adversity.

In each of these cases, the Dichotomy of Control offers a roadmap for focusing on what truly matters—your actions and intentions—while cultivating serenity and acceptance around the things you cannot change.

The Freedom of Focusing on What You Can Control

By learning to differentiate between what we can and cannot control, we free ourselves from the emotional turmoil of striving for impossible guarantees and outcomes. Instead, we become empowered to live with intention, integrity, and peace. The Dichotomy of Control is not about withdrawing from life's challenges but engaging with them more effectively by focusing on what truly matters—our own actions and attitudes. Through this practice, we can find freedom in any circumstance, knowing that we are living in accordance with nature, guided by wisdom and virtue.

Key Stoic Virtues: Wisdom, Courage, Justice, and Temperance

At the heart of Stoicism lies a set of cardinal virtues that form the foundation for a life lived in accordance with nature. These virtues—wisdom, courage, justice, and temperance—are not merely abstract ideals but practical principles that guide everyday behavior and decision-making. For the Stoics, these virtues represent the essential qualities necessary for human flourishing, or eudaimonia. They are seen as interdependent, with each one supporting and balancing the others to create a harmonious and virtuous life.

In this exploration, we will delve deeply into each of the four key Stoic virtues, uncovering how they shape the Stoic understanding of ethical living and provide a roadmap for navigating life's challenges. Through practical examples and engaging storytelling, these timeless virtues will come to life, showing how they continue to offer wisdom for our modern lives.

Wisdom (Sophia): The Guiding Virtue

The Role of Practical Wisdom in Stoicism

Wisdom (Sophia) is considered the most fundamental of the Stoic virtues, serving as the guiding principle that informs all others. In Stoicism, wisdom is not just theoretical knowledge or intellectual understanding; it is practical wisdom, or phronesis—the ability to make sound decisions based on a deep understanding of the world and human nature.

Wisdom enables us to see things as they truly are, distinguishing between what is within our control and what is not. It teaches us to align our thoughts and actions with reason, helping us to navigate complex situations with clarity and moral insight. The Stoics believed that wisdom allows us to understand the nature of life's impermanence and accept reality as it unfolds, without attachment or aversion.

Wisdom in Action: A Story of Clarity

Imagine a successful entrepreneur, Alex, facing a major financial setback. Without wisdom, Alex might panic, make rash decisions, or become consumed by anxiety over the loss. However, with the Stoic virtue of wisdom, Alex pauses to reflect on the situation calmly. They understand that while they cannot control the market forces that led to the loss, they can control how they respond—by learning from the experience, adjusting strategies, and maintaining a sense of purpose. Wisdom enables Alex to see the setback as a temporary challenge rather than a personal failure.

In this way, wisdom is the ability to maintain perspective, see the bigger picture, and make decisions that are not clouded by fear or desire. It helps us act with intention, keeping our minds aligned with what is virtuous and reasonable.

Courage (Andreia): Facing Fear and Adversity

Courage as Emotional and Physical Fortitude

Courage (Andreia) is the virtue that enables us to face fear, uncertainty, and adversity with strength and resolve. For the Stoics, courage is not limited to physical bravery but also encompasses emotional resilience—the ability to persevere in the face of hardship, loss, or discomfort without succumbing to fear or despair.

The Stoics emphasized that life is filled with challenges, and how we respond to those challenges defines our character. Courage allows us to endure difficulties with dignity, acting according to our principles even when the outcomes are uncertain or unfavorable. It is the quality that ensures we don't give up in the pursuit of virtue, even when the road is difficult.

Courage in Action: The Story of a Soldier

Consider the example of a soldier facing an overwhelming battle. The soldier feels fear, but instead of retreating, they summon the courage to defend their comrades, knowing that the outcome is uncertain and potentially fatal. This is the Stoic definition of courage—not the absence of fear, but the decision to act virtuously in spite of it.

In everyday life, courage can manifest in more subtle ways: speaking up for justice in the workplace, standing by one's values in the face of social pressure, or persevering through personal challenges like illness or loss. Stoic courage is the commitment to do what is right, regardless of external circumstances or personal risk.

Justice (Dikaiosyne): Acting with Fairness and Integrity

Justice as the Social Virtue

Justice (Dikaiosyne) in Stoicism is the virtue concerned with fairness, integrity, and respect for others. It reflects the Stoic belief that we are all part of a larger human community and that our actions should contribute to the common good. Justice calls for treating others with dignity, ensuring that we do not harm others through our actions, and upholding the principles of fairness in all our dealings.

Unlike wisdom, which is primarily focused on personal development, justice extends beyond the individual, governing our interactions with society. It asks us to recognize the inherent value in every person and to act with compassion, respect, and fairness, regardless of our own interests.

Justice in Action: A Story of Integrity

Imagine a corporate leader who discovers unethical practices within their company. Justice, as a Stoic virtue, demands that the leader address the wrongdoing, even at the risk of losing profits or facing backlash. The leader understands that protecting the well-being of employees and customers is more important than short-term gains, and they take action to correct the company's course.

Justice requires that we do what is right, not just what is easy or convenient. It means advocating for equality, protecting the vulnerable, and ensuring that our actions contribute to the betterment of society.

Temperance (Sophrosyne): The Balance of Desires

The Importance of Self-Control

Temperance (Sophrosyne), often referred to as self-control or moderation, is the virtue that helps us govern our desires and impulses. It ensures that we do not indulge in excess, whether in the pursuit of pleasure, wealth, or power. For the Stoics, temperance is essential because it keeps our desires in check, allowing us to focus on what is truly important and live in harmony with our rational nature.

Temperance teaches us to practice restraint, not as a form of deprivation but as a way to cultivate balance and inner peace. By exercising self-control, we avoid becoming enslaved by our passions, which can lead to destructive behavior, addiction, or moral compromise.

Temperance in Action: The Story of Balanced Living

Consider a politician who has access to great wealth and power. Without temperance, they might be tempted to use their position for personal gain, indulging in luxury at the expense of their responsibilities. However, with temperance, they choose to live modestly, ensuring that their focus remains on serving the public good rather than satisfying personal greed.

Temperance is about recognizing that true fulfillment does not come from indulgence but from maintaining balance. It allows us to enjoy life's pleasures without being controlled by them and to act with discipline in the face of temptation.

The Interdependence of the Stoic Virtues: A Holistic Approach

The four Stoic virtues—wisdom, courage, justice, and temperance—are not isolated qualities. They are deeply interconnected, each one supporting and balancing the others. Wisdom guides us in understanding what is virtuous, while courage gives us the strength to act on that understanding. Justice ensures that our actions are fair and compassionate, and temperance keeps our desires in check, preventing excess.

For example, consider a judge who is tasked with making a difficult ruling in a high-profile case. The judge must rely on wisdom to understand the complexities of the law and the situation. They need courage to make an unpopular decision if it is the right one. Justice compels them to treat all parties fairly, and temperance helps them remain unbiased, avoiding the influence of personal desires or external pressures.

In this way, the Stoic virtues create a holistic framework for ethical living. Together, they provide a comprehensive guide to navigating life's challenges with integrity, clarity, and balance.

The Pillars of a Virtuous Life

These four key virtues—wisdom, courage, justice, and temperance—by cultivating these virtues, we develop the character needed to face life's uncertainties with grace and strength, contribute to the welfare of others, and live in harmony with our true nature. Stoicism teaches that human flourishing depends on living according to these virtues, and by doing so, we can achieve a life of purpose, resilience, and inner peace. Whether in times of success or hardship, the Stoic virtues provide a timeless and practical guide for living with integrity and fulfillment.

Stoic Practices: Negative Visualization, Amor Fati, and Memento Mori

Stoicism, one of the most enduring and practical philosophies, offers a range of practices designed to cultivate resilience, tranquility, and wisdom. Three core Stoic exercises—Negative Visualization, Amor Fati, and Memento Mori—provide unique methods for reframing our experiences and deepening our understanding of life's impermanence, uncertainty, and challenges. These practices encourage us to not only accept the world as it is but to embrace and thrive within it, even when faced with hardship or loss.

In this exploration, we will dive into each of these Stoic practices in detail, uncovering how they work, their underlying principles, and how they can be applied to modern life. Through storytelling and practical examples, these ancient practices will be brought to life, demonstrating their continued relevance in cultivating a more balanced and resilient mindset.

Negative Visualization: Preparing for Life's Challenges

The Power of Imagining the Worst

At first glance, Negative Visualization may seem counterintuitive. After all, why would anyone want to dwell on negative outcomes or imagine worst-case scenarios? However, this practice lies at the heart of Stoic resilience. Known as **premeditatio malorum** (the premeditation of evils), Negative Visualization involves actively imagining potential misfortunes or losses as a way to prepare the mind for life's inevitable difficulties.

The goal of this exercise is not to induce anxiety but to foster acceptance and emotional preparedness. By regularly contemplating what could go wrong—whether it's the loss of a job, a health crisis, or even the death of a loved one—Stoics believe we become better equipped to face these challenges when they arise. This practice teaches us to appreciate what we have and to remain calm in the face of adversity.

Negative Visualization in Action: A Story of Gratitude

Imagine Sophia, a business owner whose company is thriving. Instead of taking her success for granted, she practices Negative Visualization by imagining what would happen if her business failed, if a major client left, or if a global economic downturn impacted her industry. This reflection doesn't leave her paralyzed with fear; instead, it reminds her to be grateful for her current situation and to develop contingency plans should the worst occur.

Negative Visualization helps Sophia appreciate her current success while staying mentally prepared for any setbacks. If a challenge does arise, she is less likely to be caught off guard, as she has already mentally rehearsed the possibility and has considered her responses. The practice does not eliminate grief or hardship but reduces the shock and emotional turmoil that often accompany life's unexpected blows.

The Gratitude Effect

Beyond mental preparedness, Negative Visualization has the added benefit of enhancing gratitude. When we imagine the loss of things we take for granted—our health, relationships, financial stability—it sharpens our appreciation for them. By regularly reflecting on the fragility of life's gifts, we become more present and less likely to complain about minor inconveniences or to feel entitled to continued comfort.

Amor Fati: Embracing Fate with Love

Loving What Happens: The Heart of Amor Fati

Amor Fati, or "love of fate," is another Stoic practice that takes acceptance to the next level. Whereas Negative Visualization prepares us for potential misfortunes, Amor Fati calls for a radical embrace of **everything that happens**, good or bad, as part of the natural order of the universe. It's not enough to simply accept fate—Stoics are encouraged to **love it**.

At its core, Amor Fati reflects the Stoic belief that everything happens for a reason, in accordance with nature, and that our task is to align ourselves with this natural flow rather than resist it. This doesn't mean passivity or resignation. Instead, it means reframing life's challenges as opportunities for growth and viewing obstacles as necessary parts of the journey.

Amor Fati in Action: The Story of Marcus Aurelius

One of the most famous Stoics, Marcus Aurelius, embodied the spirit of Amor Fati during his reign as emperor of Rome. Despite facing military conflicts, political betrayals, personal illness, and the death of multiple children, Marcus continually reminded himself to accept fate's unfolding with grace and strength. Rather than lament his misfortunes, he sought to view each hardship as an opportunity to practice virtue—whether patience, resilience, or wisdom.

For instance, during a military campaign where conditions were harsh and outcomes uncertain, Marcus wrote in his *Meditations*: "The impediment to action advances action. What stands in the way becomes the way." This mindset exemplifies Amor Fati—Marcus saw every obstacle not as a hindrance but as the path itself, a challenge to be met with determination and an open heart.

Amor Fati in Modern Life

In today's world, Amor Fati can be applied in many areas. Consider someone who is unexpectedly laid off from their job. Instead of viewing this event as a catastrophe, they could approach it with the mindset of Amor Fati: What new opportunities does this present? What can I learn from this experience? How can I grow? By embracing the situation rather than resisting it, they might find new paths opening up—perhaps a career change or a chance to pursue long-neglected passions.

Amor Fati teaches us to stop fighting reality and instead flow with it, trusting that even life's hardships are part of a greater unfolding that can lead to personal development and fulfillment.

Memento Mori: Remembering the Impermanence of Life

Confronting Mortality with Memento Mori

Memento Mori—Latin for "Remember you will die"—is a Stoic practice that encourages us to confront our own mortality. Far from being a morbid or nihilistic exercise, Memento Mori is meant to sharpen our focus on what truly matters in life. By regularly reminding ourselves of death's inevitability, we are encouraged to live with greater intention, urgency, and gratitude.

The Stoics believed that the constant awareness of death was essential for living a virtuous life. By contemplating the brevity of existence, we are more likely to prioritize our values, avoid procrastination, and cultivate a sense of purpose. Memento Mori serves as a call to action, urging us to live fully and authentically while we still can.

Memento Mori in Action: The Story of Seneca

Seneca, another prominent Stoic philosopher, often reflected on death in his writings. In his letter to Lucilius, Seneca wrote: "Let us prepare our minds as if we'd come to the very end of life. Let us postpone nothing. Let us balance life's books each day." For Seneca, the awareness of death was not a source of fear but a source of clarity—it allowed him to strip away distractions and focus on what was truly meaningful.

In his later years, when he faced political exile and the eventual command to take his own life by Emperor Nero, Seneca remained calm and composed. Having spent his life practicing Memento Mori, he faced death with acceptance, seeing it as a natural part of life's cycle.

Living with Memento Mori: A Modern Perspective

In modern times, Memento Mori might manifest in how we approach our daily lives. Consider someone who is constantly putting off spending time with their family or pursuing their dreams, thinking they'll "do it later." Memento Mori serves as a reminder that **later may never come**. It encourages us to act now, to say the things we need to say, and to live in alignment with our deepest values.

This practice is especially valuable in reducing procrastination and regrets. By remembering that life is finite, we are motivated to live each day with intention and to make decisions that reflect our true priorities.

Embracing Life Through Stoic Practices

Negative Visualization, Amor Fati, and Memento Mori; each of these three Stoic practices in its own way helps us confront life's inherent uncertainties and challenges with greater resilience, clarity, and acceptance.

Through Negative Visualization, we mentally prepare for life's hardships and cultivate gratitude for what we have. With Amor Fati, we embrace all of life—both the joys and the struggles—as necessary and meaningful parts of our journey. And through Memento Mori, we keep death in mind as a guide for living fully and intentionally. Together, these practices provide a powerful framework for navigating life's complexities, helping us to live with courage, purpose, and grace in the face of whatever fate may bring.

The Role of Virtues in Ethical Living: A Pathway to Flourishing

Virtue ethics, a central approach to ethical thinking that dates back to Aristotle, focuses on the development of moral character rather than adherence to rules or the calculation of consequences. In this framework, virtues are understood as the habits or dispositions that lead to a well-lived life. Unlike moral systems that prescribe what is right or wrong in specific situations, virtue ethics asks, "What kind of person should I be?" The answer lies in cultivating virtues that enable individuals to flourish—both personally and within society.

At the heart of virtue ethics is the idea that ethical living is about becoming a person of character—someone who consistently acts with wisdom, courage, justice, and temperance, among other virtues. This perspective presents ethical development as a lifelong journey of becoming the best version of oneself. In this exploration, we will delve deeply into the nature of virtues, how they guide ethical living, and their practical applications in everyday life.

Understanding Virtue Ethics: Character and Moral Excellence

The Origins of Virtue Ethics: Aristotle's Influence

Virtue ethics originated with Aristotle in his seminal work, the *Nicomachean Ethics*, where he introduced the concept of **eudaimonia**—often translated as flourishing or well-being. Aristotle argued that all human beings aim for eudaimonia, and the path to achieving it lies in the cultivation of virtues. For Aristotle, virtues are not inherent traits but qualities that are developed through habit and practice. Ethical living is thus about continuously developing and refining these virtues over the course of one's life.

Aristotle saw virtues as the golden mean between two extremes—excess and deficiency. For example, courage lies between recklessness (excess) and cowardice (deficiency), and generosity lies between prodigality (excess) and stinginess (deficiency). The virtuous person is someone who strikes the right balance in every situation, acting with reason and moderation.

The Nature of Virtues: Habits, Dispositions, and Excellence

In virtue ethics, a virtue is not simply a moral rule or a one-time action; it is a habit or disposition that is practiced consistently over time. Virtues are qualities of character that define how a person interacts with the world, others, and themselves. Virtue ethics views ethical behavior as a natural extension of being a virtuous person rather than following specific moral directives.

For example, honesty as a virtue is not about telling the truth in a single instance but about being a person who values and practices honesty consistently across various situations. Similarly, kindness is not a one-off action but a disposition to act with compassion and care for others, even when it's difficult or inconvenient.

By cultivating these habits, the individual not only behaves ethically but becomes ethically excellent. Ethical living, in virtue ethics, is about striving to embody the virtues and making them a core part of one's character.

Core Virtues in Ethical Living

Wisdom (Phronesis): The Guiding Virtue

In virtue ethics, wisdom (phronesis) is considered the cardinal virtue that informs and guides all other virtues. Wisdom involves practical reason and the ability to judge what is right in any given situation. Aristotle emphasized that wisdom allows us to discern the **golden mean**—the balanced and appropriate response in each context.

For instance, a wise person knows when to be generous without becoming overly indulgent and when to be assertive without slipping into arrogance. Wisdom integrates experience, ethical principles, and situational awareness to make ethical decisions that are both thoughtful and morally sound.

In modern life, wisdom manifests as the ability to navigate complex social, personal, and professional situations with a sense of balance and integrity. Whether deciding how to approach a difficult conversation or navigating a moral dilemma at work, wisdom is the virtue that allows us to see beyond immediate emotions and act with clarity and purpose.

Courage: The Strength to Act Ethically

Courage is the virtue that enables individuals to face fear, risk, and adversity while remaining true to their ethical values. It is not the absence of fear but the capacity to act in spite of it. In virtue ethics, courage is essential because ethical living often requires us to make difficult choices, confront challenges, and stand up for what is right, even when it is uncomfortable or dangerous.

For example, a person may need courage to **speak out** against injustice in the workplace, even if it threatens their job security. Similarly, it takes courage to **admit a mistake** and make amends, particularly when it involves personal or professional consequences.

Courage in virtue ethics is about maintaining moral integrity and acting according to one's virtues, even when external pressures make it tempting to do otherwise.

Justice: Fairness and the Common Good

Justice is the virtue that governs how we treat others and ensures that we act with fairness, equality, and respect. For the virtue ethicist, justice is not about blind adherence to the law but about a deep commitment to treating people equitably and with dignity.

In Aristotle's view, justice encompasses both **distributive justice** (fair distribution of goods and resources) and **corrective justice** (righting wrongs and addressing inequalities). A just person works to ensure that their actions **contribute to the common good**, recognizing that personal flourishing cannot be separated from the well-being of the broader community.

For example, in professional life, justice might manifest as ensuring that all team members have an equal opportunity to contribute to a project and be recognized for their work. In personal relationships, it means treating friends, family, and even strangers with fairness and respect, acknowledging their inherent dignity.

Temperance: Self-Control and Moderation

Temperance is the virtue of self-control, helping us regulate our desires and impulses in pursuit of the good life. Temperance ensures that we do not overindulge in pleasures or give in to destructive habits, but instead maintain a **balance** that supports ethical living.

This virtue applies not only to physical desires, such as food, drink, or comfort, but also to emotional impulses, such as anger, jealousy, or greed. Temperance allows us to act with **restraint**, ensuring that we are not controlled by fleeting desires or emotions but by our reasoned understanding of what is best for ourselves and others.

A temperate person enjoys life's pleasures but does so in moderation, ensuring that their actions align with their broader goals and values. For example, temperance helps a leader maintain humility and avoid the excesses of power, ensuring that their decisions serve the common good rather than personal ambition.

Virtues as the Foundation of Ethical Living

The Role of Virtues in Personal Development

In virtue ethics, the cultivation of virtues is a process of self-improvement and personal growth. Ethical living is seen as a lifelong practice of becoming a better person, not simply following moral rules. The virtues we develop become habits of character that guide us in every aspect of life, from personal relationships to professional endeavors.

For instance, a person practicing the virtue of honesty will naturally be truthful not only in major situations, like business dealings, but also in the small, everyday interactions of life. Over time, this practice of virtue shapes their character, making honesty a second nature rather than a conscious choice.

Virtue in the Community: Living for the Common Good

Ethical living in virtue ethics also involves recognizing that we are not isolated individuals but part of a larger community. Virtues like justice and generosity guide us to act not only in our own interest but in ways that benefit others and contribute to the common good. In this sense, virtue ethics fosters social harmony and encourages individuals to act in ways that build stronger, more just communities.

Living a Life of Virtue

Virtues Matter. Ethical Living shapes not only individual character but also the broader community. By cultivating virtues such as wisdom, courage, justice, and temperance, we engage in a lifelong journey of becoming ethical individuals who act with integrity, balance, and compassion.

Virtue ethics teaches that ethical living is not about following rigid rules or seeking rewards but about becoming the kind of person who naturally does what is right. By focusing on personal development and embodying the virtues, we move closer to living a life of flourishing, fulfillment, and meaningful contribution to the world around us.

Aristotle's Concept of Eudaimonia: The Pursuit of Human Flourishing

In Aristotle's virtue ethics, eudaimonia is central to understanding the goal of human life. Often translated as "flourishing" or "well-being," eudaimonia goes beyond mere happiness or pleasure. It represents the highest good that humans can achieve, a state of living in accordance with reason and virtue over the course of an entire lifetime. For Aristotle, eudaimonia is not a fleeting emotion but a sustained state of excellence—a life well-lived.

This notion of flourishing is deeply tied to Aristotle's understanding of human nature. According to him, every living being has a purpose or telos—a natural end it seeks to achieve. For humans, that telos is rational activity and virtuous living, both of which enable individuals to fulfill their potential. In this detailed discussion, we will explore Aristotle's nuanced concept of eudaimonia, its relationship to virtue, and how it guides ethical living. Along the way, we will uncover the profound insights Aristotle offers into what it means to lead a flourishing life.

The Nature of Eudaimonia: More Than Happiness

Eudaimonia and the Misconception of Happiness

The English word "happiness" often misrepresents the depth of eudaimonia in Aristotle's philosophy. Whereas happiness in modern contexts can refer to a subjective emotional state, eudaimonia is about objective flourishing. It is not simply feeling good, nor is it about temporary pleasure or comfort. Eudaimonia is achieved through the actualization of human potential, particularly the exercise of reason and the cultivation of virtue.

Aristotle makes a critical distinction between pleasure and flourishing. While pleasure is a natural part of life, it is not the ultimate goal. Many people may pursue pleasure, wealth, or honor, thinking these will bring happiness, but Aristotle argues that these are external goods and, while they may contribute to a flourishing life, they are not sufficient for achieving eudaimonia. True flourishing, according to Aristotle, involves fulfilling our function as rational beings and living virtuously.

Eudaimonia as an Activity, Not a State

One of the key aspects of eudaimonia is that it is not a static state or an end goal that we eventually reach. Instead, Aristotle describes eudaimonia as an activity—a way of living that is continuous and requires ongoing engagement with life. It is not something we acquire and keep but something we actively do throughout our lives. To flourish is to live in accordance with virtue every day, continuously exercising our rational and moral capacities.

For instance, a person may be wealthy or famous, but if they do not live virtuously—if they are unjust, unkind, or reckless—they are not truly flourishing in the Aristotelian sense. Similarly, someone who experiences hardship but lives virtuously, practicing wisdom and temperance in the face of challenges, is closer to eudaimonia.

The Function of Human Beings: Rational Activity

The Concept of Telos: Purpose and Function

To understand eudaimonia, Aristotle's concept of telos—the purpose or function of a thing—is crucial. Aristotle argues that everything in nature has a specific function, and for human beings, that function is rational activity. Humans are distinguished from other living beings by their capacity for reason, and it is through the proper exercise of reason that we achieve eudaimonia.

For Aristotle, the human good is tied to the function that is unique to humans. Since humans possess the ability to reason, it follows that living a rational life—one governed by thoughtful decision-making and the pursuit of virtue—is the way to fulfill our telos. Thus, eudaimonia is deeply connected to living in accordance with reason.

Rational Activity and Virtue

Aristotle sees a clear connection between rational activity and the development of virtue. Virtues are the qualities that enable us to reason well and act in accordance with our rational nature. These virtues—such as wisdom, courage, justice, and temperance—are cultivated through experience, education, and deliberate practice.

For example, the virtue of courage involves rational deliberation about how to act in the face of fear. Courage does not mean rashness or foolhardiness; it is the rational middle ground between recklessness and cowardice. Similarly, temperance involves rational control over desires, ensuring that we enjoy pleasures in moderation without being ruled by them. Aristotle emphasizes that living virtuously is not a matter of following rules but of developing good habits of thought and action.

Virtue and the Role of Practical Wisdom

Practical Wisdom (Phronesis): The Key to Virtuous Living

A critical component of achieving eudaimonia is the development of practical wisdom (phronesis). Practical wisdom is the intellectual virtue that allows us to navigate the complexities of life and make sound decisions about how to act virtuously. It is the ability to apply reason to real-world situations, finding the appropriate response in any given context.

Practical wisdom is not theoretical knowledge or abstract reasoning—it is the capacity to deliberate well about how to live a good life. For example, someone who practices phronesis knows when to speak up for justice and when to remain silent, when to show generosity, and when to practice restraint. Practical wisdom helps us find the golden mean—the right balance between extremes in any given situation.

Virtue as the Mean Between Extremes

In Aristotle's ethics, virtues are often described as the mean between two vices—one of excess and one of deficiency. This concept of the golden mean reflects Aristotle's belief that virtue lies in balance. For instance, the virtue of generosity lies between the extremes of stinginess (deficiency) and wastefulness (excess). Similarly, courage is the mean between recklessness and cowardice.

Aristotle emphasizes that finding the mean requires the exercise of practical wisdom. It is not a matter of strict rules but of understanding the context, one's abilities, and the needs of the situation. Virtue, then, is not about rigidly adhering to principles but about flexibly responding to the complexities of life in a rational and balanced way.

External Goods and the Role of Fortune

The Importance of External Goods in Flourishing

Although eudaimonia is primarily about living virtuously, Aristotle acknowledges that external goods—such as health, wealth, and friendship—also play a role in human flourishing. These goods are not the core of eudaimonia, but they provide the conditions that allow for the exercise of virtue. For example, a person in extreme poverty may find it difficult to cultivate certain virtues, such as generosity, without the material means to support themselves and others.

Aristotle also recognizes that some elements of flourishing are beyond our control. Fortune—good or bad luck—can impact our ability to live well, but it does not define us. While we may face external setbacks, true flourishing comes from how we respond to these circumstances through virtuous action. Eudaimonia, therefore, depends on both external goods and internal virtues, with the latter taking precedence.

Eudaimonia as a Lifelong Process

Flourishing as a Lifetime Achievement

Aristotle stresses that eudaimonia is achieved over the course of a lifetime, not in a single moment or a short period of success. A person can only be said to have flourished if they have lived virtuously and in accordance with reason throughout their life. This long-term perspective on flourishing means that setbacks, failures, and external misfortunes do not preclude eudaimonia, as long as the person consistently practices virtue.

This view also highlights the ongoing nature of ethical development. There is no final point at which a person becomes fully virtuous; instead, the process of becoming virtuous is continuous, involving self-reflection, adjustment, and growth. A flourishing life is one of constant striving toward excellence, guided by practical wisdom and an unwavering commitment to virtue.

Eudaimonia—The Art of Living Well

Eudaimonia is not a fleeting sense of happiness or pleasure but a deep, sustained fulfillment that comes from living in accordance with virtue and reason. It is an active process of becoming the best version of oneself through the cultivation of virtues like wisdom, courage, justice, and temperance. Aristotle's concept of eudaimonia reminds us that flourishing is not about external success or wealth but about the quality of our character and the way we engage with the world around us. By consistently practicing virtue and applying practical wisdom to life's challenges, we can achieve a state of flourishing that transcends temporary pleasures and endures over time, leading to a life of purpose, meaning, and fulfillment.

Developing Practical Wisdom (Phronesis) in Virtue Ethics: The Key to Ethical Living

In Aristotle's virtue ethics, practical wisdom, or phronesis, is regarded as the central intellectual virtue that enables individuals to navigate the complexities of life with ethical clarity and moral excellence. Unlike theoretical knowledge (episteme) or technical skill (techne), phronesis is the ability to make sound decisions in everyday situations, balancing reason, emotion, and circumstance to act virtuously. It is the essential tool that allows us to live a life of eudaimonia—human flourishing.

Practical wisdom is not about following fixed rules or rigid principles; it's about having the judgment to understand the right course of action in the ever-changing dynamics of life. Developing phronesis requires practice, reflection, and an awareness of both oneself and the world. This exploration will delve into the nature of practical wisdom, its relationship with other virtues, and how it can be cultivated to live ethically and purposefully.

The Nature of Phronesis: What Is Practical Wisdom?

Phronesis: The Bridge Between Thought and Action

Practical wisdom, or phronesis, is the capacity to deliberate well about what is good and beneficial in life, not just for oneself but for the broader community. Aristotle emphasized that phronesis is not a theoretical virtue concerned with abstract truths, but a practical virtue that connects thought with action. It allows us to make decisions that lead to virtuous actions in specific contexts.

For example, knowing that generosity is a virtue is not enough. One must also have the practical wisdom to know how and when to be generous. Is it wise to give all your money to someone in need, or is there a more thoughtful way to help them while preserving your own well-being? Phronesis is the ability to navigate these kinds of moral dilemmas.

Aristotle's View of Practical Wisdom

Aristotle defined phronesis as the virtue that helps one achieve the golden mean, the balanced approach between extremes of excess and deficiency. For example, courage lies between recklessness and cowardice, and honesty lies between brutal truthfulness and deceit. Practical wisdom helps us find that balance by considering the context, the individual involved, and the circumstances surrounding the decision.

Aristotle believed that phronesis was central to ethical living because it is the virtue that guides the exercise of all other virtues. Without practical wisdom, virtues like justice, temperance, or courage may be applied incorrectly or inappropriately. Phronesis helps us avoid moral absolutism by teaching us to respond flexibly and thoughtfully to the nuances of real-life situations.

The Role of Phronesis in Ethical Decision-Making

Navigating Complex Moral Situations

One of the hallmarks of practical wisdom is its ability to guide individuals through complex or ambiguous moral situations. Unlike rule-based ethical systems that offer clear-cut answers, virtue ethics acknowledges that life's ethical challenges are rarely black and white. Practical wisdom enables us to read the situation, understand the emotional and social dynamics at play, and act in a way that aligns with our moral values while taking the circumstances into account.

Consider a situation in which a friend asks for advice, but you know that the truth may hurt their feelings. Should you be brutally honest, or should you temper your response to protect their emotions? Practical wisdom allows you to weigh the possible outcomes, the character of your friend, and the nature of your relationship to find a path that is both kind and truthful.

Phronesis as Moral Perception

Phronesis also involves what philosophers call moral perception—the ability to perceive and interpret moral aspects of situations that might not be immediately apparent. People with practical wisdom are often attuned to the subtle moral dimensions of a scenario, recognizing ethical dilemmas where others might not.

For instance, a business leader might be faced with a choice to cut costs by laying off workers. While a purely profit-driven decision might seem logical, a leader with practical wisdom would also consider the human impact of the decision. They would recognize that ethical business leadership involves balancing financial success with fairness and responsibility toward employees.

Cultivating Practical Wisdom: From Theory to Practice

Learning Through Experience

Practical wisdom cannot be learned from books alone—it is cultivated through experience and reflection. Aristotle emphasized that phronesis is developed by engaging with real-life situations, learning from mistakes, and refining one's ability to make good judgments over time. This learning process involves recognizing patterns in human behavior, understanding emotional reactions, and discerning the right course of action in varying circumstances.

Consider the role of a doctor making a difficult decision about a patient's treatment. Over time, through years of practice and facing numerous cases, the doctor develops a sense of judgment that allows them to not only apply medical knowledge but also consider the emotional, social, and personal aspects of patient care. This is the essence of phronesis in action: applying expertise with empathy and wisdom.

The Importance of Mentorship

Aristotle also believed that mentorship plays a crucial role in cultivating practical wisdom. By observing and learning from individuals who consistently demonstrate good judgment, one can internalize the habits and dispositions that lead to wise decision-making. A mentor offers guidance, shares life lessons, and helps develop the ability to navigate ethical challenges with balance and integrity.

In modern life, seeking the advice of trusted mentors—whether they are colleagues, family members, or community leaders—can accelerate the development of practical wisdom. These relationships provide valuable perspectives that help us learn from the experiences of others and refine our own decision-making processes.

Phronesis and the Unity of the Virtues

Practical Wisdom as the Foundation of Virtue

In Aristotle's virtue ethics, phronesis is not just one virtue among many; it is the guiding virtue that ensures all other virtues are applied correctly. This means that virtues like courage, justice, and temperance rely on practical wisdom to be enacted in the right way, at the right time, and for the right reasons.

For example, the virtue of justice requires wisdom to know how to balance fairness and compassion. A wise judge doesn't just follow the letter of the law; they consider the context and individual circumstances of each case. Without practical wisdom, justice can become rigid or blind, leading to unfair outcomes.

Similarly, courage without practical wisdom can turn into recklessness, and generosity without wisdom can lead to financial ruin. Phronesis acts as the unifying force that ensures virtues are not applied in isolation but are harmonized to create a balanced, ethical life.

Practical Wisdom in Modern Life: Applying Phronesis Today

Phronesis in Leadership and Decision-Making

Practical wisdom is highly relevant in today's world, particularly in leadership roles where complex decision-making is required. In business, politics, education, and healthcare, leaders are often confronted with situations where the "right" answer is not immediately clear. Phronesis enables leaders to navigate ethical gray areas, balancing competing interests, values, and outcomes.

A leader with practical wisdom knows when to take decisive action and when to listen, when to stand firm and when to compromise. They are attuned to the broader implications of their decisions, considering how their actions will affect not only immediate stakeholders but also future generations and society at large.

Phronesis in Personal Life

Practical wisdom also plays a crucial role in our personal lives. Whether we are making decisions about relationships, family, or personal goals, phronesis helps us reflect on the long-term impact of our choices and how they align with our deeper values. It encourages us to act with integrity, balance short-term desires with long-term flourishing, and treat others with fairness and empathy.

For example, a parent might use phronesis to decide how to discipline a child, finding a balance between firmness and understanding. The wise parent knows that the goal is not just to enforce rules but to nurture the child's moral development. In this way, practical wisdom helps us make decisions that foster personal and communal flourishing.

Practical Wisdom as the Path to Ethical Mastery

Aristotle's concept of phronesis highlights that ethical living is not about adhering to rigid rules but about developing the capacity to discern the right course of action in every unique situation. Through experience, reflection, and mentorship, we can cultivate practical wisdom in our lives, allowing us to navigate complex ethical challenges with confidence and clarity. In both leadership and personal life, phronesis empowers us to live virtuously, ensuring that our actions contribute to our own flourishing and the well-being of others. By developing practical wisdom, we unlock the potential to live a truly ethical and fulfilling life.

The Dynamic Interaction of Philosophies in Daily Life: CBT, Stoicism, Buddhism, and Virtue Ethics

In the realm of self-improvement and mental well-being, several philosophical frameworks offer unique yet complementary tools to navigate life's complexities. Cognitive Behavioral Therapy (CBT), Stoicism, Buddhism, and Virtue Ethics each provide practical guidance for overcoming challenges, cultivating emotional resilience, and leading a life of purpose and ethical integrity. While these frameworks come from diverse historical and cultural backgrounds, their interaction in daily life can create a comprehensive approach to flourishing.

This exploration will provide a nuanced understanding of how these philosophies dynamically interact, weaving together elements of cognitive restructuring, acceptance, emotional management, and ethical living. In doing so, we will see how CBT's emphasis on thought patterns is reinforced by Stoic and Buddhist practices of acceptance and mindfulness, while Virtue Ethics offers a grounding in moral character that ties these approaches together in a life well-lived.

Cognitive Behavioral Therapy: Restructuring Thought Patterns

The Power of Cognitive Restructuring

Cognitive Behavioral Therapy (CBT) is a therapeutic approach that focuses on identifying and challenging negative thought patterns that contribute to emotional distress. At its core, CBT posits that our thoughts influence our emotions and behaviors, meaning that by altering dysfunctional thinking, we can alleviate anxiety, depression, and other mental health issues.

CBT is highly practical. Imagine a person struggling with anxiety who constantly worries about failure. Through CBT techniques, this person might identify the cognitive distortion of catastrophizing—assuming the worst possible outcome. By reframing these thoughts with more balanced and realistic ones, they can reduce anxiety and approach challenges with greater confidence.

CBT provides a foundation for mental clarity, allowing individuals to untangle the cognitive distortions that cloud judgment. But while it offers an effective method for managing thoughts, it doesn't always address the existential realities of life's inevitable difficulties—enter Stoicism and Buddhism, which provide complementary tools for facing life's uncertainties with equanimity.

Stoicism and Buddhism: Accepting What Cannot Be Changed

Stoic Acceptance: Focusing on What You Can Control

Stoicism, an ancient Greek philosophy, teaches that while we cannot control external events, we can control our reactions to them. This principle is encapsulated in the Dichotomy of Control—a Stoic practice that helps us focus on what is within our power (our thoughts, actions, and responses) and let go of what is not (external circumstances, the behavior of others, and natural events).

When applied in tandem with CBT, Stoicism provides a philosophical anchor for the cognitive restructuring process. For instance, if someone is dealing with rejection, CBT helps them identify irrational thoughts like, "I'm not good enough," while Stoicism adds the insight that rejection is beyond one's control and therefore should not be a source of distress. This perspective encourages the individual to accept the situation as it is, focusing instead on how they can grow from the experience.

Buddhist Detachment: Embracing Impermanence

Buddhism offers a similar approach to Stoicism but with a focus on the nature of impermanence and the practice of detachment. One of the central teachings of Buddhism is that suffering arises from clinging—to people, experiences, outcomes, and desires. By practicing non-attachment, individuals can reduce their suffering by accepting that everything in life is temporary.

In daily life, Buddhism encourages us to cultivate mindfulness and recognize when we are becoming overly attached to specific outcomes. For example, someone anxious about the future may use CBT to challenge distorted thinking patterns, but Buddhism takes this further by encouraging them to embrace uncertainty and live fully in the present moment, without clinging to expectations of what might happen next.

Virtue Ethics: Tying It All Together with Ethical Living

The Role of Virtue in Ethical Growth

While CBT helps manage thoughts and Stoicism and Buddhism offer tools for acceptance, Virtue Ethics provides a framework for ethical living. Developed by Aristotle, this philosophy emphasizes the cultivation of virtues—qualities like wisdom, courage, justice, and temperance—that enable individuals to live a life of eudaimonia (flourishing). In this way, Virtue Ethics shifts the focus from merely avoiding suffering or managing thoughts to becoming the best version of oneself.

Virtue Ethics ties together the practical insights of CBT, Stoicism, and Buddhism by providing an overarching goal: the development of moral character. For example, as someone works to challenge negative thoughts through CBT, they may realize that the virtue of courage is necessary to face their fears. Stoic practices of acceptance help them to avoid excessive worry, while Buddhist mindfulness cultivates temperance, preventing overreaction to life's challenges. Together, these practices enable them to make ethical choices and live in accordance with their values.

Virtue in Action: A Story of Balance

Imagine a person facing a difficult ethical decision at work, such as whether to confront a colleague about unethical behavior. CBT helps this individual manage their self-doubt and fear of conflict by restructuring irrational thoughts. Stoicism reminds them to focus on what is within their control—their own actions and moral stance—while letting go of the anxiety surrounding the outcome. Buddhism helps them detach from the fear of personal loss, knowing that their sense of self-worth does not depend on the approval of others.

Virtue Ethics brings these tools together, guiding the person toward the virtue of justice—the courage to speak out against wrongdoing and the wisdom to do so with kindness and balance. The combination of these philosophies empowers the individual not only to make the right decision but to do so in a way that fosters personal growth and ethical integrity.

The Dynamic Interaction in Daily Life: A Holistic Approach

Integrating Cognitive, Emotional, and Ethical Development

The dynamic interaction of these philosophies offers a holistic approach to personal growth and ethical living. CBT provides a foundation for rational thinking by helping individuals identify and challenge negative thought patterns. Stoicism and Buddhism build on this foundation by teaching acceptance, resilience, and non-attachment in the face of life's inevitable uncertainties. Finally, Virtue Ethics ties everything together by focusing on the development of moral character, ensuring that cognitive clarity and emotional resilience are used in the service of ethical living.

These philosophies do not operate in isolation; they reinforce and deepen one another. For example, the clarity gained through CBT enables better decision-making in accordance with the Dichotomy of Control from Stoicism, while the Buddhist practice of mindfulness enhances the individual's ability to recognize and challenge unhelpful thought patterns. Meanwhile, Virtue Ethics ensures that these practices are not just tools for self-help but part of a larger goal to live a life of meaning and ethical purpose.

Building Resilience and Purpose: A Story of Transformation

Consider the journey of Sarah, who struggles with feelings of inadequacy in both her personal and professional life. Through CBT, Sarah begins to identify her self-critical thought patterns and learns to challenge the belief that she must be perfect to be valued. As she gains cognitive clarity, Stoicism teaches her to focus on what she can control—her efforts and virtues—while letting go of external approval. Buddhism complements this by helping her detach from perfectionism, reminding her that nothing in life, including her own perceived failures, is permanent.

As Sarah progresses, Virtue Ethics offers her a guiding light: the pursuit of personal excellence through virtues like courage, humility, and patience. By integrating these philosophies, Sarah not only overcomes her self-doubt but transforms her life, becoming a person who lives with greater purpose, resilience, and compassion for herself and others.

Flourishing Through the Integration of Philosophy

Harmonizing Thought, Acceptance, and Ethics is the Path to Flourishing. CBT, Stoicism, Buddhism, and Virtue Ethics work together to help individuals navigate challenges, manage emotions, and develop ethical character. CBT offers the foundation for cognitive clarity, while Stoicism and Buddhism provide tools for accepting life's uncertainties. Virtue Ethics elevates this practice by encouraging us to live not just with mental and emotional well-being but with moral integrity and purpose.

By integrating these philosophies, we create a comprehensive approach to flourishing—one that empowers us to think clearly, act ethically, and embrace life's complexities with wisdom, resilience, and grace.

Having explored the foundational concepts of Cognitive Behavioral Therapy, Stoicism, Buddhism, and Virtue Ethics, we now turn to the daily practices and habits that bring these philosophies to life. Theories and frameworks provide invaluable guidance, but their true power emerges through consistent, mindful action. In this section, we will delve into practical techniques such as mindfulness and meditation, journaling for self-reflection, and the art of habit formation. These practices not only help us integrate philosophical insights into our daily routines but also foster greater clarity, emotional resilience, and personal growth. By establishing intentional habits and routines, we can cultivate virtues, challenge negative thoughts, and live more ethically and mindfully, making philosophy a living practice. Let's explore how to transform abstract concepts into everyday actions that support a flourishing life.

3. Building a Life of Mindful Action: Daily Practices for Personal Growth and Virtue

In the journey toward personal growth and ethical living, daily practices play a crucial role in transforming abstract philosophical concepts into tangible actions. The cultivation of habits such as mindfulness and meditation, journaling, and habit formation creates a foundation for lasting change, helping us apply insights from Cognitive Behavioral Therapy, Stoicism, Buddhism, and Virtue Ethics in our everyday lives. These practices not only foster self-awareness and mental clarity but also reinforce the virtues we seek to cultivate, guiding us toward a life of balance, resilience, and purpose. By engaging in these daily routines, we actively shape our thoughts, emotions, and actions, setting the stage for continual personal development and a deeper sense of fulfillment. Let's explore how these powerful tools can be integrated into our lives to enhance well-being and foster a virtuous existence.

Setting Up a Daily Meditation Practice: Cultivating Mindfulness and Inner Peace

In the pursuit of mental clarity, emotional balance, and personal growth, meditation stands as a cornerstone practice. Rooted in both Buddhist and secular mindfulness traditions, meditation is far more than a relaxation technique. It is a discipline that strengthens the mind, fosters self-awareness, and creates space for inner stillness amidst the turbulence of daily life. When practiced consistently, meditation becomes a powerful tool for cultivating mindfulness, reducing stress, and enhancing overall well-being.

However, the key to unlocking the full benefits of meditation lies not in occasional practice but in making it a **daily habit**. Building a regular meditation routine requires both intention and commitment, and understanding how to establish this practice in a sustainable way can significantly enhance the impact it has on your life. In this section, we will explore the foundations of setting up a daily meditation practice, from choosing the right techniques to creating the conditions that support long-term success.

The Foundations of Meditation: What It Is and What It Is Not

Meditation as Mental Training, Not Just Relaxation

While meditation is often associated with relaxation, its true purpose extends far beyond simply calming the mind. At its core, meditation is a form of mental training designed to cultivate mindfulness, awareness, and equanimity. Whether practiced through the lens of Buddhism or modern mindfulness, the primary goal of meditation is to sharpen our attention, deepen our understanding of the present moment, and reduce the habitual patterns of thought that lead to suffering.

Imagine your mind as a wild horse—constantly racing, distracted, and reactive to external stimuli. Meditation is like learning to tame that horse, not by force, but through gentle guidance and consistent effort. It teaches us to observe our thoughts and emotions without being swept away by them, offering a pathway to greater self-control and emotional resilience.

What Meditation Is Not: Common Misconceptions

Before diving into the practice, it's essential to address some common misconceptions about meditation. **Meditation is not about emptying the mind or achieving a state of perpetual bliss**. Thoughts will arise, distractions will occur, and discomfort may surface—this is all part of the process. The practice of meditation is not about eliminating thoughts but learning to observe them without attachment or judgment.

Moreover, meditation is not a quick fix for life's problems. While it can bring a sense of calm and clarity, its deeper purpose is to cultivate a non-reactive awareness that allows us to engage with life's challenges from a place of presence rather than automatic emotional responses.

Getting Started: How to Set Up a Daily Meditation Practice

Choosing the Right Time and Place

Establishing a daily meditation practice begins with creating the right conditions. Meditation requires focus and minimal distractions, so choosing a consistent time and place is essential for building a habit. Early mornings, before the busyness of the day begins, are often an ideal time to meditate, as the mind is typically more quiet and receptive after sleep. However, the best time to meditate is whenever you can commit to practicing regularly.

Your meditation space should be calm, clean, and free of distractions. You don't need a special room or elaborate setup—a quiet corner with a cushion or chair is sufficient. By dedicating a specific space for meditation, you begin to train your mind to associate that environment with mindfulness and stillness.

Starting Small: The Power of Short, Consistent Sessions

When beginning a meditation practice, it's important to start small. Aim for 5 to 10 minutes of meditation per day, gradually increasing the time as you become more comfortable. Short sessions help you build consistency without feeling overwhelmed, and consistency is far more important than long, infrequent sessions.

Imagine planting a seed in a garden. If you water it a little bit every day, the seed will grow steadily. However, if you only water it once a week for an hour, the plant may struggle to thrive. Meditation works in much the same way—regular, brief sessions allow the mind to acclimate to stillness and mindfulness.

Choosing a Technique: Breath Awareness and Body Scan

Two foundational techniques for beginners are breath awareness and body scanning. These practices help anchor the mind and bring attention to the present moment:

- **Breath Awareness**: This involves focusing on the natural rhythm of your breath as it flows in and out of the body. When the mind wanders, gently bring your attention back to the breath. This practice cultivates concentration and reduces mental distractions.
- **Body Scan**: In this technique, you bring awareness to different parts of the body, noticing sensations, tension, or relaxation. This helps to ground your awareness in the physical experience and develop a deep connection between mind and body.

Both of these techniques are accessible to beginners and lay the foundation for more advanced meditation practices. By focusing on the breath or bodily sensations, you train your mind to stay present and less reactive to thoughts or emotions that may arise.

Step-by-Step Guide to Breath Awareness Meditation

Below is a detailed, step-by-step guide to help you perform Breath Awareness Meditation.

1. Choose a Quiet, Comfortable Space

Find a quiet space where you won't be disturbed for the duration of your meditation. This could be a dedicated meditation corner, a room in your home, or even an outdoor space. Ensure the environment is calm and free of distractions.

Tips:

- Turn off your phone or any devices that may disrupt your meditation.
- Wear comfortable clothing that allows you to sit without discomfort.

2. Settle into a Comfortable Posture

Sit in a comfortable position, either on a cushion on the floor or in a chair with your feet flat on the ground. Your spine should be upright but not rigid, creating a stable base for your meditation.

Posture Options:

- **Cross-legged** on a cushion (if sitting on the floor is comfortable for you).
- **In a chair** with feet flat on the floor and hands resting gently on your thighs.

Make sure your body feels supported. Rest your hands on your knees or in your lap, palms facing down or up, whichever feels more natural. If you prefer, you can also lay your hands gently on your belly to feel the movement of your breath.

3. Close Your Eyes or Gaze Softly Ahead

Close your eyes gently to minimize visual distractions and encourage internal focus. If closing your eyes feels uncomfortable, you can lower your gaze to a spot on the floor about a meter in front of you and keep a soft focus.

4. Bring Awareness to Your Body and Posture

Before focusing on the breath, take a moment to **bring awareness to your body**. Notice how your body feels in this seated posture. Scan through your body slowly, noticing any areas of tension, tightness, or relaxation.

Quick Body Scan:

- Start from the top of your head and move down through your shoulders, torso, legs, and feet.
- Make small adjustments to your posture if necessary to feel more relaxed or balanced.

5. Focus on the Sensation of Your Breath

Now bring your awareness to the sensation of your breath. Breathe naturally—there is no need to control or modify your breathing. Simply observe the **natural rhythm** of the breath as it enters and leaves your body.

Where to Focus:

- **Nostrils**: Feel the coolness of the air as you inhale and the warmth as you exhale through your nostrils.
- **Chest or Abdomen**: Notice the gentle rise and fall of your chest or belly with each breath.
- **Throat**: Some people may prefer to notice the flow of air in the throat.

Choose one area to focus on, whichever feels most comfortable or noticeable to you, and keep your attention there.

6. Observe, Don't Control the Breath

Allow the breath to flow naturally, without trying to alter it. Your role is to **observe** the breath as it is—whether it's deep or shallow, fast or slow. The point is not to force a certain type of breathing but to be aware of how your body breathes in the present moment.

If your breath changes naturally as you meditate, simply notice the change without judgment or reaction.

7. Notice When the Mind Wanders

As you sit in meditation, it's natural for your mind to wander. Thoughts, emotions, and distractions will arise. When this happens, don't get frustrated or try to suppress the thoughts. Gently acknowledge that your mind has wandered, and then guide your attention back to the breath.

Common distractions:

- Random thoughts or worries.
- Physical sensations (like an itch or discomfort).
- Sounds in your environment.

When you notice these distractions, calmly bring your focus back to the sensation of breathing, allowing each distraction to pass without engaging in it.

8. Return to the Breath with Patience

Each time your mind wanders, simply bring it back to the breath, without judgment or frustration. Think of this process as a form of mental training—each time you bring your attention back to the breath, you're strengthening your ability to remain present.

Mantra for returning to focus: If it helps, you can silently say a word or phrase to yourself, like "**in**" as you inhale and "**out**" as you exhale, to help keep your focus on the breath.

9. Continue for a Set Time

Set a timer for your meditation to avoid the temptation of checking the clock. For beginners, **5 to 10 minutes** is a great starting point. Gradually, you can extend the duration as you become more comfortable with the practice.

10. Gently Transition Back to Your Day

When the meditation time is over, **do not rush to get up**. Take a moment to **gently bring your awareness back** to your surroundings. Notice how your body feels and how your breath has settled.

- Slowly open your eyes if they were closed.
- Take a few deep breaths and stretch if needed.
- Reflect briefly on how you feel after the meditation.

Tips for Building Consistency in Breath Awareness Meditation

- **Start small**: Begin with short sessions (5-10 minutes) and gradually increase the time as you build your practice.
- **Create a routine**: Meditate at the same time and place each day to build a sustainable habit.
- **Be patient**: Progress in meditation is gradual; the key is consistency, not perfection.

- **Use guided meditations**: If you find it difficult to focus on your own, use a guided meditation app or video to help guide your practice.
- **Track your practice**: Keeping a meditation journal can help you reflect on your progress and stay motivated.

By anchoring your attention on the breath, you develop greater mindfulness, focus, and emotional resilience, qualities that extend into your daily life. As you continue practicing, you'll find that meditation becomes a grounding force that brings peace and clarity, no matter how chaotic life may seem. Through daily commitment to Breath Awareness Meditation, you cultivate a deeper connection to yourself and the present moment, paving the way for lasting inner calm and mindfulness.

Step-by-Step Guide to Body Scan Meditation

Below is a detailed, step-by-step guide to help you perform a Body Scan Meditation.

1. Find a Quiet, Comfortable Space

Choose a quiet space where you can relax and focus without interruptions. The environment should be calm, with minimal distractions, allowing you to fully immerse yourself in the meditation.

Tips:

- Turn off your phone or other devices that might disturb you.
- Wear comfortable, loose-fitting clothes.
- Dim the lights or use soft lighting to create a peaceful atmosphere.

2. Choose a Comfortable Posture: Sitting or Lying Down

You can perform a Body Scan Meditation either **sitting** or **lying down**. Choose whichever position allows you to feel most relaxed and supported.

- **Lying down**: Lie on your back with your arms resting comfortably by your sides and legs extended. Your feet should be slightly apart, and your head should rest in a neutral position.
- **Sitting**: If you prefer to sit, find a comfortable chair or sit cross-legged on a cushion. Keep your back straight but not rigid, with your hands resting on your thighs or in your lap.

Tip: If you are lying down, consider using a cushion under your head or knees for added comfort, but avoid becoming so comfortable that you fall asleep.

3. Close Your Eyes and Focus on Your Breath

Once you are settled in your position, gently close your eyes to help bring your attention inward. Begin by taking a few deep breaths to relax your body and mind.

Breathing exercise:

- Inhale deeply through your nose, filling your lungs completely.
- Exhale slowly through your mouth, releasing any tension or tightness in your body.
- Take 3-5 deep breaths in this way, then allow your breathing to return to its natural rhythm.

As your breath returns to its normal pace, let it be a **gentle anchor** for your awareness, but don't try to control it. Simply observe the sensation of the breath entering and leaving your body, using it as a way to relax and focus.

4. Begin the Body Scan: Focus on the Head and Face

Now, begin the body scan by directing your attention to the **top of your head** and **face**. Slowly bring your awareness to any sensations you may notice in this area, such as warmth, tingling, tightness, or relaxation.

Guide for scanning the head and face:

- Notice the sensations in your **scalp** and the **crown of your head**.
- Bring awareness to your **forehead**, allowing any tension there to soften.
- Move down to your **eyes**, noticing whether they feel relaxed or strained.
- Bring your attention to your **jaw**, which is a common area for tension. If you notice tightness, consciously relax the muscles here.

5. Move to the Neck and Shoulders

Once you have spent time focusing on your head and face, gently shift your attention to your **neck** and **shoulders**.

- Notice if there is any tightness or discomfort in your **neck**. If you find tension, take a slow, deep breath and allow that area to soften with each exhale.
- Bring your awareness to your **shoulders**, which often carry the weight of stress. As you breathe, let go of any tension, feeling your shoulders relax and sink naturally into the floor or chair.

6. Focus on the Arms and Hands

Next, bring your attention to your **arms**, moving from the upper arms down to your **hands** and **fingers**.

- Notice the sensations in your **upper arms**—any tightness, heaviness, or lightness.
- Gradually move down to your **elbows**, **forearms**, and **wrists**.

- Finally, focus on your **hands**. Notice if they are warm or cold, tense or relaxed. Become aware of each **finger**, and observe any sensations, even subtle ones.

7. Scan the Chest and Upper Back

Now, shift your awareness to your **chest** and **upper back**.

- As you inhale, notice the natural rise and fall of your **chest** with each breath.
- Feel any sensations in the **upper back**, being mindful of any areas of tension or discomfort.
- If you find tightness, imagine each exhale softening and relaxing that area.

8. Move to the Abdomen and Lower Back

Bring your attention to your **abdomen** and **lower back**.

- As you breathe naturally, notice the gentle movement of your **abdomen**—rising with the inhale and falling with the exhale.
- Become aware of any sensations in the **lower back**, where tension may accumulate. If you detect any discomfort, let your breath soften that area.

9. Focus on the Hips, Pelvis, and Buttocks

Now, direct your attention to your **hips**, **pelvis**, and **buttocks**.

- Become aware of how these areas feel as they make contact with the chair or floor. Are they tense, relaxed, or neutral?
- Observe the sensations in your **pelvic area** without judgment, simply acknowledging any discomfort or tension.

10. Scan the Legs and Feet

Finally, bring your attention to your **legs**, moving from the **thighs** down to the **feet**.

- Start with your **upper legs**, noticing any sensations in your **thighs** and **hamstrings**.
- Move down to your **knees**, **shins**, and **calves**. Are these areas heavy, light, warm, or tense?
- Focus on your **ankles**, **feet**, and **toes**. Feel the contact between your feet and the floor. Notice any sensations, such as tingling, warmth, or relaxation.

11. Expand Your Awareness to the Entire Body

Once you've completed the scan, take a moment to expand your awareness to your **entire body** as a whole. Feel the connection between all the parts of your body and the floor or chair beneath you.

Notice how your body feels after the scan. You may feel more relaxed, more connected to your physical self, or simply more aware of any areas that were holding tension.

12. Gently Transition Out of the Meditation

When you're ready to end the meditation, **gently bring your attention back** to your surroundings. Slowly deepen your breath, and take a few moments to observe how your body feels after the practice.

- If your eyes are closed, gently open them.
- Take a few gentle stretches or wiggle your fingers and toes to reawaken your body.
- Reflect on the experience before getting up or moving on with your day.

Tips for Deepening Your Practice

- **Start with short sessions**: If you're new to Body Scan Meditation, start with 5-10 minutes and gradually extend the time as you become more comfortable.
- **Be patient with distractions**: It's normal for your mind to wander during the body scan. When you notice your attention drifting, gently bring it back to the part of the body you were focused on.
- **Use guided meditations**: If you're having trouble staying focused, try using a guided Body Scan Meditation from an app or audio recording until you become more familiar with the practice.
- **Practice regularly**: The more frequently you engage in Body Scan Meditation, the more mindful and connected you will become to your body and its sensations.

By methodically bringing attention to each part of the body, you cultivate greater **mindfulness, self-awareness**, and **stress relief**. Through consistent practice, you will develop a stronger connection between your mind and body, allowing you to carry this presence and calm into daily life. Whether used to manage stress, enhance relaxation, or simply foster mindfulness, Body Scan Meditation is a powerful tool for achieving greater balance and well-being.

Overcoming Common Obstacles: Persistence Through Discomfort

Dealing with Restlessness and Boredom

One of the most common challenges beginners face in meditation is restlessness or boredom. Sitting still, even for a few minutes, can feel uncomfortable or tedious, and the mind may rebel by wandering or urging you to quit. These moments are an opportunity to practice patience and compassion toward yourself. Instead of resisting or judging these feelings, acknowledge them and return to your breath or focus point. Over time, this practice strengthens your ability to stay grounded in the face of discomfort.

Remember, discomfort is part of the process. Much like physical exercise strengthens muscles through resistance, meditation strengthens the mind through moments of distraction and restlessness.

Managing Expectations: Progress Is Not Linear

Another obstacle to maintaining a meditation practice is the expectation of immediate results. Many people start meditating with the hope of achieving instant calm or enlightenment, only to feel frustrated when their mind remains busy or their emotions remain turbulent. It's important to recognize that progress in meditation is not linear. Some days, your mind will be calm and focused, while other days it will be chaotic.

Think of meditation as a long-term investment in your mental and emotional well-being. The benefits accumulate over time through consistent practice. Each session, no matter how difficult or distracting, contributes to the gradual development of mindfulness and inner peace.

The Benefits of a Daily Meditation Practice

Cultivating Mindfulness and Emotional Resilience

One of the most profound benefits of meditation is the cultivation of mindfulness—the ability to stay present in the moment, observing thoughts and feelings without becoming overwhelmed by them. This skill extends beyond the meditation cushion and into daily life. With regular practice, you may find yourself reacting less impulsively to stressful situations, feeling more grounded in your emotions, and gaining a deeper understanding of yourself.

For example, if you're stuck in traffic, instead of reacting with frustration or anger, meditation allows you to recognize those feelings, take a deep breath, and remain calm. Over time, this mindfulness becomes a default response, helping you navigate life's challenges with greater ease.

Enhancing Focus, Clarity, and Well-Being

Meditation also sharpens mental clarity and focus, improving your ability to concentrate on tasks and make clear decisions. This is particularly valuable in today's fast-paced world, where distractions are constant, and the mind is often pulled in many directions. By regularly training your attention through meditation, you enhance your ability to stay present and focused on what truly matters.

Additionally, meditation has been shown to reduce stress, lower anxiety, and increase overall feelings of well-being. Studies have demonstrated that consistent meditation practice can even lead to changes in the brain, improving emotional regulation and resilience.

Planting the Seed of Meditation for Lifelong Growth

A daily meditation practice is not just a tool for relaxation—it is a path toward cultivating mindfulness, emotional resilience, and self-awareness. By setting up a consistent practice, starting small, and choosing techniques that resonate with you, you plant the seed for lifelong mental and emotional growth. As you progress, meditation becomes more than a daily routine—it becomes a way of living, guiding your actions, thoughts, and interactions with greater presence and clarity. By integrating meditation into your daily life, you set the stage for flourishing, cultivating not only peace of mind but also a deeper connection to yourself and the world around you.

Mindfulness in Everyday Activities: Bringing Awareness into Daily Life

While formal meditation practices like sitting meditation or body scan meditation are crucial for cultivating mindfulness, the real power of mindfulness is revealed when it becomes integrated into the everyday activities of life. Mindfulness in everyday activities involves bringing a moment-to-moment awareness to ordinary tasks such as eating, walking, or even doing chores. It's about transforming mundane moments into opportunities for presence and deep connection with the present moment.

Mindfulness in everyday life is not about creating a special time or place for awareness but about weaving mindfulness into the fabric of daily existence. This practice can foster greater mental clarity, reduce stress, and help individuals reconnect with themselves and the world around them. In this exploration, we will delve into how mindfulness can be applied in various daily activities, providing practical tools to create a life that is not only more aware but also more meaningful.

The Concept of Mindfulness in Daily Life

Beyond the Cushion: Expanding Mindfulness Beyond Formal Practice

Traditionally, mindfulness has been associated with sitting meditation practices, where practitioners engage in structured sessions to cultivate awareness and mental clarity. However, mindfulness is not limited to a set time on the meditation cushion. In fact, its most transformative benefits occur when applied to everyday activities, allowing you to bring full awareness to the present moment, regardless of the task at hand.

The goal of mindfulness in daily activities is to make even the simplest actions—like washing dishes or walking—opportunities for deep presence. Instead of operating on autopilot, where the mind wanders or becomes preoccupied with the past or future, mindfulness encourages us to fully engage with whatever we are doing, paying attention to sensations, emotions, and thoughts as they arise.

Consider the act of brushing your teeth. Normally, you might rush through this task while thinking about the day ahead. With mindfulness, brushing your teeth becomes an opportunity to focus on the sensation of the toothbrush, the taste of the toothpaste, and the rhythm of your hand movements. This brings you into the present moment and fosters a sense of calm and focus.

The Present Moment as a Path to Clarity

At its core, mindfulness is about cultivating awareness of the present moment. Our minds have a natural tendency to drift into thoughts about the past or the future—worrying about what might happen or ruminating on what has already occurred. In everyday activities, this mental drift often leads to a sense of disconnection, where we miss out on the richness of life unfolding in the present.

By applying mindfulness to daily activities, we can step out of this mental fog and engage with what is happening right now. This presence not only makes mundane tasks more enjoyable but also reduces stress, as mindfulness encourages us to let go of unnecessary mental chatter and focus on the task at hand.

Everyday Activities as Opportunities for Mindfulness

Eating Mindfully: Savoring Each Bite

One of the most accessible ways to integrate mindfulness into daily life is through mindful eating. Often, we eat while distracted—watching TV, checking our phones, or rushing through meals to get on with the day. When we eat mindlessly, we miss the opportunity to truly savor the flavors, textures, and aromas of our food.

Mindful eating involves slowing down and paying close attention to the entire eating process. This includes observing the colors and textures of the food on your plate, noticing the smells before taking a bite, and being aware of the sensations as you chew and swallow. By bringing full awareness to the act of eating, you not only enjoy your food more but also become more in tune with your body's hunger and fullness signals.

Imagine eating a single raisin. With mindful eating, you would examine the raisin's texture, feel it in your hand, and notice its smell before placing it in your mouth. As you chew slowly, you'd pay attention to the changing flavors and sensations. This simple practice transforms eating into a meditative experience, fostering gratitude and awareness.

Walking Meditation: Moving with Intention

Another powerful way to integrate mindfulness into daily life is through walking meditation. Walking is something we do every day, but we rarely pay attention to the sensations of our feet on the ground or the movement of our body. Walking meditation is about slowing down and bringing awareness to every step, treating the act of walking as a deliberate and mindful experience.

To practice walking meditation, start by walking slowly in a quiet space. Focus on the sensation of your feet touching the ground, noticing how your weight shifts with each step. Pay attention to the movement of your legs, the sway of your arms, and the rhythm of your breath as you walk. Whenever your mind wanders, gently bring it back to the physical sensations of walking.

By engaging in walking meditation, even a simple walk through the park can become an opportunity to connect with the present and foster a sense of inner calm.

Mindful Listening: Being Present with Others

Mindfulness can also enhance your interactions with others. Mindful listening involves giving someone your full, undivided attention, without interrupting or thinking about what you'll say next. In our fast-paced world, we often listen to respond rather than to truly hear the other person.

To practice mindful listening, focus on the speaker's words, tone, and body language. Notice how you feel while listening and resist the urge to judge or mentally prepare your response. This kind of presence not only deepens your connection with others but also fosters greater compassion and understanding in relationships.

Cleaning Mindfully: Finding Joy in Mundane Tasks

Even routine tasks like cleaning or washing dishes can be transformed into opportunities for mindfulness. Instead of seeing these activities as chores to rush through, bring your full attention to the physical sensations involved.

When washing dishes, for example, focus on the feeling of the warm water, the texture of the soap, and the sound of the running tap. Rather than letting your mind wander, stay present with the task, noticing the simple joy of accomplishing something with intention and focus. This approach not only makes mundane tasks more enjoyable but also provides a sense of grounding in the present moment.

The Benefits of Mindfulness in Everyday Life

Reducing Stress and Enhancing Well-Being

One of the most significant benefits of bringing mindfulness into daily activities is the reduction of stress. When we are fully present with what we are doing, we naturally let go of worries about the future and regrets about the past. This presence fosters a sense of calm and equanimity, allowing us to approach life's challenges with greater clarity and resilience.

Mindfulness also enhances overall well-being by helping us reconnect with the simple pleasures of life—whether it's enjoying a meal, feeling the warmth of the sun, or taking a deep breath. When we are present, even the most routine activities can become sources of contentment and joy.

Strengthening Focus and Productivity

By practicing mindfulness in everyday tasks, you can also improve your focus and productivity. When you give your full attention to a task, you're less likely to become distracted or overwhelmed by competing demands. This heightened focus allows you to work more efficiently and with greater satisfaction.

Living Fully Through Mindful Engagement

Every Moment Matters. By practicing mindfulness in routine tasks—such as eating, walking, and even cleaning—you unlock opportunities for greater presence, clarity, and inner peace. These moments of mindful engagement serve as reminders that life's richness is not found in the distant future but in the here and now. Through consistent mindfulness in daily activities, you begin to cultivate a deeper sense of connection with yourself and the world around you, enhancing both your well-being and your relationships. In doing so, you transform the ordinary into the extraordinary, living a life that is fully engaged, meaningful, and present.

CBT Thought Records: Unlocking the Power of Self-Reflection for Cognitive Restructuring

In Cognitive Behavioral Therapy (CBT), one of the most effective tools for identifying and changing unhelpful thought patterns is the thought record. Thought records allow individuals to systematically examine their thoughts, emotions, and behaviors in response to specific situations. By doing so, they gain insight into the cognitive distortions that may be driving emotional distress or problematic behaviors. The ultimate goal of using thought records is to challenge and reframe those distortions, fostering a more balanced and realistic view of the world.

A CBT thought record is more than just a journaling exercise; it is a structured way to dissect automatic thoughts and identify underlying beliefs that may be contributing to negative emotional states like anxiety or depression. In this exploration, we will dive deep into the mechanics of a thought record, explain how it can be used to develop cognitive resilience, and illustrate how it fits into the broader landscape of self-reflective practices.

Understanding the Role of Thought Records in CBT

Cognitive Behavioral Therapy and the Thought-Emotion-Behavior Cycle

At the heart of CBT is the idea that thoughts, emotions, and behaviors are interrelated. Our thoughts shape our emotional responses to situations, and those emotions drive our behaviors. When someone is stuck in a negative cycle—such as feeling anxious or depressed—this can often be traced back to distorted thinking patterns.

The thought record is a tool designed to break this cycle. By recording the specific thoughts, emotions, and behaviors that arise in a challenging situation, individuals can begin to see patterns in their thinking. Often, these patterns reveal cognitive distortions, such as catastrophizing, black-and-white thinking, or personalization. Once identified, these distortions can be challenged and replaced with more balanced, reality-based thinking.

The Function of Thought Records in Cognitive Restructuring

Thought records serve the purpose of cognitive restructuring, a process through which individuals examine their negative automatic thoughts and replace them with more constructive alternatives. By encouraging reflection, thought records allow individuals to:

- **Identify triggers** that lead to negative thoughts or emotional responses.
- **Understand the connection** between thoughts and emotions.
- **Evaluate the evidence** for and against their automatic thoughts.
- **Develop alternative thoughts** that are more realistic and less distressing.

Breaking Down the Components of a Thought Record

1. Identifying the Situation: Context is Key

The first step in completing a thought record is to identify the situation that triggered the emotional response. This could be an external event, a specific conversation, or even a memory or thought that caused distress. Describing the situation in detail helps provide context and clarity for the thought analysis that follows.

For example, a person might write, "I received critical feedback from my boss during a meeting," as the situation. By capturing the context, it becomes easier to understand what prompted the cascade of thoughts and emotions.

2. Recording Emotional Reactions: Naming the Feelings

The next step is to identify and name the emotions that arose in response to the situation. It's important to be specific when describing these emotions. Instead of using vague terms like "bad" or "upset," focus on more precise emotional language, such as anxiety, sadness, anger, or frustration.

It's also helpful to rate the intensity of each emotion on a scale of 1 to 10. This rating provides a useful baseline for later reflection, especially when you revisit the situation with new insights.

In our example, the individual might record emotions like:

- **Anxiety** (7/10)
- **Frustration** (5/10)

3. Identifying Automatic Thoughts: The Mental Narrative

Once the emotional reactions have been recorded, the next step is to identify the automatic thoughts that occurred in response to the situation. These are the initial, often unfiltered thoughts that pop into our minds when faced with a stressor or trigger. Automatic thoughts are typically fleeting and can feel deeply ingrained, making them difficult to recognize without conscious effort.

Common automatic thoughts might include statements like:

- "I'm terrible at my job."
- "I'll never succeed."
- "Everyone thinks I'm incompetent."

In our example, the individual may have had automatic thoughts such as, "My boss thinks I'm incompetent," or "I'll never be able to fix this mistake."

4. Evaluating the Evidence: Is This Thought Really True?

With the automatic thoughts identified, the next step is to evaluate the evidence for and against those thoughts. This involves looking at the situation from a more objective standpoint, asking questions like:

- What facts support this thought?
- What facts contradict this thought?

- What alternative explanations could there be?

This step is critical in challenging cognitive distortions because it forces the individual to take a step back from their emotional reaction and evaluate the situation with a more balanced perspective.

For instance, the individual may find that there is no evidence to suggest that their boss thinks they are incompetent. Instead, the feedback may have been about a specific mistake that can be corrected. They might also realize that they've received praise from their boss in the past, contradicting the belief that they are "terrible" at their job.

5. Developing Alternative Thoughts: Reframing the Situation

Once the evidence has been evaluated, the next step is to generate alternative thoughts that are more realistic and balanced. These thoughts should reflect the evidence gathered and offer a less emotionally charged interpretation of the situation.

In our example, the individual might develop alternative thoughts like:

- "My boss gave me feedback to help me improve, not because they think I'm incompetent."
- "I made a mistake, but I can learn from it and do better next time."

These alternative thoughts help reframe the situation, reducing the emotional intensity and allowing for a more constructive response.

6. Reassessing Emotional Responses: Measuring the Shift

Finally, after developing alternative thoughts, it's important to reassess the emotional reactions. How do the emotions change after challenging the automatic thoughts? This step helps measure the effectiveness of cognitive restructuring and provides insight into how much emotional relief can be achieved through balanced thinking.

For example, after reframing the situation, the individual's anxiety might decrease from a 7/10 to a 4/10, and their frustration might drop to a 2/10. This shift indicates that the process of using the thought record has helped alleviate emotional distress.

How Thought Records Promote Cognitive Growth

Gaining Insight into Patterns

As individuals use thought records regularly, they begin to notice patterns in their thinking. Certain triggers may repeatedly lead to the same cognitive distortions, such as catastrophizing or all-or-nothing thinking. By tracking these patterns, individuals can become more proactive in challenging their automatic thoughts before they spiral into emotional distress.

Empowering Self-Regulation

Thought records foster a sense of self-regulation by giving individuals the tools to manage their thoughts and emotions independently. Instead of feeling overwhelmed by negative emotions, individuals can take control of their cognitive processes, leading to greater emotional resilience and mental well-being.

Enhancing Problem-Solving Skills

By encouraging individuals to evaluate situations objectively, thought records also improve problem-solving skills. Rather than being caught in the loop of negative thinking, individuals can approach challenges with a clearer, more solution-oriented mindset.

Rewriting the Mental Narrative

By using thought records, individuals can dissect negative thought patterns, challenge cognitive distortions, and replace automatic reactions with more balanced, rational interpretations. This process not only fosters emotional well-being but also empowers individuals to approach life's challenges with greater clarity and resilience. Through consistent use, thought records become a powerful tool for self-reflection and personal growth, providing a structured way to untangle the mental narratives that often lead to distress. With time, this practice can help reshape the way individuals engage with their thoughts, emotions, and the world around them, leading to a life of greater balance, emotional intelligence, and mental strength.

Stoic Reflection and Evening Review: Cultivating Virtue Through Daily Self-Examination

One of the core practices in Stoicism is the regular habit of self-reflection, particularly at the end of each day. Ancient Stoics like Seneca and Marcus Aurelius emphasized the importance of reviewing one's thoughts, actions, and emotions to align with their values and to cultivate virtue. This practice, often referred to as the Evening Review, is more than a simple reflection—it is a disciplined approach to examining how well one lived according to Stoic principles and correcting any missteps.

The Evening Review not only fosters personal growth but also strengthens one's ability to act with wisdom, courage, justice, and temperance in daily life. It is a moment of quiet introspection that encourages Stoics to evaluate their day in light of the things they can control (their actions and responses) and those they cannot (external events). In this exploration, we will dive deeply into the nature of Stoic reflection, provide practical guidance for practicing the Evening Review, and illustrate how this ancient technique can be a transformative tool for modern life.

The Foundation of Stoic Reflection

The Importance of Self-Examination in Stoicism

Stoicism is fundamentally a philosophy of action—one that aims to guide individuals toward virtuous living. To live virtuously, the Stoics understood that it wasn't enough to passively accept the teachings of wisdom; one must actively apply them in daily life. This is where the practice of self-examination becomes indispensable.

For the Stoics, reflection is a tool for maintaining moral accountability and for correcting the natural tendencies toward selfishness, impulsivity, and ignorance. Seneca, in his letters, described his practice of self-review every evening, recounting how he would ask himself about what he did well, what he did poorly, and how he could improve. By doing this consistently, he aimed to sharpen his ability to live according to reason and virtue.

This kind of moral inventory allows individuals to reflect on their actions with honesty, evaluate where they might have strayed from their values, and recommit to living with virtue the next day. It is an ongoing process that leads to greater self-awareness and a deeper understanding of what it means to live a good life.

Living According to Stoic Virtues

The goal of the Evening Review is not to judge oneself harshly but to assess whether one's thoughts and actions aligned with the four cardinal virtues of Stoicism: wisdom, courage, justice, and temperance. These virtues provide the guiding framework for ethical behavior and right action.

- **Wisdom** involves seeing things clearly and acting with understanding.
- **Courage** is the strength to face difficulties without shrinking away.
- **Justice** represents fairness and acting with consideration for others.
- **Temperance** is self-control, moderation, and the ability to balance desires.

By reflecting on how well these virtues were upheld during the day, one can develop greater moral clarity and cultivate the ability to act virtuously in future situations.

The Practice of the Stoic Evening Review

Setting the Stage for Reflection: Creating the Right Environment

Before engaging in the Evening Review, it is important to create a conducive environment for reflection. The practice requires a quiet and calm space, free from distractions, where you can think deeply about the events of the day.

While this reflection can be done mentally, many Stoics and modern practitioners find value in journaling their reflections. Writing down your thoughts creates a tangible record of your progress and allows you to see patterns over time. Choose a journal that is dedicated solely to your Stoic reflections, and keep it somewhere easily accessible.

Step 1: Recalling the Day's Events

Begin the review by mentally revisiting the events of the day. Try to recall specific situations in which you interacted with others, made decisions, or reacted emotionally. It's important to approach this process with curiosity and openness, rather than judgment. Simply recount what happened, paying attention to moments where you felt challenged or emotionally stirred.

You might ask yourself:

- What happened today?
- What situations brought up strong emotions or reactions?
- Where did I face challenges or adversity?

Step 2: Analyzing Actions and Reactions

Once you've recalled the day's events, the next step is to analyze how you responded to those situations. This is where Stoic philosophy comes into play—examine whether your thoughts and actions were aligned with the Stoic virtues.

Consider the following questions as part of your self-examination:

- **Wisdom**: Did I approach today's challenges with clarity and reason? Did I act based on understanding or emotion?
- **Courage**: Did I face difficulties with bravery, or did I shy away from uncomfortable situations?
- **Justice**: Was I fair and kind in my interactions with others? Did I treat people with respect and consideration?

- **Temperance**: Was I moderate in my desires and actions, or did I give in to excess?

For example, if you had a disagreement at work, reflect on how you handled the conflict. Did you act impulsively, or did you pause to consider the most just and fair response? If you acted out of anger, how could you approach similar situations differently in the future?

Step 3: Identifying Cognitive Distortions

Just as CBT uses thought records to challenge **cognitive distortions**, the Stoic Evening Review helps individuals identify areas where their thinking might have been irrational or unhelpful. Stoicism teaches that **it's not events that disturb us, but our judgments about them**.

As you reflect, ask yourself:

- Did I let external events affect my inner peace?
- Was I overly concerned with things outside my control?
- Did I catastrophize or make assumptions about what others were thinking?

By identifying these distortions, you can better prepare yourself to respond with reason and clarity when similar situations arise.

Step 4: Learning from Mistakes

One of the most valuable aspects of the Stoic Evening Review is the ability to learn from mistakes without self-criticism. The Stoics believed that errors are part of the human condition, and instead of feeling guilty, we should use our mistakes as opportunities for growth.

As you reflect on moments where you fell short of your ideals, ask yourself:

- What can I learn from this?
- How can I improve my response next time?
- What virtues can I cultivate to handle similar situations more effectively?

For example, if you noticed that you lacked patience in a conversation, acknowledge this without judgment and consider how you might practice temperance or understanding in the future.

Step 5: Reaffirming Commitment to Virtue

The final step in the Stoic Evening Review is to reaffirm your commitment to living in accordance with Stoic virtues. This process is not about dwelling on past mistakes but about preparing to meet the next day with greater wisdom, courage, justice, and temperance.

Consider closing your reflection with a positive statement of intention. For example:

- "Tomorrow, I will strive to act with greater patience and understanding."
- "I commit to responding to challenges with courage and composure."

By reaffirming these commitments, you set the stage for continued moral growth and resilience.

How the Evening Review Enhances Stoic Practice

Developing Greater Self-Awareness

The daily practice of reviewing one's thoughts and actions fosters greater self-awareness, a key component of Stoic philosophy. Over time, this awareness extends beyond the review itself and begins to influence how you act in the moment. By regularly reflecting on your actions, you develop the ability to observe your reactions in real time, allowing you to make more virtuous choices.

Strengthening Emotional Resilience

The Stoic Evening Review also strengthens emotional resilience. By confronting your emotions honestly and examining them through the lens of Stoic wisdom, you become better equipped to handle life's challenges with equanimity. You learn to detach from external outcomes and focus on what you can control—your thoughts, actions, and responses.

Fostering Continuous Personal Growth

Stoicism is not about achieving perfection but about engaging in the process of continuous self-improvement. The Evening Review provides a structured way to grow in virtue each day. Through this regular practice, you learn to approach mistakes with compassion, view challenges as opportunities for growth, and gradually align your life more closely with Stoic ideals.

Ending the Day with Purpose and Clarity

By taking time each evening to reflect on your actions, analyze your thoughts, and reaffirm your commitment to virtue, you engage in a lifelong process of self-improvement. The Stoic Evening Review is a powerful tool for transforming everyday experiences into opportunities for growth. Through this practice, you cultivate greater self-awareness, learn from mistakes, and become more adept at navigating life's challenges with wisdom and composure. As you continue to integrate this reflective practice into your daily routine, you will find yourself living with greater purpose, clarity, and inner peace.

Virtue Tracking and Reflection: Cultivating Moral Growth Through Self-Examination

In the quest to live a life guided by virtue, self-reflection becomes an essential tool for personal growth. While philosophies like Virtue Ethics and Stoicism emphasize the importance of virtues such as wisdom, courage, justice, and temperance, it is through regular practice and self-examination that these virtues are truly cultivated. One powerful technique for fostering moral development is the practice of virtue tracking and reflection—a journaling method that encourages individuals to assess how well they embody their chosen virtues in daily life.

Virtue tracking is more than simply recording actions; it is a structured approach to consciously monitoring and evaluating how aligned your behaviors are with your moral values. This practice helps bring abstract virtues to life by making them concrete, actionable, and observable. Through consistent reflection, individuals can identify patterns, celebrate progress, and course-correct where needed, ensuring that they are on a continuous path toward living a more virtuous life.

Understanding Virtue Tracking and Its Purpose

What is Virtue Tracking?

Virtue tracking is the practice of regularly documenting and assessing how well you live in accordance with specific virtues. Unlike general journaling, which may focus on thoughts or feelings, virtue tracking is laser-focused on the ethical dimension of your actions. It involves creating a system—whether through a formal journal or a digital log—where you record your daily or weekly reflections on how well you practiced particular virtues.

The idea of tracking virtues can be traced back to figures like Benjamin Franklin, who famously created a chart to monitor his progress in practicing 13 virtues, including temperance, sincerity, and humility. Franklin believed that by systematically focusing on one virtue at a time, he could improve himself over time. Similarly, virtue tracking in modern times allows individuals to bring intentionality to their moral development, offering a tangible way to measure ethical progress.

Why Track Virtues?

Virtue tracking serves several purposes in the development of character:

1. **Accountability**: By writing down and reviewing your actions, you hold yourself accountable to your moral goals. This prevents you from slipping into mindless behaviors that are misaligned with your values.
2. **Self-Awareness**: Regular reflection builds greater **self-awareness**, helping you to recognize both strengths and areas for improvement in your ethical life.
3. **Growth Mindset**: Rather than seeing virtues as static traits, virtue tracking encourages a **growth mindset**—the belief that virtues can be cultivated and strengthened through practice and effort.
4. **Clarity of Purpose**: It reminds you of the **values** you aim to live by and helps you align your decisions with those values, creating a clearer sense of purpose and direction in life.

Choosing and Defining Your Virtues

Identifying Core Virtues

Before you begin tracking virtues, it's important to identify the core virtues that are most meaningful to you. These virtues might come from ancient philosophical traditions like Aristotle's Virtue Ethics or the Stoic virtues of wisdom, courage, justice, and temperance. Alternatively, they may be personal virtues, such as kindness, gratitude, or compassion, that resonate deeply with your moral vision of life.

Aristotle believed that virtues were essential for achieving eudaimonia, or human flourishing. He argued that each virtue lies on a spectrum between deficiency and excess, with the right balance—what he called the "Golden Mean"—leading to virtuous action. For example, courage is the balance between cowardice (deficiency) and recklessness (excess).

Defining Virtues in Concrete Terms

Once you've identified the virtues you want to track, the next step is to define them in specific, actionable terms. A virtue like "wisdom" might feel abstract, so it's crucial to break it down into concrete behaviors that you can observe and evaluate. For instance:

- **Wisdom** could involve thoughtful decision-making, seeking knowledge, and listening to others before forming an opinion.
- **Courage** could be defined as speaking up in difficult situations, taking risks when appropriate, and facing fears without avoidance.
- **Justice** might involve treating others fairly, standing up for the rights of others, or making decisions that benefit the greater good.

By creating clear definitions, you make it easier to assess whether your actions align with the virtues you've chosen.

The Practice of Virtue Tracking

Daily and Weekly Reflection

The core of virtue tracking lies in consistent reflection on how well you lived according to your chosen virtues. There are two common approaches to virtue tracking: daily reflection and weekly reflection. Both have distinct advantages.

Daily Reflection:

- At the end of each day, spend 5-10 minutes reflecting on how you practiced your virtues. Write about specific actions or decisions that align with your virtues, as well as moments where you fell short.
- For example, if you are tracking temperance, you might reflect on whether you exhibited self-control in moments of temptation, or if you acted impulsively.

Weekly Reflection:

- In a weekly review, you take a broader view of your actions over the past seven days. This allows you to identify patterns and trends, providing insight into areas where you've consistently excelled or struggled.
- A weekly reflection might also involve setting goals for how to improve your practice of virtues in the coming week.

Using a Virtue Journal

A virtue journal is a practical way to organize your reflections and track your progress. You can structure your journal in a way that aligns with your personal needs, but here is a basic template that can help you get started:

1. **Date**: Record the date of the entry.
2. **Virtues Practiced**: List the virtues you are tracking.
3. **Daily Actions/Decisions**: Write down specific actions or decisions that reflect how you practiced each virtue.
4. **Challenges/Setbacks**: Note any situations where you struggled to act virtuously and reflect on why this happened.
5. **Lessons Learned**: Identify any insights or lessons from the day's reflection that can help you improve tomorrow.

For example:

- **Virtue: Courage**
    - **Action**: "I spoke up during a meeting today to express my concerns, even though I was nervous about how it would be received."
    - **Challenge**: "I avoided having a difficult conversation with a colleague out of fear of conflict."
    - **Lesson**: "Next time, I will prepare myself mentally for difficult conversations and remind myself that facing discomfort is part of courage."

Benefits of Virtue Tracking

Developing Self-Awareness and Moral Clarity

One of the most significant benefits of virtue tracking is the development of self-awareness. When you regularly reflect on your actions, you become more attuned to how your behaviors align—or fail to align—with your values. This process of reflection helps you cultivate moral clarity, allowing you to navigate ethical dilemmas with greater confidence and wisdom.

For instance, someone who consistently reflects on the virtue of justice may become more aware of situations where they can advocate for fairness and equity, both in their personal and professional lives.

Building Consistency in Virtuous Action

Virtue tracking also fosters consistency in living according to your values. By tracking your progress, you become more intentional about practicing virtues in daily life. Over time, this consistency strengthens your ability to act virtuously, even in challenging situations.

Consider a person who is tracking the virtue of temperance. Through daily reflection, they notice that they tend to give in to indulgence when stressed. With this insight, they can consciously work on practicing temperance by developing healthier coping mechanisms.

Encouraging Long-Term Moral Growth

The practice of virtue tracking is not a one-time activity but a lifelong commitment to moral growth. Over months and years, this habit enables individuals to make meaningful progress toward living a more virtuous life. The process of reflection and adjustment ensures that virtues are not merely ideals but habits that are continuously strengthened.

Becoming the Best Version of Yourself

This practice of reflection and growth offers a structured way to cultivate virtues by making them tangible and actionable in everyday life. Through regular self-examination, individuals develop a deeper sense of self-awareness, accountability, and moral clarity. Virtue tracking is not about achieving perfection but about committing to the ongoing process of moral development. With each reflection, you refine your ability to act with wisdom, courage, justice, and temperance, gradually becoming the best version of yourself. By integrating virtue tracking into your daily habits, you take an active role in shaping your character and leading a life of meaning and ethical purpose.

Setting and Achieving Small Goals: The Key to Sustainable Habit Formation

In the pursuit of personal growth and self-improvement, the formation of lasting habits is one of the most powerful tools available. However, many people struggle with turning their aspirations into consistent, actionable behaviors. The secret to habit formation lies in understanding how small, achievable goals can serve as the building blocks for larger changes. By focusing on setting and achieving small goals, individuals can cultivate habits that not only lead to personal success but are also sustainable in the long term.

This practice is grounded in behavioral psychology and is reinforced by success stories from every domain of life. The key idea is simple: large goals can be daunting, but by breaking them down into small, manageable steps, you create a clear path to success. Through this method, change becomes not only possible but enjoyable, as you build momentum with each small victory.

In this exploration, we will delve into the science behind habit formation, explain the importance of setting small goals, and provide strategies for ensuring those goals are both achievable and meaningful.

The Science of Habit Formation: How Small Goals Lead to Big Change

Understanding Habits as Automatic Behaviors

At its core, a habit is an automatic behavior that develops through repetition. Whether it's brushing your teeth every morning or checking your phone when you wake up, habits are formed when a behavior becomes ingrained in your routine. According to psychologist Charles Duhigg, author of *The Power of Habit,* habits are formed through a cue-routine-reward loop. The brain identifies a cue, triggers a routine, and then receives a reward for that behavior, making it more likely to repeat the next time the cue appears.

The challenge with habit formation lies in the early stages of building new routines. The brain resists change, preferring the comfort of established habits. This is where small goals come into play: they allow you to create new routines without overwhelming your brain with drastic change.

The Power of Small Wins

Small goals work because they tap into the psychology of small wins. According to research by Teresa Amabile at Harvard Business School, small wins provide a sense of progress and accomplishment, which increases motivation and engagement. When you achieve a small goal, your brain releases dopamine, the "reward" chemical that reinforces positive behavior. This creates a feedback loop that motivates you to continue working toward your larger goals.

For example, if your long-term goal is to run a marathon, you might start by setting a small goal of running for 10 minutes every morning. Achieving that goal provides a sense of success, and each time you complete it, you feel more capable of eventually reaching the marathon distance.

Setting Small, Achievable Goals: The Building Blocks of Success

Start with Clear, Specific Goals

To set effective small goals, clarity and specificity are essential. Vague goals like "exercise more" or "be healthier" are difficult to measure and even harder to achieve. Instead, aim to create goals that are specific, measurable, attainable, relevant, and time-bound (SMART).

For example:

- **Vague goal**: "I want to exercise more."
- **Specific goal**: "I will go for a 15-minute walk every morning before work."

By making your goals specific, you provide yourself with clear parameters for success. This specificity also makes it easier to track your progress, which is crucial for maintaining motivation.

Make Goals Small and Incremental

The primary advantage of setting small goals is that they are manageable. Instead of trying to change your entire routine overnight, you focus on one small change at a time. The beauty of this approach is that it reduces the cognitive load on your brain, making it easier to stick with the new behavior.

For instance, if your goal is to improve your diet, start with something small and achievable, like adding one piece of fruit to your breakfast every day. Once that becomes a habit, you can gradually increase the challenge—perhaps by incorporating more vegetables into lunch or reducing sugar intake. Over time, these small changes add up to significant improvements in overall health, without the stress of making drastic adjustments all at once.

Link New Habits to Existing Routines

One of the most effective ways to establish small habits is to link them to existing routines, a technique known as habit stacking. Habit stacking involves taking an already established habit and adding a new behavior immediately before or after it. This leverages the existing cue-routine-reward loop of the established habit to make the new habit easier to adopt.

For example, if you already have the habit of brushing your teeth every morning, you might stack a new habit—such as practicing mindfulness for two minutes—immediately afterward. Over time, brushing your teeth will act as the cue for your new mindfulness practice, making it more likely that you'll stick with it.

Achieving Small Goals: Strategies for Success

Tracking Your Progress

Tracking your small goals is essential for both accountability and motivation. Whether you use a journal, a habit-tracking app, or a simple checklist, recording your progress provides a visual reminder of how far you've come. Seeing a streak of completed goals can be incredibly satisfying and serves as a powerful motivator to keep going.

Additionally, tracking helps you identify patterns. If you notice that you consistently fail to meet a certain goal, you can reflect on what might be causing the issue and adjust accordingly.

Celebrate Small Wins

Celebrating small wins is an important part of the goal-setting process. When you achieve a small goal, take a moment to acknowledge your success. This reinforces the habit loop by associating the new behavior with a positive emotion. The celebration doesn't need to be elaborate—it can be as simple as saying, "Well done," or rewarding yourself with a short break or something you enjoy.

Celebrating these small victories keeps you engaged in the process and prevents burnout, especially when working toward long-term goals.

Adjust and Refine Goals as Needed

Flexibility is key to long-term success in habit formation. While setting small goals is important, it's equally important to adjust those goals as you make progress. Once a small goal becomes easy to achieve, it's time to level up—increase the challenge incrementally so that you continue to grow.

For example, if your initial goal was to walk for 10 minutes a day and you're consistently meeting that target, increase it to 20 minutes or add a new habit, such as stretching after the walk. The key is to strike a balance between challenging yourself and ensuring that the goals remain attainable.

The Role of Patience and Consistency in Habit Formation

Progress Takes Time

It's important to recognize that habit formation is a gradual process. According to research by Phillippa Lally, a health psychology researcher, it takes an average of 66 days to form a new habit. This means that patience and consistency are critical to success. The beauty of small goals is that they allow you to build habits slowly and sustainably, without feeling overwhelmed by the enormity of the long-term goal.

Rushing the process often leads to burnout or frustration. By focusing on small, consistent progress, you give yourself the time needed to solidify new habits and make them automatic.

Building Momentum: The Compound Effect

Once you've mastered the art of setting and achieving small goals, you'll begin to notice a compound effect. Like compound interest in finance, small efforts made consistently over time yield significant results. As you build momentum, your small wins will accumulate, creating a powerful sense of achievement and progress.

This effect is particularly noticeable when working toward long-term goals. What may seem like a small action today can, over time, lead to major transformations in health, productivity, relationships, or personal development.

The Path to Success is Paved with Small Steps

Small Steps, Big Changes. By focusing on manageable, specific goals, you lay the foundation for lasting change, avoiding the overwhelm that often accompanies large, undefined ambitions. Small goals provide the structure and motivation needed to build momentum, and through consistent practice, they become the habits that define who you are. Whether you're striving to improve your health, advance in your career, or enhance your emotional well-being, the path to success begins with small, intentional steps taken each day. By setting and achieving small goals, you transform your aspirations into reality, one habit at a time.

The Role of Consistency and Discipline in Habit Formation: The Foundation of Lasting Change

In the pursuit of self-improvement, the formation of habits is often cited as a critical element for success. However, it's not merely the setting of goals or the desire for change that leads to success. Rather, it is consistency and discipline—two forces that transform initial motivation into sustainable, long-term habits. While motivation can spark the desire for change, it is consistency and discipline that fuel the journey, ensuring that habits are established, maintained, and reinforced over time.

Consistency refers to the regularity with which a behavior is performed. It is the repeated execution of small, deliberate actions that lead to habit formation. Discipline, on the other hand, is the ability to carry out these actions, even when motivation fades or obstacles arise. Together, consistency and discipline create the foundation for lasting change, ensuring that habits are ingrained into daily routines, becoming automatic and effortless.

This in-depth exploration will cover the importance of both consistency and discipline in habit formation, explain how these two principles work together, and offer strategies for cultivating them in your daily life. Through practical examples and insights, we will see how mastering consistency and discipline can transform fleeting intentions into a powerful framework for lifelong improvement.

The Importance of Consistency in Habit Formation

Habits Are Built Through Repetition

At its core, habit formation relies on the power of repetition. Just as a river carves its path into rock over time, so too are habits etched into our brains through consistent practice. Neuroscientific research shows that as we repeat behaviors, the brain strengthens neural pathways, making the behavior more automatic over time. This process, known as synaptic plasticity, is the key to transforming conscious effort into habitual action.

For example, if you aim to develop a habit of daily exercise, it's the regular, repeated activity of exercising—whether it's for 10 minutes or an hour—that gradually conditions your body and mind to expect and crave physical activity. Each repetition reinforces the habit, making it easier to perform the next time.

Consistency Breeds Predictability and Structure

Consistency provides predictability and structure to our lives. When habits are performed consistently, they become embedded in our daily routines, reducing decision fatigue and creating a sense of rhythm. This allows us to reserve mental energy for other important tasks. A consistent morning routine, for example, can set a positive tone for the day, anchoring the mind and body in familiar, productive actions that build momentum.

A lack of consistency, on the other hand, can lead to frustration and failure in habit formation. When we approach habits in a sporadic or haphazard manner—working on them only when we feel like it—our brains struggle to establish the behavior as automatic. As a result, the habit is never truly formed, and we fall back into old patterns.

The Power of Discipline: Acting Beyond Motivation

Discipline: The Engine of Long-Term Success

Discipline is the ability to push through discomfort, distractions, or lack of motivation to achieve a goal. While motivation often fluctuates—rising when we feel inspired and waning when we encounter setbacks—discipline provides the steady drive necessary to persist.

Discipline involves cultivating the mental strength to keep going, even when faced with difficulty. Unlike motivation, which is often linked to external stimuli, discipline is internally generated and rooted in a deep commitment to personal growth. This means that even on days when you don't feel like practicing a habit, discipline pushes you to take action.

In the process of habit formation, discipline is the glue that holds everything together. Without discipline, consistency is impossible because the natural ups and downs of daily life will inevitably lead to skipped actions, and the habit will fail to take root.

Overcoming the Obstacles: The Role of Willpower

Discipline is closely tied to willpower, which is the ability to resist temptations or distractions that pull us away from our desired behaviors. While willpower can be depleted over the course of the day, just like any muscle, it can be strengthened with practice.

For instance, if your goal is to read for 30 minutes every night, discipline enables you to resist the temptation to watch TV or scroll through social media. Even though the urge to procrastinate may be strong, practicing discipline by sticking to your reading goal helps solidify the habit. Over time, as discipline grows, the need to exert willpower diminishes, and the action becomes automatic.

Strategies for Cultivating Consistency and Discipline

1. Start Small to Build Momentum

One of the most effective ways to cultivate consistency and discipline is to start small. When habits are too ambitious from the outset, they can feel overwhelming, making it difficult to stay consistent. Starting with small, manageable actions reduces the mental barrier to beginning, making it easier to show up every day.

For example, if you're aiming to start a daily meditation practice, begin with just 5 minutes a day rather than an hour. By setting a small, achievable goal, you're more likely to succeed and build momentum, which fuels both consistency and discipline. Over time, you can gradually increase the duration as the habit becomes ingrained.

2. Create Accountability Systems

Accountability is another powerful tool for maintaining consistency and discipline. Whether it's through a friend, mentor, or app, having someone (or something) to hold you accountable helps keep you on track. When we know that others are watching or expecting us to follow through, we are more likely to honor our commitments.

Accountability systems can be as simple as sharing your goals with a friend who checks in regularly or joining a group with similar objectives. The mere act of reporting progress to someone else provides an extra layer of motivation to stay consistent, even on days when your internal drive is low.

3. Use Environmental Cues to Trigger Action

The environment plays a crucial role in habit formation, particularly in supporting consistency. By designing your environment in ways that cue your desired behavior, you make it easier to act on your goals. This technique, known as habit stacking, involves linking a new habit to an existing one, or setting up external cues that remind you to take action.

For instance, if you want to develop a habit of stretching in the morning, place a yoga mat beside your bed before going to sleep. When you wake up and see the mat, it acts as a visual reminder to stretch, increasing the likelihood that you'll follow through.

4. Cultivate Self-Discipline Through Regular Practice

Discipline is like a muscle—it gets stronger with regular exercise. The more you practice self-discipline, the more resilient it becomes in the face of temptation or adversity. A practical way to build discipline is to engage in deliberate acts of discomfort—tasks that require effort or sacrifice.

For example, choosing to take cold showers or committing to a technology detox for an hour each day are simple ways to challenge your willpower and strengthen discipline. These small challenges create a mental toughness that can be applied to other areas of your life, especially when forming new habits.

5. Track Progress and Celebrate Milestones

Tracking your progress is essential for maintaining both consistency and discipline. Keeping a journal or using an app to monitor how often you practice a habit allows you to visualize your success. This not only boosts motivation but also provides a sense of accomplishment as you observe how far you've come.

Additionally, it's important to celebrate small wins along the way. Acknowledging progress, no matter how small, reinforces positive behavior and encourages you to continue. For instance, after completing a week of consistent exercise, you might reward yourself with a relaxing activity or a special treat.

The Synergy Between Consistency and Discipline

How Consistency and Discipline Work Together

While consistency ensures that habits are performed regularly, discipline is what makes consistency possible in the first place. These two forces are deeply interconnected. Without discipline, it's easy to break the chain of consistent behavior as soon as external circumstances change. Similarly, without consistency, discipline loses its focus and direction.

Think of discipline as the engine that powers your efforts and consistency as the track that keeps you moving forward in the right direction. Together, they create a dynamic system that supports long-term habit formation.

The Steady Path to Lasting Change

While motivation may be the spark that ignites your desire for change, it is consistency and discipline that build the habits necessary for lasting success. By embracing these principles, you create a framework for steady, incremental growth that transforms fleeting intentions into tangible results. Consistency provides the structure and repetition needed for habits to take root, while discipline ensures that you stay the course, even when motivation fades or challenges arise. Through small, intentional actions performed consistently and with discipline, you set the stage for profound, long-lasting transformation. Ultimately, the power to change lies in your hands—guided by the daily practice of consistency and the unwavering strength of discipline.

Incorporating Virtue into Daily Actions: A Path to Moral Excellence

Living a life rooted in virtue is a fundamental goal in many philosophical and ethical traditions, from Aristotle's Virtue Ethics to Stoic philosophy. While these traditions offer profound insights into what it means to live virtuously, the true power of virtue lies in its application—not just in moments of moral crisis but in everyday life. The practice of incorporating virtue into daily actions involves a deliberate effort to align your habits, choices, and behaviors with core values like wisdom, courage, justice, and temperance.

The key to living a virtuous life is to integrate these values into the mundane, often overlooked moments of the day. Instead of reserving virtue for extraordinary situations, the challenge is to make it a habit, woven into the fabric of your routine. By consciously incorporating virtue into daily actions, you transform the way you interact with others, make decisions, and handle challenges, leading to a life of moral integrity, purpose, and flourishing.

This in-depth discussion will explore how to bring virtues into daily life, how to use habit formation to support virtuous living, and how the consistent practice of virtue leads to personal and moral growth. Through storytelling and practical examples, we will see how small, virtuous actions shape a meaningful and fulfilling life.

The Importance of Virtue in Everyday Life

Defining Virtue in Practical Terms

In ethical philosophy, virtue is often described as the moral quality or excellence that guides individuals toward living well. Aristotle defined virtues as the golden mean between extremes—such as courage being the balance between recklessness and cowardice. Stoicism, on the other hand, emphasizes living in accordance with nature and reason, guided by the virtues of wisdom, justice, courage, and temperance.

While these definitions offer a framework for understanding virtue, the challenge lies in applying them to daily life. Virtue, in practice, means more than having good intentions—it involves taking deliberate, morally sound actions in everything you do. Virtue is reflected in how you treat others, how you respond to adversity, and how you make decisions.

Why Virtue Matters in Daily Habits

The integration of virtue into daily habits is essential because it shapes who you become over time. Habits, whether virtuous or not, are the building blocks of character. The small actions you take every day—how you treat your colleagues, how you manage stress, or how you react to criticism—ultimately define your moral character. If you consistently practice virtuous habits, you become a person who embodies those virtues.

Aristotle famously said, "We are what we repeatedly do. Excellence, then, is not an act, but a habit." In other words, living virtuously is not about isolated acts of goodness but about making virtue a habit, something you embody in every moment of your life. It is through this habitual practice that virtues become ingrained in your character, leading to a life of eudaimonia, or flourishing.

Cultivating Virtue Through Habit Formation

Building Virtuous Habits: Starting with Small Actions

Incorporating virtue into daily actions starts with the intentional development of small, virtuous habits. Just as with any other habit, building a virtue-based habit requires repetition, intentionality, and consistency. Rather than waiting for moral dilemmas or big decisions, focus on how you can practice virtues in the simple actions of daily life.

For example:

- **Practicing Courage**: Rather than waiting for a moment of life-threatening danger to practice courage, start by speaking up in meetings or expressing your true opinions, even when it feels uncomfortable.
- **Practicing Justice**: Make fairness a habit by treating people equally in your daily interactions—whether you're dealing with a colleague, a cashier, or a family member. Ensure that you listen and act with fairness and empathy.
- **Practicing Temperance**: Incorporate moderation in your daily habits by managing your consumption—whether it's food, technology, or leisure activities—and making choices that reflect self-discipline.

By starting with small, actionable habits, you build the muscle of virtue, just as you would develop any other skill. These small actions, repeated daily, become automatic, helping you embody virtue without conscious effort.

Linking Virtue to Existing Routines

A practical way to integrate virtues into your daily life is through habit stacking—attaching a new, virtuous behavior to an existing routine. This approach leverages the structure of your current habits to incorporate new virtues more easily.

For instance:

- **Before Meals**: Use the act of preparing or sitting down for a meal as an opportunity to practice gratitude, a key element of the virtue of **justice**. Take a moment to appreciate the effort that went into providing your food and acknowledge those who helped make it possible.
- **During Conversations**: Use your interactions with others as an opportunity to practice **temperance** by actively listening and refraining from interrupting. This practice builds empathy and self-restraint, aligning your behavior with the virtue of fairness.
- **Before Making Decisions**: Implement the habit of pausing before making a decision and ask yourself, "What is the virtuous action in this situation?" This practice integrates **wisdom** into your decision-making process, encouraging thoughtful, reasoned actions.

By attaching virtue-based actions to everyday routines, you make it easier to practice them consistently, ensuring that virtue becomes an integral part of your life.

Overcoming Challenges to Virtuous Living

While incorporating virtue into daily actions is powerful, it is not always easy. Life's challenges often test our commitment to virtue. Stress, frustration, and external pressures can make it difficult to stay grounded in virtuous behavior. This is where discipline and self-awareness come into play.

One of the biggest challenges is the temptation to act according to immediate gratification rather than long-term virtue. Temperance, in particular, requires resisting impulsive behaviors—whether it's indulging in anger, consuming too much, or avoiding discomfort. Developing the habit of self-restraint and mindfulness can help overcome these obstacles.

Similarly, courage often requires stepping out of your comfort zone and confronting fear. In daily life, this might mean taking responsibility for mistakes or addressing uncomfortable truths with others. Overcoming the natural instinct to avoid discomfort is key to making courage a habitual part of your life.

The consistent practice of virtue often requires a growth mindset—the belief that through effort and reflection, you can improve your character. When challenges arise, see them as opportunities to strengthen your commitment to virtue, rather than as failures.

Examples of Incorporating Virtue in Daily Life

Practicing Wisdom in Everyday Decisions

Wisdom involves making thoughtful decisions based on reason, experience, and foresight. It's about seeing the bigger picture and avoiding impulsive or emotionally-driven choices. To incorporate wisdom into daily life, start by practicing mindful decision-making.

For example, in a work setting, rather than rushing to respond to an email in anger or frustration, take a moment to reflect on the situation. Ask yourself: "What is the best response for the long term?" or "How can I respond in a way that reflects fairness and good judgment?"

In personal interactions, wisdom might involve recognizing when to offer advice versus when to listen. It's about understanding the needs of others and responding in a way that promotes growth, rather than simply reacting based on emotion.

Practicing Justice in Relationships

Justice, in the context of virtue, means treating others with fairness and respect. It's about acting in ways that promote the common good and acknowledging the rights of others.

Incorporating justice into daily actions can be as simple as ensuring you treat others with respect in conversation, giving them the space to express their thoughts and ideas without judgment. Justice also involves standing up for what is right, even in small ways. This might mean correcting an unfair situation at work or acknowledging when you've made a mistake and taking steps to make amends.

Justice requires selflessness—it involves putting others' needs alongside your own and ensuring that your actions are equitable. By practicing fairness in small, everyday situations, you build the habit of justice into your character.

The Long-Term Benefits of Incorporating Virtue into Daily Actions

Building a Life of Integrity

As you make virtue a consistent part of your daily actions, you begin to build a life of integrity. Integrity means that your actions are aligned with your values, and you are true to your principles, even when no one is watching. Over time, this leads to a deep sense of self-respect and confidence, knowing that you are living in accordance with your highest ideals.

By consistently practicing virtues, you also cultivate trust in your relationships. When others see that you act with fairness, wisdom, and compassion on a daily basis, they are more likely to respect and rely on you. This strengthens both personal and professional connections, fostering a life of meaningful relationships and social harmony.

The Path to Eudaimonia: Flourishing Through Virtue

Ultimately, the practice of incorporating virtue into daily actions leads to eudaimonia, or flourishing. In Aristotelian philosophy, eudaimonia is the highest form of human happiness, achieved through living a life of virtue. This flourishing is not a fleeting feeling of pleasure but a deep, enduring sense of fulfillment that comes from knowing you are living in alignment with your moral values.

Living virtuously every day leads to a life of purpose, where each action contributes to your personal growth and well-being. The more consistently you practice virtue, the more you flourish, both as an individual and as a member of society.

Small Virtuous Acts, Big Moral Impact

By focusing on small, consistent actions that align with virtues like wisdom, courage, justice, and temperance, you not only strengthen your moral character but also create a life of purpose and integrity. The path to moral excellence is not paved with grand, heroic acts but with the simple, virtuous habits that define your everyday interactions and decisions. Over time, these small actions lead to a life of flourishing, where virtue is not just an aspiration but a way of being. Through the deliberate practice of virtue in daily actions, you shape a life of moral greatness, inner peace, and lasting fulfillment.

Having established a solid foundation in the formation of daily habits and the integration of virtue into everyday actions, the next step in the journey of personal growth and self-improvement involves self-reflection and cognitive restructuring. To truly live a virtuous and balanced life, it's essential to examine the inner workings of the mind—particularly the thought patterns that shape how we perceive and interact with the world. By identifying and challenging negative thought patterns, such as cognitive distortions, and practicing techniques rooted in Stoic and Buddhist philosophies, we can reframe our thinking in more constructive and compassionate ways. This section will explore how recognizing and restructuring these thoughts, with the guidance of both ancient wisdom and modern psychological insights, fosters a more balanced, ethical, and fulfilling life. Let's begin by understanding how cognitive distortions affect our mindset and how we can counteract them with self-compassion and mindfulness.

4. Mastering the Mind: Self-Reflection and Cognitive Restructuring for Balanced Living

Our thoughts have a profound impact on how we experience the world, shape our emotions, and influence our actions. Yet, our minds are often prone to distortions—automatic, negative patterns that can cloud our judgment and lead to unnecessary suffering. This next section, Mastering the Mind: Self-Reflection and Cognitive Restructuring for Balanced Living, delves into the essential practices of identifying and challenging these cognitive distortions. By developing awareness of how patterns like black-and-white thinking and catastrophizing skew our perceptions, we can begin the process of cognitive restructuring. Drawing from the philosophies of Stoicism, Buddhism, and Virtue Ethics, we'll explore practical techniques to reframe negative thoughts, cultivate self-compassion, and create a more balanced and constructive mindset. This deeper understanding of our thought processes helps us live more ethically and calmly, empowering us to align our thoughts with our values and aspirations.

Identifying Negative Thought Patterns: The Power of Recognizing Cognitive Distortions

Our thoughts are powerful—they shape our perceptions, influence our emotions, and ultimately determine how we interact with the world. However, the human mind is prone to developing negative thought patterns, often referred to as cognitive distortions, that distort reality and lead to unnecessary emotional distress. Cognitive distortions are systematic errors in thinking that cause us to perceive situations in exaggerated or inaccurate ways. These distortions often occur automatically and can reinforce negative emotions like anxiety, depression, and anger, leading to dysfunctional behaviors.

This section will explore how to identify and recognize cognitive distortions, focusing on common patterns like black-and-white thinking and catastrophizing. By gaining a deep understanding of how these thought patterns operate and how they impact our well-being, we can begin the process of cognitive restructuring—challenging these distortions and replacing them with more balanced, realistic thoughts. Through this process, we reclaim control over our mindset and develop greater resilience in the face of life's challenges.

Cognitive Distortions: How the Mind Distorts Reality

What Are Cognitive Distortions?

Cognitive distortions are irrational or exaggerated patterns of thinking that cause us to view situations in a biased or inaccurate way. These distortions typically occur automatically, often without conscious awareness, and can have a significant impact on our emotions and behaviors. Cognitive distortions are a key concept in Cognitive Behavioral Therapy (CBT), which is widely used to treat emotional and psychological disorders by helping individuals identify and change these faulty thinking patterns.

These distortions are harmful because they prevent us from seeing situations objectively, leading to misinterpretations of reality. For example, a person who fails a test might immediately conclude that they are a failure as a person—an extreme distortion that ignores the possibility of learning from the experience or acknowledging past successes.

Cognitive distortions are not only linked to specific emotional struggles like anxiety or depression, but they also impact our overall sense of well-being. They create mental filters that distort reality, making challenges seem more overwhelming than they truly are.

Recognizing Common Cognitive Distortions

Black-and-White Thinking: The World in Extremes

One of the most pervasive cognitive distortions is black-and-white thinking, also known as all-or-nothing thinking. This distortion causes individuals to see situations, people, or themselves in extreme, binary terms—things are either perfect or a total failure, good or bad, with no room for nuance or middle ground.

For example:

- A student who receives feedback on an assignment might think, "If I didn't get an A, I've completely failed," rather than seeing the feedback as an opportunity for improvement.
- In relationships, black-and-white thinking might manifest as, "If my partner doesn't agree with me on everything, they don't care about me."

This type of thinking traps individuals in rigid frameworks that leave no space for imperfection, complexity, or growth. It can lead to feelings of failure, frustration, and inadequacy, even when the situation may simply require a balanced perspective.

The Impact of Black-and-White Thinking

Black-and-white thinking can have detrimental effects on mental health. People who think in extremes are more likely to experience mood swings, heightened anxiety, and low self-esteem because they view minor setbacks as complete failures. By failing to recognize the grey areas in life, individuals miss out on opportunities for growth, resilience, and self-compassion.

Catastrophizing: The Art of Imagining the Worst

Catastrophizing is another common cognitive distortion that involves expecting the worst possible outcome in any given situation. Individuals who engage in catastrophizing tend to magnify potential problems and view them as far more disastrous than they truly are. They often anticipate negative outcomes that are unlikely or out of proportion to the actual situation.

For example:

- After making a small mistake at work, a person might think, "I'll probably get fired for this," even though the mistake is minor and correctable.
- A person might fear that a minor argument with a friend means the end of the relationship, assuming that it will escalate into something irreparable.

Catastrophizing exacerbates feelings of anxiety and helplessness because it frames everyday challenges as overwhelming and unmanageable.

The Effects of Catastrophizing on Well-Being

By constantly expecting the worst, individuals who engage in catastrophizing live in a state of chronic stress and anxiety. They are more likely to avoid challenges and opportunities, fearing negative outcomes. This distortion can lead to a cycle of avoidance and procrastination, preventing growth and development. Over time, catastrophizing can contribute to feelings of hopelessness and pessimism, as the mind becomes trapped in a pattern of expecting disaster around every corner.

Breaking the Cycle: Recognizing and Challenging Cognitive Distortions

Awareness: The First Step to Change

The first step in breaking the cycle of cognitive distortions is awareness. Cognitive distortions often operate beneath the surface of conscious thought, making it difficult to recognize when they are affecting your mindset. By becoming more aware of your automatic thoughts, you can begin to identify distortions as they arise.

One effective way to increase awareness is by practicing self-reflection through techniques like journaling or mindfulness meditation. In these reflective moments, ask yourself questions like:

- What am I thinking right now?
- Is this thought based on evidence, or is it an assumption?
- Am I falling into a cognitive distortion?

Over time, developing the habit of self-reflection will help you catch distorted thoughts before they spiral out of control.

Cognitive Restructuring: Reframing Distorted Thoughts

Once you recognize a cognitive distortion, the next step is to challenge and reframe it. This process is known as cognitive restructuring, a key component of CBT. Cognitive restructuring involves evaluating the accuracy of your thoughts and replacing distorted thinking with more balanced, realistic perspectives.

For example:

- If you catch yourself engaging in black-and-white thinking, ask yourself, "Is this really a total failure, or is there some middle ground?"
- If you're catastrophizing, challenge yourself by asking, "What's the most likely outcome, and how could I handle it if things don't go as planned?"

By actively challenging cognitive distortions, you can begin to reshape your mindset, reducing the emotional intensity of negative thoughts and developing greater emotional resilience.

Integrating Stoic and Buddhist Perspectives

Stoicism: Detachment from Extremes

The ancient philosophy of Stoicism offers valuable tools for recognizing and detaching from cognitive distortions. Stoics emphasize the importance of focusing on what you can control—your thoughts, actions, and responses—while letting go of the need to control external events. By practicing detachment, you can reduce the emotional impact of distorted thinking.

For example, instead of catastrophizing about potential failures, a Stoic approach would be to acknowledge that while you cannot control every outcome, you can control your effort and your reaction. This perspective fosters equanimity and helps counteract the fear-driven thinking behind distortions like catastrophizing.

Buddhism: Mindfulness and Compassion

Buddhism teaches the practice of mindfulness—observing thoughts without attachment or judgment. This practice aligns with the goal of recognizing cognitive distortions in a non-reactive way. By observing your thoughts through a lens of compassion and detachment, you can reduce the power of distortions and develop a more balanced view of reality.

Buddhism also emphasizes compassionate self-awareness—understanding that everyone experiences difficult thoughts and emotions. Instead of being harsh or critical of yourself for falling into distorted thinking, mindfulness allows you to accept these thoughts as part of the human experience and gently guide yourself toward healthier patterns of thought.

Breaking Free from Cognitive Distortions

Cognitive distortions like black-and-white thinking and catastrophizing distort reality, leading to emotional distress and limiting your ability to navigate life's challenges with resilience. By becoming aware of these distortions, challenging them through cognitive restructuring, and integrating Stoic and Buddhist principles, you can break free from the grip of distorted thinking. As you practice identifying and reframing negative thoughts, you create space for self-compassion, emotional balance, and mental clarity. Ultimately, this process empowers you to regain control over your thoughts and lead a more centered, fulfilling life.

Practicing Self-Compassion and Detachment: A Path to Mental Clarity and Emotional Resilience

When navigating the complexities of our thoughts and emotions, two practices are essential for cultivating mental clarity and emotional resilience: self-compassion and detachment. Both practices are deeply transformative, helping individuals break free from patterns of self-criticism and overattachment to outcomes, allowing for greater peace and well-being. In modern psychology, self-compassion is recognized for its role in reducing negative thought patterns and promoting emotional healing, while detachment, rooted in both Stoic philosophy and Buddhist teachings, helps us achieve emotional balance by separating ourselves from the highs and lows of external events.

Self-compassion encourages a kinder, gentler relationship with oneself, particularly in moments of failure or difficulty. It contrasts with the tendency many have to be their own harshest critic, leading to cycles of shame and self-doubt. Meanwhile, detachment doesn't mean disengagement from life or apathy, but rather the ability to step back from emotional entanglement with circumstances that are beyond our control. Together, these practices can reshape how we interact with our thoughts, emotions, and challenges, creating a more grounded and compassionate inner life.

In this section, we'll explore the psychological and philosophical underpinnings of self-compassion and detachment, how these practices complement each other, and the techniques to apply them in daily life. Through a deeper understanding, we can transform our inner dialogue and approach life's challenges with both wisdom and compassion.

The Power of Self-Compassion: Reframing Inner Dialogue

What is Self-Compassion?

Self-compassion is the practice of treating yourself with the same kindness and understanding that you would offer to a friend in times of struggle. Developed extensively by psychologist Dr. Kristin Neff, self-compassion involves three core components:

1. **Self-kindness**: Being warm and understanding toward oneself, especially during moments of perceived inadequacy, failure, or suffering.
2. **Common humanity**: Recognizing that everyone makes mistakes and experiences difficulties, which fosters a sense of connection to others.
3. **Mindfulness**: Being aware of negative thoughts and emotions without becoming absorbed by them or exaggerating them.

For many, self-compassion feels counterintuitive. We're often conditioned to believe that being critical of ourselves will motivate improvement, but research shows that self-compassion is a far more effective tool for personal growth. When we practice self-compassion, we are more likely to bounce back from failure, make healthier decisions, and feel a greater sense of well-being.

The Impact of Self-Criticism

Self-criticism is a common cognitive distortion that exacerbates negative thought patterns. When individuals hold themselves to impossibly high standards, they are quick to condemn themselves for any perceived failure. This harsh inner voice leads to feelings of shame, inadequacy, and self-doubt, reinforcing negative beliefs and making it difficult to break free from unproductive thought patterns.

For example, if you make a mistake at work, the self-critical response might sound like, "I'm so stupid. I can't do anything right." This thought not only amplifies negative feelings but also prevents you from learning from the experience in a constructive way. In contrast, a self-compassionate response would acknowledge the mistake without judgment: "I made a mistake, but that doesn't define my worth. Everyone makes errors, and I can learn from this."

Practicing Self-Compassion: Tools for Transformation

1. Rewriting the Inner Script

A key practice in developing self-compassion is rewriting the inner script—the automatic thoughts that arise in response to challenges. When negative thoughts or self-criticism emerge, practice speaking to yourself in a gentle, encouraging way. Ask yourself, "How would I speak to a friend in this situation?" By shifting your inner dialogue, you begin to cultivate a more nurturing relationship with yourself.

For example, instead of thinking, "I'm terrible at this," you could reframe the thought as, "I'm learning, and it's okay to not be perfect. Growth takes time." This subtle but powerful shift can change how you perceive setbacks and reduce the emotional weight of challenges.

2. Self-Compassion Breaks

Dr. Kristin Neff suggests taking self-compassion breaks during moments of difficulty. This involves pausing to acknowledge your suffering, offering yourself kindness, and recognizing that you are not alone in your struggle. A self-compassion break might include three steps:

1. **Acknowledge** the pain or difficulty ("This is a moment of suffering.")
2. **Remind yourself of common humanity** ("I am not alone; everyone goes through difficult times.")
3. **Be kind to yourself** ("May I be kind to myself and give myself the compassion I need right now.")

These breaks serve as powerful reminders to treat yourself with the care and support you need, rather than compounding the struggle with self-criticism.

Detachment: Letting Go of Emotional Overinvestment

The Concept of Detachment

Detachment, particularly in Stoicism and Buddhism, refers to the ability to maintain emotional balance by not becoming overly attached to external outcomes or material conditions. It is the practice of understanding that while we cannot control external events, we can control how we respond to them.

In Stoic philosophy, detachment is tied to the principle of focusing on what is within our control—our thoughts, actions, and attitudes—while accepting that much of life is beyond our influence. By practicing detachment, we develop resilience and inner peace in the face of challenges because we are no longer emotionally tied to outcomes we cannot change.

In Buddhism, detachment is central to the understanding of non-attachment or letting go of desires that lead to suffering. According to Buddhist teachings, suffering arises from our tendency to cling to things—whether they are material possessions, relationships, or identities—that are inherently impermanent. By cultivating detachment, we reduce suffering and live with greater equanimity.

The Dangers of Overattachment

Overattachment occurs when we place too much emotional investment in things we cannot control, such as other people's reactions, outcomes of projects, or personal achievements. When we attach our sense of self-worth to these external factors, any setback or failure feels devastating. For example:

- A person who is overattached to their career success might feel completely defeated after a minor professional failure, seeing it as a reflection of their worth.
- Someone who ties their happiness to a relationship may experience deep anxiety over any potential conflict, fearing it signals the end of the relationship.

Detachment, by contrast, allows us to care deeply and engage fully with life's challenges, but without the emotional suffering that comes from clinging to outcomes.

Cultivating Detachment: Practical Techniques for Letting Go

1. Focus on What You Can Control

A central practice in cultivating detachment is recognizing the distinction between what you can and cannot control. Stoicism teaches that by focusing only on what is within our control—our thoughts, actions, and responses—we can free ourselves from unnecessary emotional turmoil.

For example, in a stressful work situation, ask yourself: "Can I control this outcome, or can I only control my response to it?" By acknowledging the limits of your control, you free yourself from the emotional burden of worrying about the outcome and can focus on performing your best.

2. Mindfulness Meditation

Mindfulness meditation, a practice rooted in Buddhism, is a powerful tool for developing detachment. Mindfulness involves observing your thoughts and emotions without judgment or attachment. By watching your thoughts as they arise and pass, you learn to see them as temporary and fleeting, rather than becoming consumed by them.

For instance, if you feel anxious about an upcoming event, mindfulness allows you to notice the anxiety without identifying with it. Instead of thinking, "I am anxious," you observe, "I am experiencing anxiety." This subtle shift in perspective helps you maintain emotional distance and reduces the intensity of the feeling.

The Synergy of Self-Compassion and Detachment

Balancing Self-Kindness and Emotional Distance

While self-compassion invites us to treat ourselves with kindness and care, detachment helps us maintain emotional balance by preventing us from becoming overly invested in external circumstances. Together, these practices offer a powerful framework for emotional resilience.

For example, if you experience failure or rejection, self-compassion allows you to respond to yourself with kindness, acknowledging the difficulty without falling into self-blame. Detachment, on the other hand, helps you step back from the emotional investment in the outcome, recognizing that it does not define your worth.

By integrating both practices, you can navigate life's challenges with both inner strength and emotional equanimity.

Building Inner Strength Through Compassion and Detachment

Compassionate Detachment: The Key to Emotional Freedom highlights the transformative power of combining self-compassion and detachment. By learning to treat ourselves with kindness and letting go of the need to control or cling to external outcomes, we free ourselves from the emotional turmoil that often accompanies life's challenges.

Self-compassion helps us break the cycle of self-criticism, fostering emotional healing and growth. Detachment allows us to maintain peace and perspective in the face of adversity. Together, these practices create a foundation of mental clarity, emotional resilience, and inner peace, enabling us to live with greater balance, purpose, and well-being. Through these practices, we learn that while life may be filled with challenges, our response to those challenges is always within our control.

Cognitive Restructuring Techniques: Challenging and Reframing Thoughts for Mental Clarity

Cognitive restructuring is a powerful psychological tool used to reshape the way we think, helping us transform negative or unhelpful thoughts into more balanced, realistic, and productive ones. This process is central to Cognitive Behavioral Therapy (CBT) and is designed to challenge automatic thoughts and cognitive distortions that can trap us in cycles of anxiety, depression, or negative self-image. At the heart of cognitive restructuring lies the practice of challenging and reframing thoughts—a skill that allows us to identify irrational beliefs, question their validity, and replace them with healthier perspectives.

Our thoughts shape our emotions, which in turn influence our behaviors. When we get caught in patterns of distorted thinking—such as catastrophizing, black-and-white thinking, or personalization—we lose the ability to see situations clearly and objectively. Cognitive restructuring offers a way out of these mental traps, providing the tools to examine our thoughts critically and shift them toward more balanced and constructive viewpoints.

In this discussion, we will delve deeply into the process of challenging and reframing thoughts, exploring its psychological underpinnings, practical techniques, and the profound impact it can have on emotional well-being and personal growth. By mastering these techniques, you can transform the way you relate to your thoughts, leading to greater mental clarity and resilience.

The Foundation of Cognitive Restructuring: Understanding Thought Patterns

The Thought-Emotion-Behavior Connection

To understand the importance of cognitive restructuring, it's essential to grasp the thought-emotion-behavior connection. According to CBT, our thoughts, emotions, and behaviors are intricately linked. Thoughts are the lens through which we interpret the world, and they directly shape how we feel. In turn, our emotions influence the actions we take. For example, if someone interprets a neutral social interaction as negative—thinking, "They don't like me"—that thought can trigger feelings of rejection or anxiety, which may lead them to avoid future social situations.

Cognitive distortions—habitual, unhelpful ways of thinking—often skew our perceptions, leading to unwarranted negative emotions and unhealthy behaviors. By becoming aware of these distortions, we can intervene in this process and change how we experience the world.

Challenging Thoughts: Breaking Down Cognitive Distortions

What Does It Mean to Challenge Thoughts?

Challenging thoughts involves critically examining automatic, often negative thoughts and testing whether they are true, helpful, or rational. Many of our thoughts occur so quickly and subconsciously that we accept them as fact without questioning their validity. Challenging these thoughts is about bringing them into conscious awareness and subjecting them to rational scrutiny.

For example, let's say you're facing an important presentation at work. Your automatic thought might be, "I'm going to fail, and everyone will think I'm incompetent." This thought leads to intense anxiety, but upon closer examination, you may recognize that it's an exaggeration or based on fear rather than reality.

Challenging this thought requires asking yourself key questions:

- **Is there evidence to support this thought?**
- **Am I exaggerating the situation?**
- **What are the actual consequences if I don't perform perfectly?**

Through this process, you begin to dismantle the irrational thinking patterns that feed negative emotions.

Identifying Cognitive Distortions

Before you can challenge a thought, it's important to recognize whether it falls into a cognitive distortion. Some common cognitive distortions include:

- **All-or-Nothing Thinking (Black-and-White Thinking)**: Viewing situations in absolute terms, such

as "I'm either a success or a failure." This leaves no room for nuance or in-between outcomes.
- **Catastrophizing**: Expecting the worst possible outcome in every situation, often imagining a scenario where things spiral out of control.
- **Personalization**: Taking responsibility for events outside your control, such as thinking "It's my fault my team didn't succeed."
- **Overgeneralization**: Making broad, sweeping conclusions based on a single event. For example, after one rejection, thinking, "I'll never be good enough."

By identifying these patterns, you can more easily challenge them and begin the process of reframing.

Reframing Thoughts: Shifting Perspective for Balanced Thinking

What is Reframing?

Reframing is the process of taking a negative or unhelpful thought and consciously shifting its perspective to a more balanced or positive interpretation. While challenging thoughts helps identify distortions, reframing allows you to replace those distortions with healthier, more productive thoughts. The goal of reframing is not to impose an artificially positive spin on every situation but to see it more realistically and in a way that fosters emotional balance.

For example:

- Initial thought: "I'm never going to get this promotion. I'm just not good enough."
- Reframed thought: "I may not get this promotion, but that doesn't mean I'm not good at my job. I can keep improving and seek other opportunities."

Reframing helps to expand your mental framework, allowing you to see situations from multiple angles rather than being locked into a singular negative interpretation. It opens up possibilities for growth, resilience, and learning.

Techniques for Reframing Thoughts

There are several techniques for reframing thoughts effectively:

1. **The Evidence Test** Ask yourself, "What is the evidence for and against this thought?" This technique helps you evaluate whether your thoughts are based on facts or assumptions. Often, negative thoughts are based on fear or incomplete information. By gathering evidence, you can create a more balanced view.
2. **The Worst-Case Scenario** When catastrophizing, it can help to ask, "What's the worst that could realistically happen?" This often leads to the realization that even the worst-case scenario is manageable. Once you've identified the worst possible outcome, ask yourself, "How likely is it to happen?" and "What could I do to cope if it did happen?"
3. **The Best-Case Scenario** In addition to considering the worst-case scenario, it's useful to explore the best-case scenario. Ask yourself, "What's the best possible outcome here?" This expands your mental focus from negative possibilities to positive ones, creating a sense of hope and motivation.
4. **Shifting Perspectives** Sometimes it helps to view the situation from an outsider's perspective. Ask, "What would I tell a friend if they had this thought?" or "How would someone else view this situation?" This creates distance from your automatic thoughts and helps you think more rationally and compassionately.

The Psychological Benefits of Challenging and Reframing Thoughts

Reduced Emotional Intensity

One of the most immediate benefits of challenging and reframing thoughts is the reduction of emotional intensity. When you dismantle cognitive distortions, the emotions tied to those distortions—such as fear, sadness, or anger—often lose their power. For example, if you challenge the belief that you're a complete failure after a single setback, the feelings of worthlessness or anxiety associated with that thought diminish, allowing you to cope more effectively.

Greater Resilience and Flexibility

Reframing encourages cognitive flexibility, the ability to adapt your thinking to different circumstances. This flexibility fosters resilience by helping you approach challenges with an open mind and a problem-solving attitude. Instead of viewing difficulties as fixed and overwhelming, reframing encourages the mindset that setbacks are opportunities for growth and learning.

Empowerment and Agency

Cognitive restructuring restores a sense of agency and control over your thoughts and emotions. Instead of feeling like a passive victim of your thoughts, challenging and reframing empowers you to take an active role in shaping your mental experience. This leads to a greater sense of empowerment and confidence in your ability to navigate difficult situations.

Applying Cognitive Restructuring in Daily Life

Practice Through Journaling

A powerful way to practice cognitive restructuring is through journaling. Writing down your thoughts allows you to capture automatic thoughts and challenge them in a structured way. Journaling also provides an opportunity to practice reframing by experimenting with alternative ways of interpreting situations.

For example:

- Situation: "I made a mistake at work."
- Initial thought: "I'm incompetent. I'll never be good at this job."
- Evidence for: "I made a mistake today."
- Evidence against: "I've been successful at my job for months. This is one mistake."
- Reframed thought: "Making mistakes is part of learning. I can use this experience to improve."

Integrating Stoic and Buddhist Principles

Stoicism and Buddhism both emphasize cognitive restructuring in their teachings. Stoicism encourages individuals to focus only on what they can control—their thoughts and actions—and to detach from external outcomes. By adopting a Stoic mindset, you can challenge thoughts that involve overattachment to things outside your control and reframe them to focus on inner strength.

Similarly, Buddhism promotes mindfulness and non-attachment, teaching us to observe thoughts without becoming emotionally invested in them. Mindfulness helps us recognize automatic thoughts as they arise, creating the mental space to challenge and reframe them in a way that aligns with inner peace.

Reframing Your Mindset for Lasting Change

By learning to challenge cognitive distortions and reframe negative thoughts, you gain control over your emotional responses and shift your mindset toward balance and clarity. This process empowers you to approach life's challenges with greater resilience, cognitive flexibility, and self-compassion. Through the ongoing practice of cognitive restructuring, you not only change the way you think but also transform the way you feel and behave, creating lasting change in both your internal world and external experiences. Ultimately, mastering the art of challenging and reframing thoughts allows you to build a life rooted in mental clarity, emotional balance, and personal empowerment.

Balancing Thoughts with Stoic and Buddhist Principles: A Path to Inner Harmony

In the modern world, it's easy to get caught up in reactive thinking, where emotions like fear, anxiety, and frustration dominate our mental landscape. Both Stoic philosophy and Buddhist teachings offer profound wisdom on how to cultivate a more balanced, resilient mindset by guiding how we respond to our thoughts and emotions. While distinct in their origins, Stoicism and Buddhism share many overlapping principles that can serve as powerful tools for cognitive restructuring, helping us challenge negative thoughts and foster emotional equilibrium.

Stoicism emphasizes focusing on what is within our control and accepting what is beyond it. This approach promotes detachment from external outcomes and encourages inner strength, making it a perfect complement to cognitive restructuring techniques that aim to reframe irrational or unhelpful thoughts. Meanwhile, Buddhism teaches the principles of mindfulness, non-attachment, and compassion, encouraging us to observe our thoughts without becoming attached to them, thereby reducing emotional suffering and fostering inner peace.

This in-depth exploration will provide a comprehensive understanding of how to integrate Stoic and Buddhist principles into cognitive restructuring practices. By learning to balance our thoughts through these time-honored philosophies, we can reshape how we interact with our mental world, allowing us to approach life with greater clarity, resilience, and harmony.

The Stoic Approach: Focus on What You Can Control

The Dichotomy of Control: A Fundamental Stoic Principle

At the heart of Stoic philosophy lies the concept of the dichotomy of control. This principle, articulated by the Stoic philosopher Epictetus, teaches that while we cannot control external events, we have complete control over our own thoughts, actions, and attitudes. For the Stoics, mental suffering often arises from the attempt to control things that are inherently uncontrollable—such as other people's opinions, life circumstances, or outcomes of events. Stoicism encourages us to focus only on what we can control, thereby freeing ourselves from the emotional turmoil that accompanies overattachment to external factors.

For example, let's say you've applied for a job and are waiting for a response. A Stoic approach would encourage you to focus on what you can control (your preparation for the interview, how you conducted yourself) and let go of what you can't control (the employer's decision). This shift in focus allows you to remain calm and centered, regardless of the outcome.

Cognitive Restructuring with the Stoic Mindset

When applying Stoic principles to cognitive restructuring, the goal is to challenge thoughts that involve overattachment to external factors and reframe them to focus on inner control. If you find yourself worrying excessively about an outcome or feeling overwhelmed by circumstances outside your control, ask yourself:

- **Is this within my control, or am I focusing on external factors?**
- **What can I control in this situation, and how can I act in accordance with my values?**

For example, if a friend cancels plans at the last minute and you feel hurt or rejected, the Stoic response would be to focus on how you interpret and respond to the situation. Instead of ruminating on your friend's behavior (which is beyond your control), you can choose to reframe your thoughts: "I can't control my friend's actions, but I can control my own response. I will use this time productively."

By consistently practicing this Stoic mindset, you can free yourself from the emotional ups and downs that arise from external circumstances, fostering greater resilience and balance.

The Buddhist Approach: Mindfulness and Non-Attachment

Observing Thoughts with Mindfulness

In Buddhist teachings, mindfulness is a central practice for cultivating a balanced mind. Mindfulness involves paying attention to the present moment with awareness and acceptance, without becoming attached to the thoughts or emotions that arise. This practice allows us to observe our thoughts from a distance, recognizing them as temporary mental events rather than absolute truths.

When a negative thought or emotion arises, the Buddhist approach encourages us to observe it with non-judgmental awareness. Instead of reacting to the thought or identifying with it, we simply notice it. This creates a sense of mental space between the thought and our emotional response, allowing us to respond to the situation with clarity rather than reactivity.

For example, if you're experiencing anxiety before a big presentation, mindfulness practice would involve acknowledging the anxious thoughts without allowing them to dominate your experience. You might think, "I notice that I'm feeling anxious right now," and in doing so, create enough distance to remain calm and focused on the task at hand.

Non-Attachment and Letting Go of Clinging

A key teaching in Buddhism is the concept of non-attachment, which involves letting go of the tendency to cling to desires, outcomes, or identities that are inherently impermanent. According to Buddhist philosophy, much of our suffering arises from our attachment to things—whether it's success, relationships, or material possessions. By practicing non-attachment, we can reduce the mental suffering that comes from trying to hold onto things that are beyond our control or transient in nature.

In the context of cognitive restructuring, non-attachment helps us to let go of fixed, rigid thoughts and adopt a more flexible, open mindset. For example, if you're feeling frustrated because a project didn't go as planned, non-attachment encourages you to accept the situation as it is rather than clinging to the desire for things to be perfect. This creates an opportunity to reframe the thought: "Even though this didn't go as planned, I can learn from the experience and move forward."

By embracing non-attachment, you become less reactive to life's inevitable changes and challenges, fostering a greater sense of peace and equanimity.

Integrating Stoicism and Buddhism: A Balanced Cognitive Framework

Reframing Thoughts with Stoic and Buddhist Principles

When we combine the principles of Stoicism and Buddhism in cognitive restructuring, we create a powerful framework for managing our thoughts and emotions. Stoicism teaches us to focus on what we can control, while Buddhism helps us cultivate mindfulness and non-attachment. Together, these philosophies provide a balanced approach to thought management that emphasizes mental clarity, emotional resilience, and inner peace.

For example, if you're feeling overwhelmed by a difficult situation at work, you can apply the Stoic principle of focusing on what you can control while using Buddhist mindfulness to observe your thoughts without becoming attached to them. Instead of spiraling into negative thinking, you might reframe the situation by acknowledging, "I can't control every aspect of this project, but I can control my effort and how I respond to challenges." At the same time, you practice mindfulness by noticing the anxious thoughts without identifying with them, allowing them to pass through your mind like clouds in the sky.

The Importance of Acceptance and Compassion

Both Stoicism and Buddhism emphasize the importance of acceptance—accepting what is, rather than resisting reality. In Stoicism, this is reflected in the practice of amor fati—the love of fate—which encourages individuals to embrace all aspects of life, including challenges and setbacks, as opportunities for growth. In Buddhism, acceptance is tied to the concept of impermanence, recognizing that everything is constantly changing and that suffering arises when we try to resist this natural flow.

Additionally, self-compassion plays a crucial role in balancing thoughts. While Stoicism emphasizes rational control, it is essential to temper this approach with the Buddhist practice of compassion—toward yourself and others. When we make mistakes or experience difficult emotions, self-compassion allows us to respond with kindness rather than self-criticism. This balance of rational control and compassionate acceptance leads to a more integrated and harmonious inner life.

Practical Techniques for Balancing Thoughts

1. Stoic Journaling

One way to incorporate Stoic principles into cognitive restructuring is through Stoic journaling. At the end of each day, reflect on moments when you felt overwhelmed or emotionally reactive. Write down the thoughts you had during those moments and ask yourself:

- Was I focusing on things within my control?
- How could I have responded differently based on what I can control?
- What virtues (such as courage, patience, or wisdom) could I have applied to this situation?

This practice helps you internalize the Stoic mindset and reframe your thoughts for future challenges.

2. Buddhist Meditation on Non-Attachment

Incorporate Buddhist meditation practices to observe and release attachment to your thoughts. Sit in meditation and focus on your breath. When thoughts arise, practice noticing them without judgment or attachment. Label the thought as "just a thought" and return to your breath. Over time, this practice trains the mind to see thoughts as temporary and passing, reducing emotional reactivity and fostering detachment.

Achieving Cognitive Balance Through Ancient Wisdom

Inner Equilibrium: Harmonizing Thoughts with Stoic and Buddhist Wisdom captures the essence of applying these two ancient philosophies to cognitive restructuring. By balancing Stoic rational control with Buddhist mindfulness and non-attachment, we create a powerful framework for managing our thoughts and emotions. This integration allows us to challenge unhelpful thoughts, detach from external outcomes, and cultivate greater peace and resilience in the face of life's challenges.

The combination of Stoic and Buddhist principles empowers us to transform our mental landscape, turning reactive and distorted thinking into balanced, constructive thoughts. Through the ongoing practice of these techniques, we achieve not only mental clarity but also a deeper sense of harmony within ourselves and with the world around us.

Using Virtue Ethics to Guide Thought Processes: Cultivating Ethical Thinking and Emotional Balance

In the journey of self-reflection and cognitive restructuring, Virtue Ethics offers a compelling and timeless approach for guiding our thought processes toward moral clarity and emotional well-being. Rooted in the teachings of Aristotle and further developed by scholars such as Alasdair MacIntyre and Philippa Foot, Virtue Ethics emphasizes the importance of cultivating moral character through the habitual practice of virtues such as wisdom, courage, justice, and temperance. Unlike other ethical frameworks that focus primarily on rules or consequences, Virtue Ethics is concerned with who we are as individuals and how our thoughts, choices, and actions reflect our moral development.

When applied to cognitive restructuring, Virtue Ethics becomes a powerful tool for reshaping the way we think by aligning our thought processes with virtuous living. It offers a structured yet flexible approach to evaluating our thoughts not only for their logical consistency but also for their moral implications. Are our thoughts promoting compassion, fairness, or courage? Are they reflecting wisdom or impulsiveness? By using virtue as a guide, we can challenge harmful thought patterns and cultivate a mindset that fosters personal growth, ethical living, and emotional balance.

In this exploration, we will delve deeply into the principles of Virtue Ethics and how they can be applied to cognitive restructuring. Through practical examples and insights, you'll gain a full understanding of how aligning your thoughts with virtues leads to a more fulfilling and harmonious life.

The Core of Virtue Ethics: Cultivating Moral Excellence

Virtue Ethics encourages us to ask, "What kind of person am I becoming through the way I think?" It emphasizes that the quality of our thoughts has a direct impact on the quality of our actions and, ultimately, our character. Therefore, cognitive restructuring through the lens of Virtue Ethics involves assessing whether our thoughts are helping us become more virtuous or leading us away from ethical behavior.

How Virtue Guides Thought Processes: A Framework for Ethical Thinking

The Role of Phronesis: Practical Wisdom in Decision-Making

One of the key virtues in Virtue Ethics is phronesis, or practical wisdom. Phronesis is the ability to make good decisions in specific situations by balancing intellectual reasoning with ethical considerations. When restructuring our thought processes, phronesis acts as a guide for evaluating whether our thoughts are leading to ethical actions and rational decisions.

For example, if you're struggling with a difficult choice—whether it's a professional decision or a personal dilemma—practical wisdom asks you to consider both the moral and practical implications of your options. Are you acting with integrity, or are you being swayed by short-term gains? Are your thoughts driven by fear or by a genuine desire to do what is right? By aligning your thought process with practical wisdom, you learn to approach challenges in a way that reflects both reason and virtue.

Evaluating Thoughts Through the Four Cardinal Virtues

To guide your thought processes ethically, consider evaluating your thoughts through the lens of the four cardinal virtues—wisdom, courage, justice, and temperance. Each of these virtues provides a framework for reframing and challenging harmful or irrational thought patterns.

1. **Wisdom (Sophia)**: Are my thoughts grounded in reason and knowledge? Wisdom calls for thoughtful consideration of the facts before jumping to conclusions. It asks us to challenge impulsive thinking and consider the long-term implications of our thoughts and actions.
     - Example: You may think, "I'll never succeed in this project." Reframing through wisdom might involve asking, "Is this based on evidence, or am I reacting emotionally? What steps can I take to approach this project with more knowledge?"
2. **Courage (Andreia)**: Am I avoiding difficult truths or challenges out of fear? Courage requires facing reality with bravery, even when it is uncomfortable. This virtue challenges us to reframe thoughts of avoidance or self-doubt into thoughts that promote resilience.
     - Example: Instead of thinking, "I'm not good enough to take on this role," courage reframes this as, "Taking on new challenges is difficult, but I can face the uncertainty and learn from the experience."
3. **Justice (Dikaiosyne)**: Are my thoughts fair, both to myself and others? Justice encourages us to think about the impact of our thoughts on our relationships and interactions. Are we treating ourselves and others with fairness and respect?
     - Example: If you're caught in a thought pattern of resentment toward a colleague, justice prompts you to reframe: "Am I being fair to this person, or am I projecting my frustrations onto them? How

can I approach this situation with fairness and empathy?"
4. **Temperance (Sophrosyne)**: Are my thoughts balanced and moderate? Temperance calls for self-restraint and the avoidance of extreme thinking. This virtue encourages us to move away from polarized thinking (e.g., "all-or-nothing" thoughts) and find balance in our perspectives.
    - Example: If you're thinking, "I always mess things up," temperance invites you to consider a more balanced view: "I make mistakes sometimes, but I also succeed in many areas. What can I learn from this experience to improve?"

Applying Virtue Ethics to Cognitive Restructuring: Practical Techniques

1. Virtue-Based Journaling

One effective way to integrate Virtue Ethics into cognitive restructuring is through virtue-based journaling. This practice involves reflecting on your thoughts and actions at the end of each day and asking yourself questions aligned with the virtues:

- **Wisdom**: Did my thoughts today reflect careful reasoning, or did I jump to conclusions?
- **Courage**: Did I avoid challenges, or did I face them with resilience?
- **Justice**: Was I fair in my thoughts about others and myself?
- **Temperance**: Did I allow my thoughts to become extreme, or did I maintain balance?

By regularly reflecting on your thoughts through this virtuous lens, you can begin to reshape your habitual thought patterns in alignment with ethical living.

2. Reframing Challenges as Opportunities for Virtue

When faced with a difficult situation or negative thought pattern, consider reframing it as an opportunity to practice virtue. For instance, if you're feeling anxious about a presentation, view the situation as a chance to practice courage and wisdom. Instead of seeing anxiety as a sign of weakness, frame it as an opportunity to grow in resilience and to apply thoughtful preparation.

By consciously reframing challenges as opportunities to develop virtue, you shift the focus away from fear or failure and toward personal growth and ethical development.

The Ethical Impact of Thought Restructuring: Building Moral Character

From Thought to Action: How Virtuous Thinking Shapes Behavior

Virtue Ethics teaches us that the way we think directly shapes the way we act. Our thoughts are the precursors to our decisions and behaviors, and by aligning our thoughts with virtue, we ensure that our actions are consistent with our ethical principles. As you practice cognitive restructuring through the lens of Virtue Ethics, you not only improve your mental well-being but also strengthen your moral character.

For example, reframing self-doubt as an opportunity to practice courage encourages you to take bold actions in the face of fear. Restructuring thoughts of resentment into thoughts of fairness and justice helps you foster more compassionate relationships. In this way, virtuous thinking leads to virtuous action, creating a positive feedback loop that promotes both personal and ethical growth.

Shaping Your Mind and Character Through Virtue

By aligning your thoughts with the cardinal virtues—wisdom, courage, justice, and temperance—you can cultivate a mindset that not only challenges negative thought patterns but also promotes moral excellence and personal flourishing. This virtuous approach to thinking encourages self-reflection, ethical decision-making, and emotional resilience, leading to a life of greater purpose and harmony. Through the consistent application of Virtue Ethics in your thought processes, you develop not only a clearer and more balanced mindset but also a stronger sense of character. Ultimately, guiding your thoughts with virtue leads to more ethical actions, deeper relationships, and a more fulfilling life grounded in moral integrity.

As we continue to explore cognitive restructuring and self-reflection, we now turn our attention to an equally vital aspect of personal growth: emotional regulation and resilience. Thought patterns have a direct impact on our emotional states, and understanding how to manage emotions effectively is crucial for mental well-being. In this next section, we will delve into various techniques and philosophical practices that offer powerful tools for navigating emotional challenges. Drawing from Cognitive Behavioral Therapy (CBT), Stoicism, and Buddhism, we will explore practical strategies for recognizing and managing emotions, from anxiety to anger, while cultivating resilience in the face of life's inevitable ups and downs. By learning to balance emotional awareness with mental calmness and acceptance, we can develop the skills necessary to thrive in the midst of adversity. Let's begin by examining how CBT techniques can help us become more aware of our emotions and regulate them effectively.

5. Mastering Emotional Resilience: Techniques for Emotional Regulation and Inner Calm

Emotions play a profound role in shaping our experiences, influencing how we respond to challenges, relationships, and everyday events. Yet, learning how to effectively regulate and understand these emotions is essential for achieving mental and emotional well-being. In this section, Mastering Emotional Resilience: Techniques for Emotional Regulation and Inner Calm, we will explore a range of strategies from Cognitive Behavioral Therapy (CBT), Stoicism, and Buddhism to help manage emotions like anxiety, depression, and anger. By cultivating emotional awareness and developing tools such as detachment from outcomes and mindfulness, we can navigate life's inevitable emotional turbulence with greater clarity, balance, and resilience. Each of these philosophical and therapeutic approaches offers unique insights into how we can not only manage our emotions but also grow through them, fostering a sense of inner calm and strength. Let's begin by understanding how CBT techniques can help us identify and regulate our emotional responses.

Emotional Awareness and Identification: The Foundation of Emotional Management

Emotions often serve as our body's first response to the world around us, shaping how we perceive and react to situations. However, for many people, emotions can feel overwhelming or difficult to understand, leading to impulsive reactions or unresolved inner turmoil. In Cognitive Behavioral Therapy (CBT), emotional awareness and identification are foundational skills for managing emotions effectively. These skills involve becoming attuned to the full spectrum of emotions, understanding their sources, and learning how to respond to them in a healthy, constructive manner.

By increasing emotional awareness, you can begin to recognize the emotions you are experiencing as they arise and identify the specific thoughts and circumstances triggering them. This heightened self-awareness empowers you to intervene before emotions spiral into unhealthy behaviors, such as anger, avoidance, or negative self-talk. The process of emotional identification further allows you to name and categorize your emotions with precision, preventing vague feelings from lingering in the background and influencing your decisions unconsciously.

In this discussion, we will explore the intricacies of emotional awareness and emotional identification, highlighting their importance in CBT for fostering emotional regulation and resilience. Through this comprehensive approach, you will gain deeper insight into how to manage your emotional responses, enabling you to handle life's challenges with greater balance and clarity.

Understanding Emotional Awareness: Why It Matters

Emotional Awareness as the First Step to Control

Emotional awareness refers to the ability to recognize and understand your emotions as they occur. Without emotional awareness, emotions can dominate our thoughts and actions in ways that feel automatic and uncontrollable. People often experience strong emotional reactions, such as anger or sadness, without fully understanding why those emotions have arisen. This lack of awareness can lead to reactive behaviors that undermine relationships, personal goals, and overall well-being.

For example, imagine that you're feeling overwhelmed at work. Without emotional awareness, you might become irritable with your colleagues, interpreting the situation as their fault rather than recognizing that the overwhelm stems from your own emotional state. In contrast, by cultivating emotional awareness, you can pause and acknowledge, "I'm feeling overwhelmed because of my workload," and take steps to manage the feeling before it leads to conflict or frustration.

In CBT, emotional awareness is the first step toward developing emotional intelligence, a critical skill for navigating both personal and professional environments. By becoming aware of your emotions, you gain control over how you react to them, making it possible to choose thoughtful, deliberate responses rather than impulsive ones.

The Connection Between Emotions and Thoughts

A fundamental principle of Cognitive Behavioral Therapy is that thoughts, emotions, and behaviors are interconnected. Emotional awareness allows you to recognize not just the feelings you're experiencing but also the thoughts that are driving those emotions. For example, if you feel anxious before a public speaking engagement, the underlying thought might be, "I'm going to embarrass myself." By becoming aware of both the thought and the emotion, you gain the ability to challenge the thought and reframe it into something more helpful, like, "I've prepared well, and I can handle this."

This connection between thoughts and emotions is vital because emotions are often fueled by distorted thinking patterns, such as catastrophizing, overgeneralization, or black-and-white thinking. By identifying the emotion first, you can trace it back to the underlying thought and work to restructure that thought using CBT techniques.

Emotional Identification: The Power of Naming Emotions

Why Naming Emotions is Crucial

Once you become aware of your emotions, the next step is emotional identification—the process of naming and labeling those emotions with accuracy. Many people struggle with vague feelings that they can't quite define, which can lead to emotional confusion. For instance, you might feel a sense of unease without realizing that it stems from a combination of anxiety and frustration. Without identifying the exact emotions involved, it becomes difficult to address the underlying causes.

Research in psychology has shown that naming your emotions—sometimes referred to as affect labeling—can significantly reduce their intensity. By labeling your emotions, you engage the prefrontal cortex, the part of the brain responsible for logical reasoning and emotional regulation. This process of naming emotions helps shift activity away from the amygdala, which is responsible for triggering emotional reactions like fear or anger. As a result, the simple act of labeling your emotions can help calm your mind and allow for clearer thinking.

For example, instead of saying, "I'm upset," emotional identification requires that you be more specific: "I'm feeling anxious because of the upcoming deadline, and I'm also feeling disappointed because I didn't meet my own expectations." This specificity allows you to better address each emotion individually, leading to more effective emotional regulation.

Developing a Vocabulary for Emotions

To practice emotional identification effectively, it's essential to develop a broad emotional vocabulary. Many people default to a small set of emotional labels, such as "happy," "sad," or "angry," without recognizing the wide range of emotions that exist. For example, emotions like shame, guilt, pride, envy, and contentment are often experienced but rarely labeled accurately. Without the right vocabulary, it becomes difficult to fully understand your emotional landscape.

In CBT, therapists often provide emotion wheels or emotion charts that list a variety of emotions, helping individuals identify their specific feelings with greater nuance. By expanding your emotional vocabulary, you become better equipped to differentiate between subtle variations in your emotional experience. This depth of emotional identification leads to more precise emotional management and the ability to respond to life's challenges with greater emotional intelligence.

Practical Techniques for Enhancing Emotional Awareness and Identification

1. Mindfulness Meditation for Emotional Awareness

One of the most effective ways to develop emotional awareness is through the practice of mindfulness meditation. In mindfulness, you focus your attention on the present moment, observing your thoughts, emotions, and bodily sensations without judgment. As emotions arise, you practice naming them as they come and go, such as "I'm feeling anxious," or "I notice sadness."

Mindfulness trains your mind to observe emotions as transient experiences rather than overwhelming forces. By regularly practicing mindfulness, you become more attuned to your emotional states, allowing you to recognize emotions as they arise before they escalate.

2. Journaling for Emotional Identification

Journaling is a powerful tool for developing both emotional awareness and emotional identification. By writing down your emotions and reflecting on the situations that triggered them, you gain deeper insight into your emotional patterns. Journaling also encourages you to label your emotions with specificity, helping you clarify exactly what you're feeling and why.

A typical journaling practice might involve writing down the following:

- The situation that triggered the emotion
- The initial emotion you felt
- Any additional emotions that accompanied it
- The thoughts you had in response to the emotion
- How you acted based on the emotion

Over time, journaling helps you identify emotional triggers, understand how your thoughts influence your emotions, and track patterns that need to be addressed.

The Benefits of Emotional Awareness and Identification

Improved Emotional Regulation

When you are aware of and can accurately identify your emotions, you're better equipped to regulate them. Emotional regulation involves recognizing an emotion, understanding its source, and choosing a healthy response. Without emotional awareness, emotions often lead to impulsive reactions, such as lashing out in anger or withdrawing in sadness. By practicing emotional awareness and identification, you gain the ability to pause, reflect, and choose thoughtful actions.

Enhanced Emotional Intelligence

Emotional awareness and identification are central components of emotional intelligence, the ability to recognize, understand, and manage your own emotions while empathizing with the emotions of others. People with high emotional intelligence tend to have better interpersonal relationships, greater mental resilience, and a stronger ability to navigate life's emotional complexities.

The Key to Mastering Your Emotions

Use emotional awareness and emotional identification as foundational tools in emotional management. By honing these skills, you take the first step toward understanding the intricate connection between your thoughts, emotions, and behaviors, allowing you to respond to life's challenges with greater clarity and control. As you develop the ability to name and categorize your emotions with precision, you enhance your capacity for emotional regulation, leading to more thoughtful decisions and healthier relationships. Ultimately, emotional awareness and identification empower you to transform reactive emotional responses into conscious, intentional actions, creating a life of greater emotional resilience and personal growth.

Strategies for Managing Anxiety, Depression, and Anger: A CBT Approach to Emotional Regulation

Anxiety, depression, and anger are three of the most common and powerful emotions that individuals struggle with daily. Each can significantly impact mental well-being, interpersonal relationships, and overall quality of life if left unchecked. Cognitive Behavioral Therapy (CBT) offers evidence-based techniques to help manage and alleviate the symptoms of these emotions, helping individuals regain control and achieve emotional balance. Understanding and addressing the thought patterns that drive these emotional states is key to managing them effectively.

In this comprehensive exploration, we will delve into the CBT strategies specifically designed for managing anxiety, depression, and anger. These techniques focus on identifying cognitive distortions, restructuring negative thoughts, and developing coping mechanisms that promote resilience and emotional regulation. Through a thorough understanding of how these strategies work, you will gain insight into their practical application, allowing you to not only manage these emotions but also transform them into opportunities for growth.

Managing Anxiety: Breaking the Cycle of Fear

The Nature of Anxiety: Understanding the Thought-Emotion Connection

Anxiety is a natural emotional response to perceived threats, uncertainties, or potential dangers. It often manifests as excessive worry, fear, or nervousness, particularly in situations where the outcome is unknown or feared. From a CBT perspective, anxiety is driven by cognitive distortions—irrational thought patterns that magnify the perceived risk or threat in a given situation. These distorted thoughts trigger an emotional response (anxiety), which in turn leads to physical symptoms like a racing heart, sweating, or restlessness, creating a cycle that can feel difficult to break.

For example, someone who experiences social anxiety might have the thought, "Everyone will judge me if I speak up in this meeting." This thought fuels the emotional response of fear, which then leads to avoidance behaviors, such as remaining silent. Over time, these avoidance behaviors reinforce the belief that social situations are dangerous, perpetuating the anxiety cycle.

CBT Techniques for Managing Anxiety

1. Thought Challenging and Reframing

The first step in managing anxiety through CBT is to identify the cognitive distortions fueling the anxiety. Common distortions include catastrophizing (expecting the worst possible outcome) and fortune-telling (predicting negative future events). Once these thoughts are identified, they can be challenged and reframed using evidence-based reasoning.

For example, someone experiencing work-related anxiety may think, "If I make a mistake, I'll lose my job." CBT encourages the person to ask themselves, "What evidence do I have that making one mistake will result in job loss? Have I ever made mistakes before without losing my job?" By gathering evidence and considering more balanced outcomes, they can reframe the thought into something more manageable, such as, "Making mistakes is part of learning, and I can take steps to correct any errors."

2. Exposure Therapy

Another key CBT strategy for managing anxiety is exposure therapy. This involves gradually exposing oneself to the feared situation in a controlled and safe manner, allowing the anxiety to naturally decrease over time as the brain learns that the feared outcome is unlikely to occur. For example, someone with a fear of public speaking might begin by practicing speaking in front of a small, trusted group before gradually increasing the size of the audience.

3. Relaxation Techniques

Anxiety often has a physical component, with symptoms such as rapid heart rate, tension, or shallow breathing. Relaxation techniques like deep breathing or progressive muscle relaxation help calm the body's physical response to anxiety, making it easier to manage the emotional and cognitive aspects. Deep breathing, for example, activates the parasympathetic nervous system, which helps counter the "fight or flight" response triggered by anxiety.

Managing Depression: Lifting the Weight of Hopelessness

The Cognitive Triad: How Depression Warps Thinking

Depression is often characterized by persistent feelings of sadness, hopelessness, and a lack of motivation. According to CBT, depression is fueled by negative thought patterns that affect how individuals view themselves, the world, and the future. This is known as the cognitive triad. People with depression often experience thoughts such as, "I'm worthless," "The world is a terrible place," or "Things will never get better."

These negative thoughts lead to emotional symptoms (such as sadness or apathy) and behavioral symptoms (such as withdrawal or inactivity), creating a cycle that reinforces the depressive state. Over time, this negative feedback loop can make it difficult for individuals to engage in activities that would normally bring them pleasure or a sense of accomplishment.

CBT Techniques for Managing Depression

1. Behavioral Activation

One of the most effective CBT techniques for depression is behavioral activation. This strategy involves identifying activities that the individual once found enjoyable or meaningful and gradually reintroducing them into their routine. Behavioral activation helps counter the withdrawal and inactivity that often accompany depression by encouraging the individual to engage in positive, mood-boosting behaviors, even when they don't initially feel like it.

For example, a person struggling with depression may have stopped exercising, socializing, or pursuing hobbies. Behavioral activation helps them create a plan to re-engage with these activities in small, manageable steps. Even though they may not feel motivated at first, the act of participating in positive activities can gradually lift their mood.

2. Cognitive Restructuring

Cognitive restructuring is a central CBT technique for addressing the distorted thoughts that fuel depression. This involves identifying negative automatic thoughts (such as "I'm a failure") and challenging them by examining the evidence for and against them. The goal is to replace these negative thoughts with more realistic and balanced alternatives.

For instance, someone who thinks, "I never do anything right," might be encouraged to look for counter-evidence: "What about the time I helped a friend through a difficult situation, or when I succeeded at work?" By reframing these thoughts, the individual can begin to break the cycle of negative thinking that perpetuates depression.

3. Scheduling Positive Activities

CBT also encourages individuals with depression to create a schedule of positive activities that they can look forward to. This helps counter the lack of motivation and feelings of hopelessness that often accompany depression. Scheduling enjoyable activities—whether it's taking a walk, meeting a friend for coffee, or reading a favorite book—can provide a sense of purpose and lead to small, achievable goals that boost mood and confidence over time.

Managing Anger: Harnessing and Redirecting the Emotion

The Nature of Anger: A Response to Perceived Injustice

Anger is a natural emotional response to perceived injustice, unfairness, or frustration. However, when anger becomes overwhelming or uncontrolled, it can lead to destructive behaviors and damaged relationships. In CBT, anger is understood as being fueled by irrational beliefs and cognitive distortions that exaggerate the sense of injustice or personal slight.

For example, someone might interpret a minor disagreement as a major personal attack, leading to an angry outburst. In this case, the underlying thought might be, "They're disrespecting me on purpose," even if the actual situation doesn't support this conclusion. The intense emotional response of anger is therefore disproportionate to the situation.

CBT Techniques for Managing Anger

1. Identifying and Challenging Trigger Thoughts

The first step in managing anger through CBT is to identify the trigger thoughts that lead to anger. Often, these thoughts involve personalization (believing that everything is a personal attack), overgeneralization (believing that this one incident reflects a larger pattern), or mind-reading (assuming you know what others are thinking). Once these thoughts are identified, they can be challenged.

For example, instead of thinking, "They did this to upset me," CBT encourages the individual to ask, "Is there any evidence that they intended to upset me, or am I jumping to conclusions?" By examining the facts more closely, the individual can challenge the distorted thought and reframe it, such as, "They might not have realized their actions bothered me."

2. Anger Management Techniques

Anger management techniques such as time-outs or assertiveness training are also key components of CBT for anger. Taking a time-out involves stepping away from the situation to allow the individual time to cool down before responding, preventing emotional escalation. Assertiveness training helps individuals express their feelings and needs calmly and clearly without resorting to aggression.

For instance, instead of lashing out in anger, an individual might say, "I feel frustrated because it seems like my input isn't being considered." This approach allows for healthy communication and prevents the anger from damaging relationships.

3. Relaxation and Stress-Reduction Techniques

Since anger is often accompanied by physiological arousal (such as a racing heart or clenched muscles), CBT incorporates relaxation techniques to help calm the body's stress response. Deep breathing, progressive muscle relaxation, or visualization exercises can help reduce the intensity of the physical symptoms of anger, making it easier to manage the emotion itself.

Transforming Emotions Through CBT

From Reaction to Regulation: Mastering Anxiety, Depression, and Anger underscores the powerful role that Cognitive Behavioral Therapy (CBT) plays in managing these intense emotional states. By addressing the cognitive distortions that drive anxiety, depression, and anger, CBT offers practical tools for identifying, challenging, and reframing unhelpful thoughts. Whether through behavioral activation for depression, thought challenging for anxiety, or anger management techniques, CBT empowers individuals to take control of their emotional lives.

By learning to understand the thought patterns that underlie these emotions and applying targeted strategies to reshape them, individuals can move from emotional reactivity to thoughtful regulation. This transformation leads to a greater sense of emotional resilience, improved relationships, and a higher quality of life overall.

Stoic Practices for Emotional Resilience: Practicing Detachment from Outcomes

One of the most powerful principles in Stoic philosophy is the concept of detachment from outcomes. This practice is rooted in the idea that while we have control over our actions, decisions, and attitudes, we do not have control over external events or their results. Learning to detach from outcomes means accepting the uncertainty of life and focusing on what lies within our control—our thoughts, values, and actions. In doing so, we develop emotional resilience, as we become less disturbed by events outside our influence and more focused on the virtues we cultivate through our behavior.

The Stoics, including Epictetus, Seneca, and Marcus Aurelius, repeatedly emphasized that striving for outcomes over which we have no control is a source of unnecessary suffering. Instead, they advised focusing on our efforts and internal states—what they called "living in accordance with nature"—which allows us to maintain inner peace regardless of how external circumstances unfold. Practicing detachment from outcomes doesn't mean becoming indifferent or apathetic. Rather, it involves maintaining a sense of tranquility by embracing the process and letting go of the fixation on results.

In this comprehensive exploration, we will dive deep into the Stoic practice of detachment from outcomes, understanding how it fosters emotional resilience, and how it can be integrated into daily life to build a mindset of strength, adaptability, and inner peace.

Understanding the Stoic Concept of Detachment

What Does It Mean to Detach from Outcomes?

At the heart of Stoicism lies the distinction between what we can and cannot control. According to Epictetus, "Some things are up to us, and some things are not up to us." The things within our control include our thoughts, intentions, and actions—essentially, our inner world. The things outside our control include external circumstances, the actions of others, and the ultimate outcomes of our efforts. Detachment from outcomes is the practice of accepting this distinction and focusing solely on what is within our sphere of influence.

Detaching from outcomes means relinquishing the emotional investment in how things turn out. This doesn't imply that we stop caring about what we do. Instead, it means that our sense of self-worth and emotional equilibrium are not contingent upon success or failure. For example, a Stoic might pursue a job promotion with full dedication, but if they do not get the promotion, their emotional well-being remains intact because they know that the outcome was beyond their control. They take satisfaction in knowing they put forth their best effort and acted according to their principles.

Why Attachment to Outcomes Leads to Suffering

From a Stoic perspective, attachment to outcomes is a primary source of emotional distress. This attachment can manifest as anxiety about future events, frustration over setbacks, or disappointment when things don't go as planned. When we tie our happiness or sense of self-worth to results that are not fully within our control, we become vulnerable to external forces—forces we have no power to change.

Consider someone who invests significant emotional energy in being liked by others. They may constantly worry about how they are perceived, and if someone criticizes them or doesn't respond favorably, their sense of self-esteem is shaken. The Stoic response would be to recognize that while we can control our own actions—such as being kind, honest, and thoughtful—we cannot control how others respond. By detaching from the need for approval, the individual can maintain inner peace, knowing that their worth is not dependent on others' opinions.

This attachment to outcomes often creates a cycle of suffering. When we desire specific outcomes—be it success, recognition, or approval—we set ourselves up for disappointment if those outcomes are not achieved. Moreover, even if we achieve them, the relief is temporary, as new desires or anxieties soon arise. Detachment from outcomes frees us from this cycle by fostering contentment with the process, rather than the result.

The Power of Focusing on What You Can Control

The Stoic Dichotomy of Control

The dichotomy of control, articulated by Epictetus, is central to practicing detachment. It teaches us to distinguish between things that are within our control—our own thoughts, beliefs, and actions—and those that are not, such as other people's actions, external events, or even the eventual consequences of our efforts.

This distinction helps us realize that much of what causes emotional turmoil is beyond our control. Once we internalize this principle, we can redirect our energy toward what we *can* influence: the way we respond to challenges, how we treat others, and how we interpret situations. In this way, practicing detachment leads to empowerment and clarity, as it eliminates the futile effort of trying to control the uncontrollable.

For instance, consider an athlete who trains rigorously for a competition. While the athlete can control their preparation, mindset, and effort during the event, they cannot control factors such as weather, the performance of their competitors, or the final outcome. By focusing on what is within their control—training with dedication and competing with integrity—the athlete can approach the event with confidence. Whether they win or lose, they find satisfaction in their effort, knowing they did their best. The outcome becomes secondary to the virtues they practiced along the way.

Living in Accordance with Nature

A core Stoic idea is that we must live in accordance with nature—that is, align our actions with the natural order of the universe and accept the inherent uncertainty of life. Detachment from outcomes embodies this principle by recognizing that life is full of unpredictable events, and trying to control or resist this natural uncertainty leads to frustration.

Stoics believe that our well-being depends on accepting the world as it is and not as we wish it to be. When we detach from outcomes, we accept the possibility that things may not go as planned, but we remain anchored in our virtues and values, which are always within our control. This shift in focus creates emotional resilience, as we no longer tie our happiness to external circumstances but to our own actions and character.

Practical Techniques for Practicing Detachment from Outcomes

1. Negative Visualization: Preparing for Uncertainty

Negative visualization is a Stoic practice in which you imagine the worst-case scenario before embarking on any task or pursuit. This is not done to invite pessimism but to prepare the mind for all possible outcomes. By imagining potential setbacks or failures, you become emotionally prepared to face them if they occur, reducing the shock or disappointment when things don't go as planned.

For example, if you're preparing for a job interview, take a moment to visualize the possibility that the interview might not go well, or that you may not get the job. By mentally preparing for this outcome, you reduce the emotional impact if it happens, and instead, you can focus on how you can improve or handle the situation with grace.

2. Amor Fati: Loving Fate

Another powerful Stoic practice is amor fati, which translates to "love of fate." This concept encourages embracing whatever happens as necessary and beneficial, regardless of whether it aligns with our desires. By cultivating a mindset that welcomes all outcomes—good or bad—we free ourselves from emotional turmoil. Amor fati is about seeing every event as an opportunity for growth and development, rather than something to be resisted or lamented.

If, for example, a business venture fails, practicing amor fati would involve accepting the failure as part of your path and looking for the lessons or new opportunities that arise from it. Rather than viewing the outcome as a setback, it becomes a valuable part of your journey.

3. Letting Go of Attachment Through Mindfulness

Although mindfulness is commonly associated with Buddhism, it aligns with Stoic principles of detachment. Mindfulness teaches us to remain fully present in the moment and to observe our thoughts and emotions without becoming attached to them. By practicing mindfulness, we can become aware of when we are overly fixated on a particular outcome and gently redirect our focus to the present effort.

For instance, if you find yourself obsessing over the result of a project at work, mindfulness can help you step back, recognize the unproductive nature of this attachment, and refocus your attention on doing the task well in the present moment. Through mindfulness, you learn to appreciate the process itself, rather than becoming entangled in the uncertainty of outcomes.

Emotional Resilience Through Detachment

The Inner Freedom of Detachment

When we practice detachment from outcomes, we cultivate an inner freedom that is unshakable by external events. Stoic philosophers often described this state as ataraxia, or tranquility of the mind. By embracing uncertainty and letting go of the need for specific results, we become emotionally resilient to whatever life brings.

Emotional resilience doesn't mean that we are unaffected by life's challenges—it means that we recover more quickly from setbacks and maintain a sense of inner peace, regardless of external circumstances. Detachment from outcomes fosters this resilience by helping us recognize that our true power lies in our actions and intentions, not in controlling results.

Detachment in Practice: A Path to Strength and Adaptability

Consider a leader facing an uncertain business venture. Rather than fearing failure, they focus on what they can control: making thoughtful decisions, treating their team with respect, and working diligently. If the venture succeeds, they remain calm, knowing their efforts contributed to the outcome. If it fails, they also remain calm, recognizing that they did their best. In both cases, they are resilient, adaptable, and internally fortified because their emotional state is tied to their actions, not external results.

The Freedom in Letting Go

Master Emotional Resilience Through the Power of Detachment from Outcomes. Stoic wisdom teaches us to focus on what we can control and release our emotional attachment to external events. By practicing detachment from outcomes, we cultivate a mindset of inner freedom and strength, allowing us to face life's uncertainties with grace and resilience. Whether we experience success or failure, we find peace in knowing that we have acted with integrity, wisdom, and effort—all of which are within our control. Through techniques such as negative visualization, amor fati, and mindfulness, we develop the ability to embrace whatever happens without losing our emotional equilibrium. This freedom from attachment not only fosters emotional resilience but also leads to a deeper sense of fulfillment and tranquility in our daily lives. As the Stoics teach us, it is not the outcome that defines us, but how we approach and respond to life's challenges.

Developing Equanimity: The Stoic Path to Mental Calmness

In a world filled with constant change, unpredictability, and emotional highs and lows, the ability to maintain equanimity—or mental calmness—is an invaluable skill. Equanimity, a central concept in Stoic philosophy, refers to the capacity to remain composed and undisturbed by external events, whether they are positive or negative. In Stoicism, equanimity is not about suppressing emotions but about cultivating the inner strength to stay balanced in the face of life's inevitable challenges and uncertainties.

The Stoics believed that true resilience comes from the ability to regulate one's internal state, regardless of what happens externally. For the Stoic philosopher Marcus Aurelius, life was filled with turmoil—wars, personal losses, and political responsibilities—yet he maintained a sense of calm through the practice of Stoic principles. He emphasized that our response to external events, rather than the events themselves, defines our emotional state. Epictetus similarly taught that while we cannot control what happens to us, we can control how we react, and therein lies our power to achieve mental calmness or ataraxia.

In this exploration of Stoic practices for emotional resilience, we will examine the importance of developing equanimity, the methods through which it can be cultivated, and how this state of mental calmness leads to a more peaceful and fulfilling life. By integrating these practices into daily life, you can build emotional resilience and develop a mindset that remains steady in the face of adversity.

Equanimity in Stoicism: The Power of Mental Calmness

What Is Equanimity in Stoic Thought?

In Stoicism, equanimity is the state of remaining emotionally steady and untroubled by external circumstances. The Stoics viewed equanimity as the key to living a life of virtue, free from the emotional turbulence that arises from desires, fears, and attachments to external outcomes. Achieving equanimity involves understanding what is within our control and what is not, and developing the wisdom to focus solely on what we can influence.

Stoic equanimity is closely linked to the idea of ataraxia, which can be translated as tranquility of the mind. This mental state is characterized by inner peace, achieved through the practice of reason and self-discipline. It is not the absence of emotion but the ability to remain emotionally balanced—free from irrational fear, anxiety, or elation—regardless of external conditions.

For the Stoics, equanimity is the natural outcome of practicing virtue. By cultivating virtues like wisdom, courage, and justice, we train our minds to respond to challenges with composure and clarity, rather than being driven by emotional impulses. Equanimity becomes a reflection of a well-ordered mind, one that is capable of maintaining calm even in the midst of external chaos.

The Value of Equanimity in Daily Life

In modern life, equanimity offers a profound antidote to stress, anxiety, and frustration. The daily pressures of work, relationships, and unforeseen events can easily throw us off balance if we are emotionally reactive to every challenge. Stoicism teaches that by developing equanimity, we can maintain our inner peace regardless of what life throws our way.

For instance, consider someone who faces constant criticism at work. Without equanimity, they might internalize these critiques, becoming anxious, defensive, or angry. However, by practicing Stoic equanimity, they can acknowledge the criticism without letting it disturb their mental calm. They recognize that while they can control how they respond and improve their performance, they cannot control others' opinions or actions. This mindset allows them to stay focused on what matters and remain emotionally steady, even in difficult situations.

Equanimity also enhances our ability to make rational decisions. When we are emotionally agitated, our ability to think clearly and act wisely is compromised. By cultivating mental calmness, we create the space needed for thoughtful reflection, allowing us to respond to situations from a place of reason rather than emotion. This leads to better choices and more harmonious interactions with others.

Practicing Equanimity: Stoic Techniques for Mental Calmness

1. Understanding the Dichotomy of Control

The foundation of equanimity in Stoicism is the dichotomy of control, a principle famously outlined by Epictetus. This concept teaches that there are two categories of things in life: those that are within our control and those that are not. According to Stoicism, the key to equanimity is to focus only on what is within our control and to accept with grace the things that are not.

What is within our control?

- Our thoughts, attitudes, and actions
- How we interpret events
- The effort we put into our tasks and relationships

What is outside our control?

- The actions of others
- External events, such as natural disasters, illness, or political changes
- The ultimate outcomes of our efforts

For example, imagine you are preparing for a major presentation. You can control how much effort you put into preparing, your attitude during the presentation, and how you respond to any difficulties that arise. However, you cannot control the audience's reaction or whether external factors, like technical issues, will disrupt your performance. By accepting this, you free yourself from the anxiety of trying to control the uncontrollable and can focus fully on your efforts.

2. Negative Visualization: Preparing the Mind for Adversity

Another Stoic technique that fosters equanimity is negative visualization, also known as premeditatio malorum (premeditation of evils). This practice involves mentally rehearsing potential difficulties or setbacks that could occur in life, not to dwell on negativity, but to prepare the mind to face challenges with calmness and composure.

For example, you might visualize losing a job, experiencing financial hardship, or facing illness. By imagining these scenarios, you train your mind to accept that difficulties are a natural part of life. When such challenges arise, they feel less shocking because you have already prepared yourself emotionally. Negative visualization helps cultivate gratitude for what you have while simultaneously building resilience for what might come.

This practice aligns with the Stoic belief that life is unpredictable, and adversity is inevitable. By rehearsing possible challenges, you reduce the emotional impact when they occur, enabling you to respond with equanimity rather than panic or despair.

3. Practicing Self-Distancing: Gaining Perspective

Another powerful Stoic technique for maintaining equanimity is self-distancing—the ability to step back from your emotions and view situations from a more objective perspective. When we are emotionally entangled in a situation, it can be difficult to think clearly or maintain composure. By distancing ourselves from the immediate emotional reaction, we can gain a broader perspective and respond more rationally.

One method of self-distancing is to ask yourself, "How would I advise a friend in this situation?" or "How would I view this event a year from now?" This shift in perspective helps reduce the emotional intensity of the moment, allowing you to act with greater clarity and calmness.

The Stoics often used this technique to remind themselves of the transient nature of life's difficulties. Marcus Aurelius, in his *Meditations*, frequently reflected on the insignificance of daily struggles in the grand scheme of things, encouraging himself to stay calm and grounded by viewing events from a higher vantage point.

4. Cultivating Mindfulness in the Present Moment

Although mindfulness is typically associated with Buddhist practices, it is highly compatible with Stoic equanimity. Mindfulness involves focusing on the present moment with nonjudgmental awareness, allowing us to fully experience life without being overwhelmed by thoughts of the past or anxieties about the future.

By practicing mindfulness, we develop the ability to observe our emotions and thoughts without becoming consumed by them. In moments of emotional turbulence, mindfulness helps us stay grounded, preventing us from reacting impulsively. Instead, we can pause, reflect, and choose how to respond.

For example, when faced with an unexpected disappointment, such as the cancellation of an important event, mindfulness allows us to acknowledge the initial feelings of frustration without letting them spiral into anger or despair. Instead, we observe the emotions as they arise, accept them, and then let them pass, maintaining mental calmness throughout.

Equanimity in Action: Applying Stoic Principles to Daily Life

Facing Setbacks with Grace

One of the most practical applications of equanimity is learning how to handle setbacks with grace. Whether it's a missed opportunity, a failed project, or a personal loss, Stoic equanimity helps us maintain emotional balance by focusing on what we can control and accepting what we cannot.

For example, if you're passed over for a promotion at work, the initial emotional reaction might be disappointment or frustration. However, by practicing equanimity, you can shift your focus to what you can control: continuing to work diligently, improving your skills, and maintaining a positive attitude. You let go of resentment because you recognize that the decision was not fully within your control.

Building Emotional Resilience in Relationships

Equanimity also plays a crucial role in managing relationships. Conflicts and misunderstandings are inevitable in any relationship, but by maintaining mental calmness, we can navigate these challenges with patience and empathy. When someone says or does something hurtful, equanimity allows us to pause before reacting, preventing impulsive outbursts or emotional escalation.

In relationships, equanimity fosters emotional resilience by helping us focus on our own actions and responses rather than trying to control others. We learn to communicate calmly, set boundaries when needed, and approach conflicts with a level-headed mindset, which strengthens relationships over time.

Cultivating Calm in the Storm

The Stoic Art of Equanimity: Finding Peace Amid Life's Challenges summarizes the profound impact that equanimity has on emotional resilience and well-being. By embracing Stoic principles, such as the dichotomy of control, negative visualization, and self-distancing, we cultivate a mindset that allows us to remain calm and composed, regardless of external circumstances. Equanimity empowers us to face life's inevitable adversities with grace, fortitude, and clarity.

Through the practice of mental calmness, we develop a profound inner strength that cannot be shaken by the unpredictability of life. Whether we are navigating personal challenges, professional setbacks, or the complexities of relationships, equanimity enables us to maintain our balance and act in accordance with our highest virtues. In this way, equanimity becomes not only a tool for emotional resilience but also a pathway to living a more peaceful and fulfilling life.

Understanding and Accepting Impermanence: A Buddhist Approach to Suffering

One of the central teachings of Buddhism is the concept of impermanence (*anicca* in Pali), which refers to the idea that all things—both material and mental—are in a constant state of flux. Everything that arises must also pass away, including our thoughts, emotions, relationships, and even our physical bodies. This reality of impermanence is not just a philosophical idea; it is a profound truth that has deep implications for how we experience life and manage suffering.

Suffering (*dukkha*), according to Buddhism, arises when we resist the natural flow of impermanence. We suffer when we cling to things that are transient, whether they are material possessions, personal identities, or emotional states. The more tightly we hold on, the more painful it becomes when these things inevitably change or disappear. Understanding and accepting impermanence is a key step in alleviating this suffering. Instead of resisting change, Buddhism teaches us to embrace it, recognizing that nothing in life is fixed or permanent. This understanding fosters emotional resilience, allowing us to live with a greater sense of peace, freedom, and equanimity.

In this discussion, we will explore the Buddhist approach to suffering and impermanence. We will examine how the Four Noble Truths and the Three Marks of Existence (impermanence, suffering, and non-self) lay the foundation for understanding life's transitory nature. We will also discuss practical ways to accept and work with impermanence in daily life, exploring how doing so can help us build emotional resilience and find greater meaning in the present moment.

The Buddhist View of Impermanence: An Ever-Changing Reality

The Nature of Impermanence: Everything is in Flux

Impermanence is a fundamental principle in Buddhism that states everything in the universe is subject to change. This includes not only physical objects but also our emotions, thoughts, relationships, and identities. Nothing remains static, and everything is in a constant process of arising, decaying, and passing away. For Buddhists, recognizing impermanence is essential for understanding the true nature of existence.

The Buddha taught that clinging to things as if they were permanent leads to suffering because the reality is that everything we attach ourselves to will eventually change or disappear. Whether it's our youth, loved ones, or material possessions, all things are temporary, and their inevitable change or loss can cause pain if we are not prepared to let go. The refusal to accept impermanence lies at the heart of human suffering.

For example, think about how often people try to hold on to happiness, wishing it would last forever. Yet, as anyone who has experienced joy knows, happiness is fleeting. Trying to cling to happiness, just like clinging to youth or success, results in frustration because these states are impermanent by nature. This insight into impermanence is not meant to cause despair but to shift our perspective toward the transient nature of life.

The Three Marks of Existence: Impermanence, Suffering, and Non-Self

Impermanence is one of the Three Marks of Existence, which also include suffering (dukkha) and non-self (anatta). Together, these three marks describe the fundamental characteristics of all things in the universe. Impermanence refers to the fact that everything changes, suffering arises from attachment to impermanent things, and non-self points to the idea that there is no unchanging, permanent self that endures over time.

The recognition of these truths is central to Buddhist teachings. The Buddha emphasized that understanding impermanence helps us confront the nature of suffering directly. By doing so, we develop the wisdom needed to navigate life's inevitable difficulties with greater ease and emotional resilience.

The Four Noble Truths: A Framework for Understanding Suffering

The First Noble Truth: The Reality of Suffering

The First Noble Truth states that suffering is an inherent part of life. This suffering comes in many forms, from physical pain to emotional distress, to the deeper existential suffering that arises from trying to hold on to things that are inherently impermanent. The Buddha's teaching on suffering is not meant to be pessimistic but rather realistic. Life contains joy, beauty, and happiness, but it also contains loss, change, and decay—all of which lead to suffering when we try to resist them.

The Second Noble Truth: The Cause of Suffering

The Second Noble Truth reveals that the cause of suffering is craving (tanha)—the desire for things to be other than they are. This craving is often rooted in our inability to accept impermanence. We crave permanence in our relationships, material wealth, and emotional states, and when these things change, as they inevitably do, we experience suffering.

For example, we may become attached to a certain lifestyle or social status, but as circumstances change—such as losing a job or moving to a new city—our attachment to the past creates emotional turmoil. We want things to stay as they were, but the reality of impermanence prevents that from happening.

The Third Noble Truth: The End of Suffering

The Third Noble Truth offers hope by teaching that it is possible to end suffering by overcoming attachment and accepting impermanence. When we stop clinging to things as if they are permanent and recognize the transitory nature of all experiences, we free ourselves from much of the suffering that afflicts us. This doesn't mean we stop caring or enjoying life, but that we approach life with a deeper understanding of its changing nature.

The Fourth Noble Truth: The Path to Liberation

The Fourth Noble Truth provides a path for overcoming suffering, known as the Eightfold Path. This path includes ethical conduct, mental discipline, and wisdom—practices that help cultivate mindfulness, equanimity, and acceptance of impermanence. By following this path, we develop the ability to face life's challenges with clarity and resilience, reducing our suffering and increasing our inner peace.

Accepting Impermanence: A Path to Emotional Resilience

Letting Go of Attachment: The Key to Peace

One of the most challenging yet transformative aspects of the Buddhist approach to impermanence is learning to let go of attachment. In Buddhist teachings, attachment refers to our tendency to cling to things, people, or experiences as if they are permanent sources of happiness. However, because all things are subject to change, attachment inevitably leads to suffering.

Letting go of attachment does not mean withdrawing from life or becoming indifferent. Rather, it involves cultivating a sense of non-attachment, where we can engage fully with life's experiences while recognizing that they are temporary. Non-attachment allows us to appreciate the present moment without trying to hold on to it. This mindset fosters emotional resilience, as we become less disturbed by the inevitable changes in our lives.

For example, in relationships, we often become attached to the idea of permanence, expecting our loved ones to always be there for us. But life is unpredictable, and people change or move away. By accepting impermanence, we can love deeply without the fear of loss, knowing that change is natural and inevitable. This approach frees us from the anxiety of trying to control what cannot be controlled.

Impermanence and Mindfulness: Staying Grounded in the Present

Mindfulness, a cornerstone of Buddhist practice, is a powerful tool for cultivating an acceptance of impermanence. Mindfulness involves paying full attention to the present moment, observing thoughts, emotions, and sensations without judgment. Through mindfulness, we become aware of the constant flow of change that characterizes all aspects of life.

By practicing mindfulness, we develop the ability to notice how our thoughts and feelings are transient. For example, when a negative emotion like anger arises, mindfulness allows us to observe it as a temporary experience. We see how the emotion appears, intensifies, and eventually fades away. This direct experience of impermanence helps reduce our attachment to both positive and negative emotions, making it easier to navigate the ups and downs of life.

Through mindfulness, we also learn to savor the present moment, knowing that it is fleeting. Whether we are enjoying a meal, spending time with loved ones, or simply sitting in nature, mindfulness encourages us to fully immerse ourselves in the experience without clinging to it. This practice deepens our appreciation of life's beauty while fostering emotional resilience in the face of its challenges.

Practical Ways to Embrace Impermanence

1. Practice Gratitude for the Present Moment

One way to embrace impermanence is by cultivating gratitude for the present moment. Recognizing that everything is temporary helps us appreciate what we have while we have it. Whether it's a friendship, a beautiful sunset, or a period of good health, gratitude allows us to savor these experiences without becoming attached to their continuation. Practicing gratitude in this way helps us accept change with grace and resilience.

2. Reflect on Change as a Constant

Regularly reflecting on the impermanent nature of all things helps us internalize this truth. This can be done through meditation or journaling, where we contemplate the transient nature of our thoughts, feelings, and experiences. By reflecting on change as a constant, we become more accepting of life's unpredictability and better equipped to handle difficult transitions.

3. Engage in Compassionate Detachment

Compassionate detachment involves caring deeply for others while understanding that we cannot control their actions or outcomes. It allows us to love and support people without becoming attached to their presence in our lives or their behavior. This approach reduces suffering in relationships, as we accept that people, like everything else, are subject to change.

Embracing Impermanence for Greater Peace

Impermanence is the Key to Freedom from Suffering. It is a profound Buddhist teaching that accepting life's transitory nature is essential for reducing suffering and achieving emotional resilience. By understanding that all things—material possessions, relationships, emotions, and even our sense of self—are impermanent, we begin to loosen our grip on the illusion of permanence. Through practices like mindfulness, gratitude, and compassionate detachment, we can cultivate a mindset that embraces change rather than resists it. This acceptance of impermanence not only fosters inner peace but also allows us to engage more fully with life, free from the anxiety and suffering that arise from attachment. In doing so, we build the emotional resilience necessary to navigate life's inevitable changes with grace and tranquility.

Practices for Reducing Suffering through Mindfulness: A Buddhist Approach

At the heart of Buddhist philosophy is the belief that suffering is an inevitable part of the human experience. The Buddha identified the root of this suffering as our attachment to desires, cravings, and illusions about the world. However, he also taught that suffering can be alleviated through mindful awareness. Mindfulness (*sati* in Pali), one of the core practices in Buddhism, offers a path to reducing suffering by helping us become fully present, non-judgmental, and accepting of whatever arises in our lives.

Mindfulness is more than just a mental exercise; it is a way of being. By cultivating a deep awareness of our thoughts, emotions, and bodily sensations, we can break free from the habitual patterns of craving and aversion that fuel suffering. Rather than becoming entangled in our thoughts or reacting impulsively to emotions, mindfulness teaches us to observe them with detachment and curiosity. In this state of heightened awareness, we can clearly see the transient nature of all things, which, in turn, allows us to let go of clinging and reduce our emotional distress.

In this discussion, we will explore Buddhist practices for reducing suffering through mindfulness, delving into the specific techniques that cultivate this awareness and foster emotional resilience. We will examine how mindfulness allows us to confront difficult emotions, reduce mental agitation, and ultimately transcend suffering by aligning with the present moment. By understanding these practices, we can cultivate a greater sense of inner peace and live with more balance and clarity.

Mindfulness as the Antidote to Suffering

The Link Between Mindfulness and Suffering

Buddhism teaches that suffering arises from attachment—our tendency to cling to things we want and avoid things we dislike. Whether it's material possessions, relationships, or even our self-image, we habitually grasp at things in the hope of finding security or happiness. Yet, because all things are impermanent, these attachments inevitably lead to suffering when they change or disappear. Mindfulness directly addresses this source of suffering by allowing us to observe our desires, thoughts, and emotions without becoming attached to them.

Mindfulness creates a space between stimulus and response. When we encounter something pleasant, we might normally react with craving, wanting to hold on to it for as long as possible. When we encounter something unpleasant, we might react with aversion, seeking to push it away or avoid it. These habitual responses create suffering because they keep us caught in a cycle of craving and resistance. Mindfulness disrupts this cycle by cultivating non-attachment—the ability to experience life's ups and downs without clinging to or avoiding them.

For example, if we experience physical pain, we may react by tensing up, becoming mentally distressed, and trying to avoid or resist the pain. However, through mindfulness, we can observe the sensation of pain without layering it with emotional reactions. We notice the pain, acknowledge it, but refrain from becoming attached to the desire to eliminate it. This shift in perspective helps reduce the mental suffering that often accompanies physical discomfort.

Mindfulness and the Four Foundations of Awareness

In Buddhism, mindfulness is often practiced through the Four Foundations of Mindfulness, outlined in the *Satipatthana Sutta*. These foundations guide practitioners in observing the body, feelings, mind, and mental objects with awareness. Each foundation serves as a focal point for developing mindfulness, leading to a deeper understanding of impermanence and the cessation of suffering.

1. **Mindfulness of the Body**: This involves observing physical sensations, such as the breath, bodily movements, or sensations of tension or relaxation. By focusing on the body, we become more grounded in the present moment and less distracted by mental chatter.
2. **Mindfulness of Feelings**: This foundation encourages us to become aware of pleasant, unpleasant, and neutral feelings as they arise. Instead of reacting to feelings with craving or aversion, we observe them with detachment, recognizing their transient nature.
3. **Mindfulness of the Mind**: Here, we observe our mental states—whether they are calm, agitated, joyful, or anxious. This awareness helps us see how our mind influences our emotions and behavior, allowing us to make more skillful choices in how we respond.
4. **Mindfulness of Mental Objects**: This includes observing thoughts, perceptions, and mental constructs. By becoming mindful of our mental objects, we recognize that thoughts are just thoughts—impermanent, fleeting, and not necessarily reflective of reality. This insight helps reduce identification with negative or distressing thoughts.

By cultivating mindfulness in these four areas, we deepen our understanding of how suffering arises and how we can let go of the attachments and aversions that fuel it.

Practical Mindfulness Techniques for Reducing Suffering

1. Mindfulness of Breathing: Anchoring the Mind

One of the most accessible mindfulness practices for reducing suffering is mindfulness of breathing (*anapanasati*). This practice involves paying close attention to the sensation of the breath as it enters and leaves the body. The breath acts as an anchor, keeping the mind grounded in the present moment. By returning to the breath whenever the mind wanders, we train ourselves to stay present and aware, even in the face of discomfort or emotional turbulence.

For example, when feeling anxious, we might notice our breath becoming shallow or erratic. Mindfulness of breathing allows us to bring our attention back to the breath, slowing it down and calming the body. As we observe the breath without judgment, we create space to let go of the anxious thoughts that might otherwise spiral into greater distress.

Over time, mindfulness of breathing strengthens our ability to remain calm and centered, even when external circumstances provoke emotional reactions. This practice helps reduce suffering by fostering equanimity and detachment from the mental chatter that often exacerbates emotional pain.

2. Observing Thoughts and Emotions with Non-Judgment

A key aspect of mindfulness is learning to observe thoughts and emotions without identifying with them or reacting impulsively. Often, suffering arises not from the initial experience of pain or discomfort but from the secondary suffering that comes from our reactions—such as frustration, fear, or self-criticism. Mindfulness helps us observe these reactions as passing mental events, rather than as facts or defining aspects of our identity.

For example, if we experience anger in a situation, mindfulness allows us to notice the sensation of anger without acting on it. We observe how the body tightens, how the mind races with angry thoughts, and how emotions rise and fall like waves. Instead of becoming consumed by anger, we watch it with curiosity, allowing it to run its course without escalating into harmful behavior. This approach helps reduce the suffering that often accompanies intense emotions.

Mindfulness teaches us that thoughts and emotions are not permanent, nor are they inherently "bad." They are simply phenomena that arise and pass away. By observing them without judgment, we weaken their grip on us, allowing us to respond more skillfully to life's challenges.

3. Body Scan Meditation: Releasing Tension and Resistance

Another mindfulness practice for reducing suffering is the body scan meditation. This practice involves slowly bringing awareness to different parts of the body, noticing any sensations of tension, pain, or relaxation. The body scan helps us become more attuned to the physical manifestation of emotions and stress, allowing us to release tension that we may not even be consciously aware of.

For instance, when we are stressed, we may unconsciously clench our jaw, tighten our shoulders, or hold tension in the stomach. By systematically scanning the body and bringing mindful awareness to these areas, we can consciously relax them, releasing both physical and emotional tension. This practice reduces suffering by helping us let go of the resistance and aversion that often intensifies physical discomfort.

The body scan also helps us reconnect with the present moment. By focusing on bodily sensations, we break free from the mental narratives that often fuel anxiety or rumination. The practice grounds us in the here and now, providing relief from the mental and emotional suffering that arises from worrying about the future or dwelling on the past.

Cultivating Mindfulness in Daily Life: A Path to Lasting Peace

Mindfulness in Everyday Activities

While formal meditation practices are powerful tools for cultivating mindfulness, it is equally important to integrate mindfulness into our everyday activities. Mindfulness in daily life involves bringing present-moment awareness to routine tasks such as eating, walking, or even washing the dishes. By paying attention to the sensations, thoughts, and emotions that arise during these activities, we train ourselves to stay connected to the present moment, reducing the tendency to become lost in unhelpful thoughts.

For example, instead of rushing through a meal while distracted by a phone or TV, mindfulness encourages us to savor each bite, noticing the textures, flavors, and sensations of eating. This simple practice not only enhances our appreciation of the present moment but also reduces the stress that comes from constantly being "on autopilot."

By practicing mindfulness in mundane activities, we create opportunities throughout the day to reconnect with the present and reduce the mental chatter that often leads to suffering.

The Power of Mindfulness in Alleviating Suffering

Buddhist teachings remind us that suffering is not caused by the events of life but by our attachment to them. Through mindfulness practices—whether it's observing the breath, watching thoughts and emotions with detachment, or practicing mindful awareness in daily activities—we develop the capacity to reduce suffering by staying anchored in the present moment. Mindfulness doesn't eliminate life's challenges, but it transforms how we relate to them. Instead of becoming overwhelmed by emotions or entangled in thoughts, mindfulness offers us the space to respond with clarity, calmness, and acceptance. This shift in perspective is the key to transcending suffering and living with greater peace, resilience, and freedom.

Integrating Emotional Regulation and Resilience Practices: A Unified Approach for Daily Life

In navigating the complexities of modern life, we often encounter emotional challenges such as anxiety, depression, anger, and general emotional turbulence. While these challenges are an inherent part of being human, there are various time-tested strategies from different philosophical and psychological traditions that help us manage and transcend them. Cognitive Behavioral Therapy (CBT), Stoicism, and Buddhism each offer practical tools for regulating emotions, building resilience, and cultivating mental calmness. By integrating these disciplines, we can create a powerful, holistic approach to emotional regulation and resilience that helps us navigate life's ups and downs with greater ease.

These approaches—CBT's focus on identifying and managing emotional triggers, Stoicism's emphasis on mental calmness and detachment from outcomes, and Buddhism's teachings on impermanence and mindfulness—are complementary. When practiced together, they can help us build emotional awareness, reduce suffering, and develop resilience to life's challenges.

Let's explore how these practices can be combined in daily life, showing how they intersect and reinforce one another for a more balanced and fulfilling emotional life.

Emotional Awareness and Identification: The First Step in All Practices

Cognitive Behavioral Therapy: Recognizing Thoughts and Emotions

One of the foundational elements of CBT is learning to identify and become aware of our emotional responses to situations. Often, we experience emotions like anxiety, anger, or sadness without recognizing the specific thoughts and beliefs that triggered them. In CBT, this process is known as emotional awareness and involves carefully observing our emotions and the cognitive distortions (such as catastrophizing or black-and-white thinking) that often accompany them.

For instance, if you experience anxiety before a presentation, CBT encourages you to identify the thoughts behind the anxiety, such as "I'm going to fail" or "Everyone will think I'm incompetent." By becoming aware of these thoughts, you can challenge and reframe them, replacing negative thoughts with more realistic and constructive ones.

Stoicism: Observing Without Attachment

The Stoic practice of detachment from outcomes complements CBT's focus on emotional awareness by helping us observe our emotions without becoming attached to or overwhelmed by them. Stoicism teaches that external events and their outcomes are often beyond our control, but how we interpret and respond to them is entirely within our control. By practicing detachment, we learn to observe our emotions without allowing them to dictate our actions or sense of self-worth.

For example, in the context of the same presentation, a Stoic approach would involve recognizing that while you can control your preparation and effort, you cannot control the audience's reaction. Practicing detachment helps you focus on what is within your control—your actions and your internal state—rather than becoming anxious about an outcome that is outside your influence.

Buddhism: Mindful Awareness of Emotional States

In Buddhism, emotional awareness is cultivated through mindfulness, where we develop the ability to observe our emotions as they arise and pass without judgment. Buddhist practices emphasize non-attachment, allowing us to see emotions as temporary phenomena that don't define us. This aligns well with both CBT's identification of cognitive distortions and Stoicism's practice of detachment.

For example, if you feel anger arise in a stressful situation, mindfulness encourages you to observe the sensations in your body, the thoughts in your mind, and the overall experience of anger without trying to suppress or indulge it. This awareness fosters acceptance, helping you avoid reactive behavior and instead respond calmly.

Managing Anxiety, Depression, and Anger: A Multi-Faceted Approach

Cognitive Behavioral Techniques: Challenging and Reframing Thoughts

Once we become aware of our emotions, CBT offers concrete strategies for managing them, particularly anxiety, depression, and anger. One key technique is cognitive restructuring, where you challenge distorted thoughts (e.g., "I always fail") and replace them with more balanced, realistic ones (e.g., "I have succeeded before, and even if I struggle this time, it's a learning experience"). This reframing helps diminish the intensity of negative emotions.

CBT also encourages behavioral activation, where you engage in meaningful activities to counter depressive or anxious feelings. For example, if anxiety keeps you isolated, engaging in small, manageable social activities can help you gradually build confidence and reduce anxiety over time.

Stoicism: Developing Equanimity and Acceptance

Stoic practices provide an invaluable tool for managing anxiety and anger through the cultivation of equanimity—a state of mental calmness and emotional balance. Stoics teach that by recognizing the limits of our control and focusing on our internal responses, we can remain calm even in the face of external challenges. For example, if you're dealing with anger over an unfair situation, Stoicism encourages you to step back, assess the situation objectively, and focus on maintaining your integrity and virtue, rather than reacting impulsively.

In moments of anxiety, Stoicism's negative visualization technique—imagining the worst-case scenario—can reduce fear. By contemplating and accepting the possibility of failure or hardship, we become less anxious because we are emotionally prepared to face it.

Buddhist Practices: Mindfulness and Compassion

From a Buddhist perspective, the key to managing difficult emotions like anxiety, depression, and anger is to practice mindfulness and compassion. Mindfulness helps you become aware of the impermanence of all emotional states—anxiety will not last forever, and anger will eventually subside. This awareness helps you avoid becoming overwhelmed by emotions, as you learn to observe them with detachment.

Additionally, compassion—both for yourself and others—helps alleviate suffering. When you are mindful of your emotions, you can respond to yourself with kindness, acknowledging that anxiety, sadness, or anger are natural human experiences. This compassionate approach reduces self-criticism and fosters emotional healing.

Integrating Detachment and Acceptance: Overcoming Suffering

Stoic Detachment: Letting Go of Outcomes

Stoicism's emphasis on detaching from outcomes aligns with both CBT and Buddhism by encouraging us to let go of the need for control over external events. In everyday life, this means practicing emotional resilience by focusing on what is within our control—our actions, thoughts, and intentions—and accepting what is not. Detachment doesn't mean indifference; it means accepting life's uncertainties and changes without being emotionally destabilized by them.

For example, in a professional setting, if a project doesn't go as planned, practicing Stoic detachment helps you remain calm and centered, knowing you did your best even if the outcome wasn't ideal. This mindset frees you from unnecessary stress and anxiety.

Buddhist Impermanence: Accepting the Transience of Emotions

The Buddhist understanding of impermanence teaches that all emotions, no matter how intense, are temporary. Emotions like anger, sadness, and even joy arise and pass away. Accepting this impermanence allows us to engage with emotions more skillfully. Instead of becoming attached to positive emotions or resisting negative ones, we learn to let them flow through us without resistance, which reduces their power over us.

For example, when feeling anxious, a Buddhist approach would be to mindfully acknowledge the anxiety without trying to eliminate it. By observing the anxiety and recognizing it as impermanent, we reduce our suffering because we no longer identify with the emotion or view it as something permanent that defines us.

A Unified Daily Practice for Emotional Resilience

By weaving together the principles from CBT, Stoicism, and Buddhism, we create a holistic daily practice that strengthens emotional regulation and resilience:

1. Morning Mindfulness and Breathing Practice (Buddhism)

Start your day with **mindfulness of breathing**. Spend 10-15 minutes in quiet meditation, focusing on the sensation of your breath. This practice helps center your mind, anchoring you in the present moment. It also sets a calm, aware tone for the day, preparing you to respond to challenges with clarity and detachment.

2. Identifying and Reframing Negative Thoughts (CBT)

As you go through your day, practice emotional awareness by noticing any anxiety, frustration, or sadness that arises. Use **cognitive restructuring** to challenge distorted thoughts. If you find yourself thinking, "I'm going to fail," reframe this thought to something more constructive, like "I've prepared well, and I'll handle whatever comes my way."

3. Applying Stoic Detachment (Stoicism)

Throughout the day, especially in high-stress situations, practice Stoic detachment by reminding yourself of the dichotomy of control—**focus only on what you can control** (your actions and reactions) and **let go of what you cannot** (outcomes or others' opinions). This will help you maintain equanimity, allowing you to stay calm and collected in the face of adversity.

4. Evening Reflection and Journaling (Stoicism & CBT)

End your day with Stoic reflection or CBT thought journaling. Reflect on your actions, emotional responses, and how well you maintained your emotional awareness and detachment. Consider what you can improve and celebrate your successes. This evening practice reinforces your emotional resilience, providing insight into how you can better respond to emotions moving forward.

Integrating Wisdom for a Resilient Mind

By blending the insights of Cognitive Behavioral Therapy, Stoicism, and Buddhism, we create a unified approach to emotional regulation and resilience. Each discipline contributes a unique set of tools for understanding, managing, and transforming our emotional experiences. CBT offers practical techniques for identifying and challenging negative thoughts, Stoicism fosters emotional resilience through detachment and mental calmness, and Buddhism provides the framework for accepting impermanence and reducing suffering through mindfulness.

When practiced together, these approaches empower us to face life's challenges with greater clarity, emotional balance, and inner peace. This integration of wisdom from ancient and modern sources enables us to live more consciously, respond to emotions more skillfully, and find serenity in a world of constant change.

As we turn from the practices that cultivate emotional regulation and resilience, we now focus on how these inner skills shape our outer lives—particularly in how we navigate ethical choices and live in alignment with our values. The next step in this journey is to explore the intersection of **Virtue Ethics**, **Stoicism**, and **Buddhism** in guiding ethical living and decision-making. By applying core virtues to everyday life, we learn to act with integrity, compassion, and wisdom. Whether facing ethical dilemmas or simply making daily choices, these frameworks provide powerful tools for aligning our actions with our deeper principles. In this next section, we'll dive into how these traditions offer guidance on cultivating virtues, making moral decisions, and applying these insights in real-world situations.

6. Living with Integrity: Virtue Ethics, Stoicism, and Buddhist Wisdom for Ethical Decision-Making

Ethical decision-making is at the heart of living a life aligned with one's values, and both ancient and modern philosophies provide profound guidance on how to navigate the moral complexities of daily life. Virtue Ethics, Stoicism, and Buddhism offer distinct yet complementary paths for cultivating integrity, compassion, and wisdom in our choices. By identifying and developing core virtues, we create a foundation for making decisions that reflect our highest ideals. In this section, we'll explore how these traditions shape ethical living—from applying virtues like justice, courage, and compassion, to navigating ethical dilemmas with practical wisdom. We will also delve into real-life case studies to see how these ethical frameworks can guide us in the most challenging moments of life, helping us live with purpose and moral clarity.

Identifying and Cultivating Core Virtues: Building a Life of Ethical Excellence

At the heart of Virtue Ethics lies the idea that a good life is not defined by rules or consequences, but by the cultivation of character—the development of personal virtues that guide us in our actions, decisions, and relationships. Unlike other ethical systems that focus on external outcomes or fixed principles, Virtue Ethics emphasizes the importance of nurturing internal qualities like courage, wisdom, justice, and temperance to lead a flourishing and morally rich life. Rooted in the teachings of Aristotle, this approach offers a roadmap for how we can develop these virtues through practice, reflection, and intentional living.

Virtues are not innate traits but habits of excellence that we acquire through deliberate cultivation. Aristotle described virtues as the "golden mean" between extremes of excess and deficiency. For instance, courage is the balance between recklessness and cowardice, and generosity lies between stinginess and wastefulness. Living virtuously means consistently choosing the middle ground in a way that aligns with reason, reflection, and the needs of the situation. Identifying and cultivating these core virtues is essential for living a life that is not only ethically sound but also deeply fulfilling.

In this exploration of virtue ethics, we will delve into the process of identifying our core virtues and nurturing them in everyday life. We will also examine how the development of virtues shapes our ethical decision-making and provides a stable foundation for navigating moral complexities. By weaving these virtues into the fabric of daily living, we grow not just as ethical individuals but as contributors to the well-being of those around us.

What Are Core Virtues? A Guide to Ethical Character Development

Understanding Virtues: Aristotle's "Golden Mean"

The central premise of Virtue Ethics is that moral excellence arises from the cultivation of virtues, or character traits, that guide us toward living a flourishing life. Aristotle identified virtues as the "mean" between two extremes: one of excess and one of deficiency. Each virtue, then, is about finding the appropriate balance in various situations. For example:

- **Courage** lies between recklessness (too much fearlessness) and cowardice (too much fear).
- **Temperance** strikes a balance between indulgence and self-denial.
- **Generosity** falls between stinginess and wastefulness.

The challenge of living ethically, according to Aristotle, is learning to discern the appropriate middle ground in any given situation. This requires practical wisdom (*phronesis*), or the ability to make sound judgments based on experience, knowledge, and reflection.

Developing virtues is not about following rigid rules but about cultivating habits that allow us to act ethically across different contexts. As Aristotle famously said, "We are what we repeatedly do. Excellence, then, is not an act but a habit." Through repeated practice, we can engrain virtuous behaviors into our character, making ethical action a natural and instinctive part of who we are.

Identifying Core Virtues: What Matters Most?

When we speak of cultivating virtues, we must first ask: What are my core virtues? Identifying the virtues that resonate most deeply with us requires self-reflection and an understanding of what kind of person we aspire to be. While Aristotle highlighted several key virtues—courage, justice, temperance, wisdom—it's essential to recognize that the virtues we prioritize may shift depending on our personal values, cultural background, and life experiences.

For example, someone whose career is dedicated to social justice may place a high value on the virtue of justice, while someone focused on creative work may prioritize creativity as a virtue. Similarly, patience might be a core virtue for those who engage in caregiving or teaching, where long-term perseverance and empathy are required. This individualized approach to identifying core virtues allows us to align our ethical development with our personal goals and values.

The Process of Cultivating Virtues: Practice, Reflection, and Growth

Cultivating Virtue: Developing Ethical Habits

Once we identify our core virtues, the next step is to begin cultivating them in daily life. Aristotle taught that virtues are developed through habitual practice. Just as a muscle grows stronger with repeated use, virtues become ingrained in our character through consistent application. Every time we choose courage in the face of fear or patience when dealing with frustration, we strengthen that virtue.

For instance, if courage is a core virtue you wish to cultivate, you might start by taking small risks in your personal or professional life—speaking up in meetings, trying something new, or standing up for yourself or others in difficult situations. Each time you act with courage, you reinforce the habit, and over time, courageous behavior becomes more natural.

Reflection is also critical in the cultivation of virtue. As we navigate daily challenges, taking time to reflect on our actions, decisions, and motivations helps us assess where we are growing and where we need improvement. This can be done through journaling, meditation, or thoughtful conversations with mentors. Reflecting on situations where we may have fallen short of our virtues allows us to learn and course-correct, ensuring that we continually refine our ethical habits.

The Role of Mentorship in Ethical Growth

In Virtue Ethics, the process of cultivating virtue is often aided by the guidance of mentors or role models who embody the virtues we seek to develop. Aristotle suggested that the best way to learn how to live virtuously is to observe and emulate those who already possess moral excellence. These role models can offer insights, provide accountability, and serve as examples of how to navigate moral complexities with integrity.

For example, if you aspire to develop the virtue of justice, you might look to figures like Mahatma Gandhi or Martin Luther King Jr., who exemplified courage and fairness in the face of societal challenges. By studying their actions and the principles that guided their decisions, you gain a clearer understanding of how to apply justice in your own life.

Living with Virtue: The Impact of Ethical Habits on Decision-Making

Virtues as a Compass for Ethical Decisions

One of the most significant benefits of cultivating virtues is that they serve as a moral compass for decision-making. In situations where ethical dilemmas arise, having well-developed virtues allows us to navigate choices with clarity and confidence. Instead of relying on external rules or worrying about the consequences, we can ask ourselves: What would a person of courage, wisdom, or justice do in this situation?

For example, in a professional setting, you might face a decision where speaking the truth could put you at risk of losing favor with colleagues. In this case, the virtue of courage would guide you to speak honestly, even if it involves personal sacrifice, because courage involves standing up for what is right in the face of fear. Similarly, in a conflict where fairness is questioned, the virtue of justice would guide you toward ensuring that all parties are treated equitably, regardless of personal bias or pressure.

The Ripple Effect: How Virtue Cultivation Enhances Relationships and Community

Virtue cultivation not only improves personal decision-making but also has a profound impact on our relationships and communities. As we grow in virtues like compassion, patience, and justice, we become more empathetic and fair in our interactions with others. This builds trust, deepens connections, and fosters a sense of mutual respect.

In leadership roles, for instance, the virtue of wisdom allows us to make decisions that benefit the greater good, while compassion helps us understand and respond to the needs of others with kindness. The practice of virtues creates a ripple effect, influencing those around us and contributing to the overall well-being of society.

Cultivating a Life of Virtue

Build a Life of Ethical Excellence. Living a morally rich and fulfilling life is not about rigid adherence to rules or chasing outcomes but about consistently cultivating the core virtues that shape our character. By identifying the virtues that matter most to us, and by practicing them daily with intentionality, we create the foundation for ethical decision-making and meaningful relationships.

Through reflection, mentorship, and consistent practice, we grow into the virtuous individuals we aspire to be. This journey of virtue cultivation not only helps us lead a life of integrity but also contributes to the greater good, as we bring our ethical excellence into every interaction and decision. Living with virtue is not a final destination but an ongoing process—one that continually refines our character and deepens our capacity for ethical living.

Making Ethical Decisions Guided by Virtue: The Path to Moral Excellence

At the core of Virtue Ethics lies the belief that ethical decision-making is not about following a strict set of rules or calculating the consequences of actions but about developing and embodying virtues that guide our choices in life. This approach, championed by Aristotle, focuses on cultivating character traits—such as courage, justice, wisdom, and compassion—that allow individuals to make ethical decisions naturally, as an extension of their virtuous character. When we are guided by virtue, our decisions are rooted in a commitment to ethical excellence, rather than external pressures or immediate gains.

Making ethical decisions guided by virtue means that we do not rely on external standards to dictate our choices; rather, we look inward, asking ourselves how a person of strong moral character would act in any given situation. This approach requires self-awareness, practical wisdom (*phronesis*), and the ability to reflect on the complexities of each unique circumstance. Virtue Ethics teaches us that morality is not one-size-fits-all—what is ethical depends on the situation, the people involved, and the virtues we cultivate to guide our actions.

In this section, we will explore how to apply Virtue Ethics in daily life, specifically in the context of making ethical decisions. We will examine the key steps in aligning decisions with core virtues, the role of practical wisdom in navigating ethical dilemmas, and how a virtue-based approach can be used in real-world situations. Ultimately, the goal is to demonstrate that ethical decisions guided by virtue create a more meaningful and morally coherent life.

What Does It Mean to Make Ethical Decisions Guided by Virtue?

The Role of Virtue in Ethical Decision-Making

Virtue Ethics shifts the focus of moral decision-making from rules and outcomes to the development of virtuous character. Ethical decisions guided by virtue reflect the habits and qualities of a person who has cultivated moral excellence. Rather than thinking in terms of "what is the right action?" Virtue Ethics asks, "What kind of person do I want to be, and how would a virtuous person act in this situation?"

For example, if you are faced with a decision about whether to speak up against injustice in your workplace, a rules-based ethical approach might evaluate the situation by considering workplace policies or the consequences of whistleblowing. Virtue Ethics, however, would focus on the virtues of courage and justice, guiding you to ask: "Is this action consistent with the person I strive to be? Would someone who values fairness and courage stand up for what is right, even if it involves personal risk?"

In this way, making ethical decisions guided by virtue encourages us to act in ways that are aligned with our highest ideals. It asks us to cultivate virtues that become second nature, allowing us to navigate ethical challenges with integrity, regardless of external circumstances.

Practical Wisdom (*Phronesis*): The Key to Ethical Judgment

Practical wisdom, or *phronesis*, is central to making ethical decisions in Virtue Ethics. Aristotle argued that virtues alone are not enough—one must also possess the wisdom to know how to apply them appropriately in different situations. Practical wisdom is the ability to balance competing virtues, recognize the moral complexities of a situation, and make judgments that are aligned with both virtue and context.

For instance, consider a situation where you must decide whether to tell the truth about a mistake that could negatively impact your team. The virtue of honesty might suggest that you should immediately confess the error. However, the virtue of loyalty might encourage you to protect your team members from harm. Practical wisdom helps you discern how to balance these competing virtues, allowing you to act in a way that is both honest and respectful to your colleagues.

In Virtue Ethics, practical wisdom is developed through experience, reflection, and learning from both success and failure. It involves an ongoing process of moral discernment, where we learn to apply our virtues in ways that fit the nuances of each ethical dilemma. This dynamic decision-making process allows for flexibility while maintaining a strong moral foundation.

Steps to Making Ethical Decisions Guided by Virtue

Step 1: Reflect on Your Core Virtues

The first step in making ethical decisions guided by virtue is to identify the core virtues that align with your values and moral aspirations. These virtues serve as a compass for decision-making, helping you navigate complex situations with integrity. By reflecting on the virtues that are most important to you—whether it's honesty, courage, compassion, or fairness—you establish a moral framework that will guide your choices.

For example, someone who values empathy and kindness might prioritize compassion when making decisions about how to treat others, while someone who values courage might focus on standing up for what is right, even in the face of opposition.

Once you have identified your core virtues, the next step is to reflect on how these virtues can guide your decision-making in specific situations. Consider how a person who embodies these virtues would act, and strive to model your behavior on these ethical principles.

Step 2: Apply Practical Wisdom (*Phronesis*) to Navigate Complexity

No ethical decision is made in a vacuum. Life is filled with competing demands, conflicting interests, and moral gray areas. In these situations, applying practical wisdom is essential to making decisions that reflect both virtue and context.

Practical wisdom allows you to balance competing virtues and make decisions that are appropriate for the situation. For example, if you are in a leadership position and must decide between prioritizing the well-being of your employees and meeting business objectives, practical wisdom helps you evaluate the situation holistically. You might recognize that while responsibility to the organization is important, the virtue of justice calls for ensuring fair treatment of your employees.

Practical wisdom is not a rigid formula but a flexible, context-sensitive approach to ethical decision-making. It involves considering the broader consequences of your actions, the needs of those involved, and the most virtuous way to address these challenges.

Step 3: Act in Alignment with Virtue

Once you have reflected on your core virtues and applied practical wisdom to navigate the complexities of the situation, the next step is to take action in alignment with virtue. Ethical decision-making is not just about thought and reflection; it requires courageous and compassionate action that reflects your moral values.

Acting with virtue means having the moral courage to stand by your principles, even when it is difficult. Whether it's making an unpopular decision, addressing an uncomfortable truth, or taking responsibility for a mistake, acting in alignment with virtue is the ultimate expression of ethical decision-making.

For instance, in a situation where telling the truth might cause short-term discomfort or conflict, the virtue of honesty guides you to be truthful, even if it means facing difficult consequences. In this way, living virtuously means prioritizing moral integrity over immediate convenience or personal gain.

Virtue in Action: Real-World Applications of Ethical Decision-Making

Case Study: Balancing Honesty and Compassion in Leadership

Consider a situation in which a manager must provide feedback to an underperforming employee. The virtues of honesty and compassion might appear to conflict. Honesty demands transparency about the employee's shortcomings, while compassion requires consideration of the employee's feelings and dignity.

Using practical wisdom, the manager can balance these virtues by offering constructive feedback that is both truthful and empathetic. Rather than delivering harsh criticism, the manager can frame the conversation in a way that encourages growth and supports the employee's development. In this way, the manager acts ethically by being honest while also demonstrating care and respect.

Case Study: Courage and Justice in Social Advocacy

In the realm of social justice, activists often face the ethical dilemma of choosing between courage (speaking out against injustice) and prudence (acting strategically to avoid harm). For example, an activist may need to decide whether to lead a protest against an unjust policy, knowing that there may be personal or professional risks involved.

By reflecting on the virtues of courage and justice, and applying practical wisdom, the activist can make an ethical decision that balances the need for courageous action with the long-term strategy for achieving justice. This balance allows for a thoughtful approach that serves both personal integrity and the broader cause.

Ethical Living Guided by Virtue

By identifying and cultivating our core virtues, we create a moral foundation that guides us in making ethical decisions in every aspect of life. Through the practice of practical wisdom, we learn to navigate complex situations with moral clarity, balancing competing virtues and responding to the unique demands of each dilemma.

When we align our actions with our virtues, we live a life of greater moral coherence, contributing not only to our personal growth but also to the well-being of those around us. Ethical decisions guided by virtue are not merely about following rules; they are about becoming the kind of person who embodies ethical excellence in every choice, action, and interaction. This path, though challenging, leads to a life of integrity, purpose, and fulfillment.

Integrating Stoic and Buddhist Ethics: The Practice of Compassion, Justice, and Wisdom

Stoicism and Buddhism, though originating from different cultures and historical contexts, offer remarkably complementary paths to ethical living and decision-making. At the heart of both traditions lie the virtues of compassion, justice, and wisdom, which guide individuals toward moral excellence and inner peace. By integrating the teachings of Stoicism and Buddhism, we gain access to a rich tapestry of ethical principles that can help us navigate the complexities of modern life with clarity, purpose, and empathy.

In both philosophies, the cultivation of these virtues is seen as central to leading a life aligned with nature, reason, and human flourishing. Stoicism emphasizes the importance of living according to reason and accepting the things we cannot control, while Buddhism teaches us to embrace compassion and wisdom as a means of alleviating suffering—our own and that of others. When combined, these ethical frameworks offer a holistic approach to morality, one that addresses both the individual's internal state and their responsibility to the wider world.

In this exploration of integrating Stoic and Buddhist ethics, we will delve into the practices that cultivate compassion, justice, and wisdom in daily life. We will examine how each tradition approaches these virtues, and how they can be woven together into a unified approach to ethical living. By understanding and practicing these virtues, we create a foundation for ethical decisions that not only benefit ourselves but also contribute to the well-being of others.

Compassion: The Heart of Ethical Action

Stoic Compassion: Rational Love for Humanity

While Stoicism is often associated with detachment and self-control, it is equally grounded in the idea of compassion—or what the Stoics called *sympatheia*. For the Stoics, compassion is not driven by emotional impulses but by a rational understanding of the interconnectedness of all people. Stoics believed that we are all part of a greater whole, the *cosmos*, and that we share in the same divine spark of reason. This perspective fosters a deep sense of responsibility toward others, motivating us to act with kindness and understanding, even in challenging situations.

Stoic compassion is rooted in recognizing the shared human condition. Marcus Aurelius, in his *Meditations*, frequently reminds himself to act with patience and empathy, noting that others act out of ignorance or misunderstanding, and that we must offer them the same forgiveness we would want for ourselves. Stoicism teaches us to avoid resentment or anger and instead respond with reasoned compassion, seeing others as fellow participants in the human struggle.

For example, if someone acts unjustly toward you, the Stoic response would be to understand that their actions stem from ignorance of virtue. Instead of reacting with anger, Stoicism encourages a compassionate response that seeks to educate or gently correct, based on the understanding that all human beings are fallible.

Buddhist Compassion: Alleviating Suffering Through Kindness

Buddhism, particularly through the practice of metta (loving-kindness), places compassion at the very core of ethical living. In Buddhism, compassion means the active desire to alleviate the suffering of all beings. This is not limited to emotional sympathy but extends to the wisdom of recognizing the interconnectedness of all life and acting to reduce suffering wherever it is found. Karuna, the Pali word for compassion, is cultivated through mindfulness and meditation, allowing us to respond to the world with a heart that is open and free from judgment.

Buddhist compassion requires us to understand the impermanence of all things and to recognize that suffering is universal. Through mindfulness, we observe our own suffering and that of others with clarity, allowing us to respond with empathy and kindness. The practice of compassion meditation or metta involves extending wishes of well-being, peace, and happiness to others, starting with oneself and gradually expanding to include friends, strangers, and even enemies.

For example, if you encounter someone who is hostile or aggressive, the Buddhist practice of compassion would encourage you to recognize their suffering and respond with kindness. Instead of reacting with defensiveness or anger, compassion allows you to see their pain and offer a response that seeks to alleviate it, even if that means simply maintaining calm in the face of hostility.

Integrating Stoic and Buddhist Compassion

Both Stoicism and Buddhism teach that compassion is not just a feeling but an ethical imperative grounded in wisdom. Where Stoicism emphasizes the rational aspect of compassion—understanding that we are all part of a larger whole—Buddhism highlights the emotional depth of compassion, encouraging us to engage in practices that open our hearts to the suffering of others.

By integrating Stoic and Buddhist compassion, we develop a balanced approach to kindness: one that is both deeply empathetic and rooted in rational understanding. This combination allows us to remain emotionally present with others' suffering while maintaining the clarity needed to offer practical help. Compassion, in this sense, becomes an act of both the heart and the mind, guiding us toward ethical actions that reduce suffering in ourselves and others.

Justice: Acting Fairly in a Complex World

Stoic Justice: The Virtue of Fairness and Duty

For the Stoics, justice is one of the four cardinal virtues (alongside courage, temperance, and wisdom). Justice, in Stoic terms, refers to treating others fairly, fulfilling our social roles, and acting with integrity in all relationships. The Stoics believed that justice arises from the recognition that we are all part of a shared human community, and that our actions should contribute to the common good. Justice is not just about following laws or rules but about fulfilling our duties to others as rational, moral beings.

Stoicism teaches that we must act justly not for the sake of reward or recognition but because it is our duty as human beings. This commitment to justice requires us to consider the welfare of others in our decision-making processes and to act with fairness, even when it is difficult or inconvenient.

For example, a Stoic leader would make decisions based not on personal gain but on what is fair and equitable for all involved. This might mean sacrificing short-term profit for the long-term well-being of employees, or making unpopular choices that serve the greater good.

Buddhist Justice: Compassionate Action in Service of Others

In Buddhism, the concept of justice is closely tied to compassion and right action. The Eightfold Path provides a framework for ethical behavior, with principles such as right livelihood, right speech, and right action guiding individuals to live in ways that do not cause harm and that promote fairness and kindness. Justice in Buddhism is about creating harmony and reducing suffering, not just for oneself but for all beings.

Buddhist justice emphasizes the importance of acting with compassion and wisdom, ensuring that our actions are aligned with the goal of alleviating suffering. In this sense, justice is not a matter of legal fairness alone but of acting in ways that contribute to the well-being of others, whether through generosity, non-harm, or speaking truthfully.

For example, a Buddhist approach to justice might involve advocating for the rights of marginalized communities, not out of obligation to external rules but out of a deep-seated desire to reduce suffering and promote harmony in the world.

Integrating Stoic and Buddhist Justice

Both Stoicism and Buddhism view justice as more than legal fairness—it is a moral duty to act in ways that promote the common good. Stoicism emphasizes the rational, duty-bound nature of justice, while Buddhism infuses justice with compassion and a focus on reducing suffering. Together, these traditions offer a powerful ethical framework for living justly in the world.

By integrating Stoic and Buddhist views of justice, we learn to balance fairness with compassion, ensuring that our actions are not only rationally just but also sensitive to the needs and suffering of others. This approach to justice encourages us to act with integrity and empathy in all situations, fostering a more equitable and compassionate world.

Wisdom: The Foundation of Ethical Living

Stoic Wisdom: Aligning with Nature and Reason

For the Stoics, wisdom is the cornerstone of all virtues. It is the ability to see things clearly, understand the nature of reality, and make decisions based on reason and virtue. Stoic wisdom involves recognizing what is within our control and what is not, and aligning our actions with what is natural and rational. Wisdom guides us in navigating life's challenges with equanimity, helping us to remain calm in the face of adversity and make decisions that are aligned with our highest values.

Wisdom in Stoicism also involves understanding the interconnectedness of all things and acting in ways that benefit both ourselves and others. It requires self-awareness, reflection, and a deep understanding of the nature of human existence.

Buddhist Wisdom: Seeing Reality as It Is

In Buddhism, wisdom (*prajna*) is the understanding of the true nature of reality, particularly the concepts of impermanence, suffering, and non-self. Buddhist wisdom involves seeing beyond the illusions of the ego and recognizing the interconnectedness of all beings. This wisdom leads to compassion, as we come to understand that suffering is universal and that we have the power to alleviate it through our actions.

Buddhist wisdom is cultivated through practices such as meditation and mindfulness, which help us observe reality without distortion or attachment. Through wisdom, we develop the ability to respond to life's challenges with clarity and compassion, making ethical decisions that are rooted in an understanding of the impermanent and interconnected nature of life.

Integrating Stoic and Buddhist Wisdom

Both Stoicism and Buddhism place a high value on wisdom as the foundation of ethical living. Stoic wisdom focuses on aligning with nature and reason, while Buddhist wisdom emphasizes seeing the true nature of reality and acting with compassion. By integrating these forms of wisdom, we develop a comprehensive approach to ethical decision-making that combines rational clarity with deep empathy for the suffering of others.

Together, Stoic and Buddhist wisdom help us navigate the complexities of life with grace and moral integrity, allowing us to act in ways that are both rational and compassionate.

Ethical Dilemmas: Balancing Virtue and Practicality in Stoic and Buddhist Ethics

Navigating ethical dilemmas is one of the most challenging aspects of moral decision-making. In complex situations, individuals often face competing values, limited resources, or conflicting obligations. This is where the integration of Stoic and Buddhist ethics offers a compelling approach. Both traditions provide frameworks for navigating ethical dilemmas by balancing the ideals of virtue with the realities of practicality. Stoicism emphasizes reason and self-control in the face of adversity, while Buddhism centers on compassion and mindfulness, providing clarity in morally complex situations.

Ethical dilemmas arise when there are no easy answers, when we are pulled between two or more virtuous paths that seem to conflict. How do we choose between courage and caution, between truth and kindness, or between justice and personal loyalty? Stoicism teaches us to focus on what we can control and to act in accordance with reason and virtue, while Buddhism encourages us to act with compassion and mindfulness, always mindful of the impermanence of all things. Together, these philosophies help us find the balance between moral ideals and the practical constraints of the real world.

In this discussion, we will explore how Stoic and Buddhist teachings can guide us through ethical dilemmas by providing tools to weigh virtue against practicality. We will look at the role of practical wisdom in decision-making, the ethical challenges of balancing competing virtues, and how Stoicism and Buddhism complement each other in helping us navigate the complexities of life. Through real-world examples, we will see how these philosophies offer practical yet morally sound solutions to difficult choices.

The Nature of Ethical Dilemmas: When Virtue Conflicts with Reality

The Challenge of Ethical Dilemmas

Ethical dilemmas are situations where there is no clear right answer, often because two or more virtues come into conflict. For example, you might face a dilemma where honesty conflicts with compassion—should you tell a painful truth to someone, or spare their feelings by withholding information? Similarly, a dilemma may involve a conflict between justice and loyalty—should you act in accordance with fairness, even if it means betraying a friend or colleague?

Both Stoicism and Buddhism recognize the complexity of such dilemmas and offer different but complementary approaches to resolving them. These philosophies emphasize that life is full of ambiguity, and that the ideal solution often lies in balancing competing values rather than adhering to rigid rules.

Stoic Perspective: Focus on Control and Virtue

In Stoicism, ethical dilemmas are approached by focusing on what is within your control and responding with virtue. The

Stoics teach that we cannot control the external world, but we can control how we respond to it. When faced with an ethical dilemma, the Stoic approach is to remain calm, use reason to assess the situation, and act according to virtues such as courage, justice, and wisdom.

For example, consider a situation where you must decide whether to tell a difficult truth that may cause harm to someone. From a Stoic perspective, you would focus on what is within your control—your ability to communicate the truth with compassion and kindness—while accepting that the outcome is beyond your influence. The goal is not to avoid discomfort or difficulty but to act with integrity in a way that reflects your highest virtues.

Buddhist Perspective: Compassion and Mindfulness

In Buddhism, ethical dilemmas are often addressed through the lens of compassion and mindfulness. Buddhist ethics emphasize the importance of understanding the consequences of your actions, not just for yourself but for others. When faced with a moral conflict, the practice of mindfulness allows you to see the situation with clarity, free from emotional reactivity or attachment. Compassion, on the other hand, ensures that your actions aim to alleviate suffering, even in difficult circumstances.

For instance, if you are in a position where telling the truth may cause pain, the Buddhist approach would encourage you to consider the broader implications of your actions. You would mindfully weigh the short-term harm against the long-term benefits, acting in a way that seeks to minimize suffering for all involved. This doesn't mean avoiding hard truths but rather finding the most compassionate way to communicate them.

Balancing Virtue and Practicality: The Role of Practical Wisdom

Practical Wisdom (*Phronesis*) in Stoicism

Practical wisdom, or *phronesis*, is essential in Stoic ethics for resolving dilemmas. Aristotle originally described practical wisdom as the ability to navigate complex moral situations by balancing virtues and understanding the context. Stoicism adopts this idea, emphasizing that ethical decisions require judgment that aligns with virtue but is also sensitive to the practical realities of the situation.

Practical wisdom in Stoicism involves stepping back from the situation to view it objectively, assessing the virtues at play, and deciding on a course of action that reflects both moral integrity and pragmatic concerns. For example, when deciding whether to stand up for justice in a situation where it might cause harm to yourself, practical wisdom would help you weigh the importance of justice against the potential consequences and act accordingly.

Buddhist Skillful Means (*Upaya*)

Buddhism offers a similar concept in the form of skillful means (*upaya*), which refers to the ability to choose the most effective and compassionate way to address a given situation. Rather than relying on fixed rules, Buddhism encourages practitioners to adapt their actions based on the specific circumstances, ensuring that the outcome promotes the greatest good.

Skillful means involves understanding the impermanence of situations and recognizing that different contexts may require different responses. For example, in one situation, compassion might mean being gentle and kind, while in another, it might involve being firm to prevent greater harm. In this way, Buddhist ethics are flexible, adapting to the practical needs of the moment while remaining grounded in compassion and wisdom.

Integrating Practical Wisdom and Skillful Means

By combining Stoic practical wisdom with Buddhist skillful means, we gain a holistic approach to navigating ethical dilemmas. Stoicism offers the rational clarity to assess virtues and context, while Buddhism brings compassion and mindfulness to ensure that our actions are aligned with the well-being of others. Together, these traditions provide a comprehensive toolkit for resolving moral conflicts in a way that is both virtuous and practical.

Navigating Ethical Dilemmas: Real-Life Applications

Example 1: Balancing Honesty and Compassion

Imagine a scenario where you must decide whether to tell a close friend the truth about a serious mistake they are making, knowing that it could damage your relationship. The dilemma involves balancing the virtue of honesty with the practical need for compassion and maintaining the friendship.

A Stoic approach would emphasize your duty to act with integrity and speak the truth, regardless of the potential discomfort. However, practical wisdom would guide you to consider how to deliver the truth in a way that minimizes harm and preserves the relationship. A Buddhist approach would similarly encourage you to act with compassion, perhaps choosing a moment when your friend is more open to hearing difficult feedback and framing the conversation in a way that reduces suffering.

By integrating Stoic honesty and Buddhist compassion, you can find a way to communicate the truth that is both kind and constructive, ensuring that your ethical decision reflects both virtue and practicality.

Example 2: Justice vs. Loyalty

Consider a workplace situation where you discover unethical behavior by a colleague who is also a close friend. The ethical dilemma arises between the virtue of justice (reporting the unethical behavior) and loyalty (protecting your friend).

From a Stoic perspective, justice is a higher virtue, and your responsibility is to act in the interest of fairness, regardless of personal loyalty. However, practical wisdom would encourage you to assess the situation carefully, considering the long-term consequences for your friend and the organization.

Buddhist ethics would introduce the dimension of compassion, guiding you to find a solution that upholds justice while also considering the impact on your friend's well-being. Perhaps the best course of action is to speak privately with your friend first, offering them the chance to correct their behavior before involving others.

Virtue Meets Practicality in Ethical Decision-Making

Balance Virtue and Practicality. Stoic and Buddhist ethics offers a path to navigating the moral complexities of life. Ethical dilemmas, by their very nature, force us to weigh competing virtues and make difficult choices. By integrating the rational clarity and virtue-centered approach of Stoicism with the compassionate and flexible principles of Buddhism, we can find practical solutions that remain true to our moral ideals.

In this approach, practical wisdom and skillful means become essential tools for navigating ethical dilemmas. They help us act with integrity, balancing the pursuit of virtue with the practical realities of the situation. Ultimately, the integration of Stoic and Buddhist ethics provides a framework that not only helps us make ethical decisions but also fosters a life of moral clarity, compassion, and purpose.

Ethical Case Studies: Applying Virtue Ethics, Stoicism, and Buddhism to Real-Life Scenarios

The true test of any ethical framework lies not in theory but in practice. Virtue Ethics, Stoicism, and Buddhism all offer profound wisdom for navigating the moral complexities of life. However, understanding how these philosophies work in the real world requires more than abstract knowledge—it demands application. By examining real-life scenarios through the lens of these ethical traditions, we can see how their principles shape decision-making and behavior in tangible, impactful ways. Whether it's a difficult choice at work, a personal moral dilemma, or a situation of societal importance, these philosophies provide a nuanced approach to ethical living that is rooted in character, wisdom, and compassion.

In this exploration of case studies, we will analyze how Virtue Ethics, Stoicism, and Buddhism can be applied to real-world situations, helping us make ethical decisions that reflect both our highest values and the practical realities we face. We will see how the cultivation of virtues like courage, justice, and compassion guide individuals toward morally sound actions, and how principles such as practical wisdom in Stoicism or skillful means in Buddhism help resolve ethical dilemmas. Each case study will illustrate the strengths and challenges of applying these philosophies in everyday life, providing a deep and practical understanding of their relevance.

Life Scenario 1: The Ethical Dilemma of Honesty vs. Kindness

Case Overview: Telling a Difficult Truth

Imagine you are in a situation where you need to deliver difficult feedback to a close friend or colleague. The truth may hurt their feelings, damage their self-esteem, or even strain your relationship. The ethical dilemma here involves balancing the virtue of honesty with the virtue of compassion. How do you decide whether to tell the truth, knowing it may cause harm, or to protect the other person's feelings by withholding or softening the truth?

Virtue Ethics: Balancing Honesty and Compassion

Virtue Ethics, particularly in the Aristotelian tradition, would ask you to consider the golden mean—the balance between excess and deficiency. In this case, pure honesty without compassion could be brutal, while too much compassion without honesty could be dishonest and avoidant. The virtuous response lies in finding the middle path between these two extremes. By acting with both honesty and kindness, you fulfill your ethical duty while maintaining a respectful relationship.

For example, instead of bluntly stating the harsh truth, a virtuous person might frame their feedback in a way that is constructive and aimed at helping the other person improve. This allows you to be truthful without abandoning compassion, embodying both virtues in your decision-making.

Stoicism: Duty and Control

In Stoicism, the focus would be on what is within your control and acting according to virtue, regardless of the emotional reactions of others. A Stoic approach to this dilemma would emphasize truthfulness and justice—two central Stoic virtues. Telling the truth would be seen as a duty, and any emotional fallout would be something beyond your control.

However, practical wisdom (*phronesis*) also plays a role here. Stoics would advocate for delivering the truth in a manner that is tactful and reasoned, focusing on how the truth can be conveyed in the most helpful way. Stoicism would not encourage cruelty or bluntness, but rather the rational expression of honesty that contributes to the greater good of both individuals.

Buddhism: Compassionate Communication

Buddhism would approach this scenario through the lens of compassion and mindfulness. Buddhism teaches that all beings experience suffering, and the goal is to alleviate that suffering through kind and mindful action. When faced with delivering difficult news, a Buddhist perspective would encourage you to consider not only the content of your message but also the way it is delivered.

Buddhist ethics would promote skillful means (*upaya*), finding a way to communicate the truth in a way that reduces harm and promotes understanding. This might involve carefully choosing the time and place for the conversation, using gentle language, and remaining mindful of the other person's emotional state. In this way, you fulfill the ethical requirement to be honest while also honoring the commitment to compassion.

Life Scenario 2: Leadership and Responsibility

Case Overview: Balancing Profit and People

Imagine you are a manager in a company and face a decision between laying off a portion of your workforce to increase profit margins or finding an alternative solution that might be more costly but saves jobs. The ethical dilemma here revolves around the tension between justice and responsibility. How do you balance the financial responsibility to the company with the ethical obligation to protect the livelihoods of your employees?

Virtue Ethics: Acting with Justice and Prudence

From a Virtue Ethics perspective, this situation requires balancing the virtues of justice and prudence. Justice demands that you act fairly toward your employees, considering their well-being and the broader social consequences of your decision. Prudence, or practical wisdom, requires you to make decisions that are well-reasoned and balanced, taking into account the long-term impacts on both the company and the employees.

A virtuous leader would seek a solution that aligns with both justice and responsibility, perhaps exploring creative alternatives to layoffs, such as temporary pay cuts or reassigning employees to different roles. This approach allows the leader to maintain fairness while also acting prudently in the best interests of the organization.

Stoicism: Duty to the Greater Good

In Stoicism, the focus would be on fulfilling your duty to both the organization and the employees. Stoicism teaches that you cannot control the external market forces that may necessitate difficult decisions, but you can control how you respond to them. The Stoic leader would act with justice, ensuring that any layoffs are done with fairness and integrity, while also recognizing the broader duty to ensure the survival of the organization for the greater good.

Stoicism emphasizes the importance of reason over emotion. A Stoic leader would not be swayed by personal attachments but would instead act in accordance with reasoned judgment, ensuring that the decision is ethical and in line with the long-term well-being of both the company and its employees.

Buddhism: Compassionate Leadership

From a Buddhist perspective, this scenario would be approached with an emphasis on compassion and interconnectedness. Buddhist ethics would encourage the leader to consider the suffering that layoffs might cause and to seek a solution that minimizes harm. This could involve exploring alternatives that balance the financial needs of the company with the well-being of the employees.

Buddhist practice encourages mindfulness in decision-making, ensuring that the leader is fully aware of the consequences of their actions. Compassion would guide the leader to make decisions that consider the broader impact on the employees' lives, perhaps choosing to sacrifice short-term profits to protect the livelihoods of those who depend on the company for their well-being.

Life Scenario 3: Personal Integrity vs. Social Pressure

Case Overview: Standing Up for Your Values

Imagine you are in a social situation where your personal values conflict with the behavior or expectations of the group. For instance, you may be asked to participate in an activity that goes against your ethical beliefs, such as lying to protect a friend or engaging in behavior that you consider harmful. The dilemma here involves the tension between personal integrity and social pressure. How do you maintain your ethical principles in the face of external expectations?

Virtue Ethics: Courage and Integrity

In Virtue Ethics, maintaining personal integrity is a central component of living a virtuous life. The virtue of courage plays a crucial role here, as it requires standing up for your beliefs even when it is uncomfortable or unpopular. Integrity, another key virtue, demands that you remain true to your moral principles, regardless of the social consequences.

A virtuous person would navigate this situation by acting with courage and integrity, even if it means facing criticism or social isolation. This might involve calmly explaining your position and choosing not to participate in activities that violate your ethical beliefs, while still maintaining respect for those around you.

Stoicism: Detachment from External Approval

Stoicism offers a powerful framework for resisting social pressure. The Stoic philosophy teaches that we should not be swayed by the opinions of others or external approval. Instead, we should focus on what is within our control—our own actions and ethical choices. Detachment from external outcomes allows us to maintain inner peace and act according to virtue, regardless of how others perceive us.

In this scenario, a Stoic would rely on reason and virtue to guide their actions, acting with courage and wisdom to uphold their ethical principles. Social disapproval or pressure would be seen as irrelevant, as the Stoic values inner integrity over external validation.

Buddhism: Mindfulness and Right Action

In Buddhism, the concept of right action is part of the Eightfold Path and emphasizes acting in ways that are ethical, compassionate, and free from harm. When faced with social pressure to act unethically, a Buddhist would practice mindfulness, remaining aware of their thoughts and feelings while considering the ethical implications of their actions.

Buddhism encourages practitioners to act with compassion and non-attachment to social approval, focusing instead on doing what is right and aligned with ethical principles. This might involve politely declining to participate in unethical activities while maintaining compassion for those who may not share the same values.

Learning from Ethical Case Studies

Analyzing Real-Life Scenarios Through the Lens of Virtue Ethics, Stoicism, and Buddhism provides us with a deeper understanding of how these philosophical traditions can be applied in practical situations. Each case study illustrates how these ethical frameworks offer unique yet complementary tools for navigating moral dilemmas. Virtue Ethics encourages us to cultivate character and balance competing virtues, Stoicism teaches us to focus on what we can control and act with reason, and Buddhism emphasizes mindfulness, compassion, and reducing suffering. Together, these traditions guide us toward ethical living in a complex world. By applying these principles in real-life situations, we not only strengthen our moral character but also contribute to the well-being of others, creating a more just and compassionate society.

As we transition from ethical decision-making and real-life applications, we now turn our attention to a critical component of personal development: building and sustaining motivation. Ethical living, while rooted in virtue and wise decision-making, requires ongoing motivation to stay aligned with our values and goals. In the next section, we will explore how to identify personal values and set meaningful goals that align with a virtuous life. Drawing on Cognitive Behavioral Therapy (CBT), Stoic resilience, and mindfulness practices from Buddhism, we will discuss practical strategies for overcoming obstacles and setbacks, ensuring that we can maintain motivation through adversity. This section will provide a roadmap for not only setting goals but also sustaining the drive to achieve them in the face of life's inevitable challenges.

7. Fueling the Journey: Building and Sustaining Motivation with Virtue, Resilience, and Mindfulness

Motivation is the driving force that propels us toward our goals and sustains our efforts in the face of adversity. Yet, motivation can be elusive—easily worn down by challenges, setbacks, and the complexities of life. In this section, we will explore how to cultivate and sustain motivation by aligning personal goals with virtue and ethical living, and how to leverage Cognitive Behavioral Therapy (CBT) techniques to break down goals into manageable steps. Additionally, we'll look to Stoic strategies for handling adversity with resilience and strength, as well as Buddhist mindfulness practices that help us reframe setbacks as learning opportunities. Together, these approaches offer a holistic framework for staying motivated, ensuring that we remain focused on our path of personal growth, no matter the challenges we face.

Identifying Personal Values and Goals: Aligning Ambitions with Virtue and Ethical Living

Understanding and defining our personal values and goals is a fundamental step in building a life that is not only fulfilling but also aligned with virtue and ethical principles. However, the process goes beyond simple goal-setting; it involves a deep exploration of what truly matters to us and how our goals align with the ethical frameworks we aspire to embody. When our goals are rooted in our core values, they become powerful motivators that guide us through challenges and sustain our efforts over time. This alignment creates a sense of coherence between our daily actions and the larger narrative of our lives, transforming ordinary ambitions into a journey of personal growth and moral integrity.

In this section, we will explore how to identify personal values, how to set goals that align with these values, and how the integration of Virtue Ethics, Stoicism, and Buddhist principles can provide a structured approach to ethical goal-setting. Through this process, we will see how aligning our ambitions with virtues such as wisdom, compassion, and courage can serve as a compass, ensuring that our pursuit of success remains anchored in ethical living.

The Foundation of Motivation: Identifying Personal Values

What Are Personal Values?

Personal values are the core beliefs and principles that define who we are and what matters most to us. They act as an internal compass, guiding our decisions, behaviors, and the goals we pursue. While values vary from person to person, they generally include concepts such as honesty, integrity, freedom, compassion, justice, and growth. These values are shaped by our upbringing, culture, experiences, and, significantly, by our philosophical and ethical perspectives.

To illustrate, let's consider two individuals: Alex and Sarah. Alex values independence and creativity, while Sarah values community and service. These values will influence the kinds of goals they set—Alex might strive to start his own business, while Sarah may seek a career in public service. Understanding these core values is essential because they are the foundation upon which all meaningful goals are built.

Discovering Your Core Values: A Guided Reflection

Identifying personal values involves introspection and reflection. Here's a step-by-step method:

1. **Reflect on Peak Experiences**: Think back to moments in your life when you felt the most fulfilled, energized, or at peace. What was happening? What values were

being honored in those moments? Perhaps it was a moment of courage when you stood up for someone, or a sense of achievement when you completed a challenging project.
2. **Examine Moments of Discontent**: Consider situations when you felt frustrated, disheartened, or unfulfilled. Often, these experiences reveal values that were violated or not respected. For example, if you felt disappointed in a job where you lacked autonomy, it might indicate that independence is a core value for you.
3. **Prioritize and Clarify**: After reflecting, create a list of your most significant values. Narrow them down to your top five and define what each value means to you. This will clarify your priorities and help you set goals that align with these values.

Aligning Goals with Virtue: An Ethical Framework for Motivation

Why Align Goals with Virtue?

While setting goals based on personal values is important, aligning them with virtue takes the process a step further. Virtue provides a moral and ethical dimension to our ambitions, ensuring that our pursuits contribute not only to personal fulfillment but also to the greater good. When our goals are infused with virtues like wisdom, justice, courage, and compassion, they transcend personal gain and become acts of ethical living.

For instance, if your value is growth, you might set a goal to achieve a higher degree of education. By aligning this goal with the virtue of wisdom, you ensure that your pursuit of knowledge not only benefits yourself but also equips you to contribute positively to society. Similarly, if you value freedom, aligning your goal with justice could lead you to advocate for the rights of others, making your pursuit not just a personal endeavor but a virtuous one.

The Role of Virtue Ethics: Cultivating Character Through Goal-Setting

Virtue Ethics, rooted in the philosophy of Aristotle, emphasizes the development of good character through the cultivation of virtues. Aristotle argued that true happiness (*eudaimonia*) is achieved through living a life of virtue and fulfilling one's potential. By aligning goals with virtue, we are not only setting ambitions but also developing our character.

Consider the goal of becoming a leader in your field. To align this with virtue ethics, you would not only focus on acquiring the necessary skills but also on cultivating the virtues that define ethical leadership: courage to make difficult decisions, justice to treat people fairly, and humility to serve rather than dominate. In this way, your goal becomes an avenue for moral development and ethical living.

Stoicism and the Focus on Inner Goals

Stoicism offers another perspective on aligning goals with virtue by emphasizing the importance of focusing on what is within our control—our thoughts, actions, and responses—rather than external outcomes. This approach encourages us to set inner goals that align with virtues such as resilience, discipline, and equanimity, rather than attaching our sense of fulfillment to external success.

For example, if your goal is to achieve financial stability, a Stoic approach would emphasize cultivating the virtues of prudence and self-control rather than fixating on financial figures alone. This shift in focus ensures that even if circumstances beyond your control affect your financial situation, you remain fulfilled through your commitment to virtue and personal growth.

Buddhist Perspective: Integrating Compassion and Non-Attachment

In Buddhism, aligning goals with virtue involves integrating the principles of compassion and non-attachment. Buddhist ethics encourage us to pursue goals that alleviate suffering for ourselves and others while maintaining an awareness of the impermanent nature of all things. This approach promotes the cultivation of virtues such as loving-kindness (*metta*) and *wisdom*.

If you set a goal to improve your physical health, a Buddhist approach would encourage you to align this goal with the virtue of compassion, not only caring for your own well-being but also inspiring others around you to do the same. Additionally, practicing non-attachment helps you pursue your goal without becoming overly fixated on specific outcomes, ensuring that your motivation remains steady, even in the face of setbacks.

Setting Goals That Reflect Ethical Living: A Step-by-Step Approach

Step 1: Identify Core Values and Virtues

Begin by reflecting on your core values, as discussed earlier. Identify how these values connect to specific virtues. For instance, if community is a core value, it may connect to virtues such as compassion, justice, or generosity. Clarifying these connections provides a foundation for setting goals that are both personally meaningful and ethically aligned.

Step 2: Define Long-Term and Short-Term Goals

Next, set long-term goals that align with your values and virtues. For example, if you value learning, a long-term goal could be to become an expert in your field, aligning with the virtue of wisdom. Break down this goal into short-term, actionable steps—such as taking courses, seeking mentorship, or dedicating specific time blocks for study. This structure ensures that your daily actions align with your broader ethical aspirations.

Step 3: Integrate Stoic and Buddhist Principles

When setting goals, integrate Stoic and Buddhist principles to create a balanced approach. From a Stoic perspective, focus on goals related to inner growth, such as developing resilience or improving self-discipline, rather than purely external achievements. This ensures that your motivation remains consistent, regardless of external circumstances.

From a Buddhist perspective, practice setting goals with an attitude of non-attachment. For instance, if you pursue a career advancement, align this with the virtue of compassion, seeing it as an opportunity to make a positive impact. Approach the goal with the understanding that success and failure are impermanent, allowing you to maintain motivation without becoming overly attached to outcomes.

Values and Virtues as the Compass for Meaningful Goals

Align Your Goals with Virtues and Ethical Living. Our ambitions are more than just personal achievements—they have become pathways to moral growth and fulfillment. By grounding our goals in core values and integrating the wisdom of Virtue Ethics, Stoicism, and Buddhist principles, we create a holistic approach to motivation that is both resilient and ethically sound. Whether we aim to achieve professional success, cultivate relationships, or enhance personal well-being, aligning these pursuits with virtue transforms them into meaningful endeavors. In this way, we not only progress toward our goals but also deepen our connection to a life of integrity, wisdom, and compassion. Virtue becomes the compass that guides our ambitions, ensuring that every step we take leads us closer to a fulfilling and ethically aligned life.

Breaking Down and Achieving Goals: The CBT Approach

Setting meaningful goals aligned with our values is a crucial step in personal development, but achieving those goals requires effective strategies. Cognitive Behavioral Therapy (CBT) offers a practical and evidence-based approach for breaking down and achieving goals, ensuring that ambitions are not only set but also accomplished. CBT emphasizes the connection between thoughts, emotions, and behaviors, helping individuals understand and manage the mental and emotional barriers that can impede progress. By applying CBT techniques, we can develop a structured plan for reaching our goals, navigate obstacles effectively, and maintain motivation throughout the journey.

Next, we will explore how CBT's practical tools can be utilized to set clear, achievable goals, break them down into manageable steps, and monitor progress. We will look into how CBT strategies such as SMART goals, behavioral activation, and cognitive restructuring provide a framework for achieving personal aspirations while managing the emotional and cognitive challenges that often arise. Through this detailed exploration, we will see how CBT not only facilitates goal attainment but also promotes psychological resilience and growth.

The Power of CBT: Turning Ambitions into Action

The CBT Model: Thoughts, Emotions, and Behaviors

Before diving into the specifics of goal-setting, it's essential to understand the CBT model itself. CBT is based on the premise that our thoughts, emotions, and behaviors are interconnected. When pursuing goals, negative thought patterns can create emotional barriers such as anxiety, fear of failure, or self-doubt, leading to avoidance or procrastination. By addressing and restructuring these thoughts, CBT helps individuals change their emotional responses and adopt behaviors that align with their goals.

For example, someone who sets a goal to pursue a new career path may experience thoughts like, "I'm not qualified enough" or "I'll never succeed." These thoughts can lead to feelings of anxiety or discouragement, causing avoidance behaviors like procrastination. CBT intervenes by helping the individual challenge these negative thoughts and replace them with more realistic and supportive beliefs, such as, "I have the ability to learn and grow, and I can take steps to build my skills." This shift in thinking enables the person to take concrete actions toward their goal.

Applying CBT Principles to Goal-Setting

CBT's approach to goal-setting involves breaking down large, overwhelming goals into smaller, achievable steps. This method, combined with the restructuring of negative thoughts, ensures that individuals stay motivated and are able to make consistent progress. Let's explore how this is done in detail.

Step 1: Setting SMART Goals

What Are SMART Goals?

A cornerstone of the CBT approach is the use of SMART goals, which are goals that are Specific, Measurable, Achievable, Relevant, and Time-bound. The SMART framework provides clarity and structure, making it easier to track progress and maintain motivation. By transforming vague aspirations into precise goals, SMART planning reduces uncertainty and increases the likelihood of success.

For example, instead of setting a broad goal like "I want to get healthier," a SMART goal would be, "I will exercise for 30 minutes, three times a week, for the next three months." This goal is specific (exercise for 30 minutes), measurable (three times a week), achievable (within the person's capabilities), relevant (related to health), and time-bound (over three months).

Breaking Down the SMART Framework

1. **Specific**: Goals should be clear and unambiguous. Instead of "I want to improve my skills," specify the exact skill you want to develop, such as "I want to improve my public speaking skills."
2. **Measurable**: Define how progress will be measured. For public speaking, this could mean attending and presenting at a set number of speaking events or classes.
3. **Achievable**: Goals should be realistic, given your current resources and abilities. If you have never done public speaking before, it's more realistic to start with small presentations than to aim for a large-scale event immediately.
4. **Relevant**: The goal should align with your broader values and objectives. If you value **personal growth**, improving public speaking is relevant as it builds confidence and enhances professional opportunities.

5. **Time-bound**: Setting a deadline creates urgency and helps maintain focus. For instance, "I will complete a public speaking course within six months."

The Importance of SMART Goals in CBT

The process of setting SMART goals in CBT helps reduce overwhelm and provides a clear path forward. By focusing on manageable and measurable steps, individuals are better able to see their progress and maintain motivation. The SMART approach also offers flexibility—goals can be adjusted if circumstances change, ensuring that individuals remain engaged and realistic about their ambitions.

Step 2: Breaking Down Goals into Manageable Steps

Behavioral Activation: Turning Goals into Actions

A key technique in CBT for achieving goals is behavioral activation, which involves breaking down goals into smaller, manageable tasks that can be accomplished step by step. Behavioral activation is particularly effective because it emphasizes action over avoidance, helping individuals build momentum and maintain motivation.

For instance, if someone's long-term goal is to write a book, the task might seem overwhelming. Through behavioral activation, the person would break down the goal into smaller steps, such as:

1. **Research**: Spend one week gathering information and resources on the topic.
2. **Outline**: Spend two weeks drafting an outline of the book's structure.
3. **Writing Sessions**: Dedicate one hour every morning to write a specific section, such as the introduction.

By breaking the goal into smaller, time-specific actions, the process becomes less daunting, and each step completed builds a sense of accomplishment.

The CBT Focus on Reinforcement

CBT emphasizes the importance of reinforcement in sustaining motivation. Celebrating small achievements along the way, such as finishing the outline or completing a chapter, reinforces positive behavior and helps maintain enthusiasm. Reinforcement might involve giving oneself a reward, like taking a break or enjoying a favorite activity, after completing a task. This practice creates a positive feedback loop that encourages continued effort.

Step 3: Cognitive Restructuring to Overcome Obstacles

Identifying and Challenging Negative Thoughts

Even with well-defined goals and actionable steps, obstacles often arise—many of which are rooted in negative thought patterns. Cognitive restructuring, a core CBT technique, helps individuals identify and challenge these thoughts to prevent them from derailing progress. Common thoughts that might arise include:

- "I'm not good enough to achieve this goal."
- "If I can't do it perfectly, there's no point in trying."
- "I'll never succeed, so why bother?"

In CBT, these thoughts are called cognitive distortions—inaccurate or exaggerated ways of thinking that can lead to negative emotions and avoidance behaviors. Cognitive restructuring involves examining these thoughts, challenging their validity, and replacing them with more balanced, realistic alternatives.

For example, if someone feels overwhelmed by a goal, they might think, "I'll never be able to finish this." CBT would guide them to reframe this thought into something more constructive, such as, "I may not be able to finish everything at once, but I can complete it step by step."

Practicing Self-Compassion and Flexibility

CBT also integrates self-compassion to help individuals manage setbacks. It's important to recognize that obstacles are a normal part of any journey, and setbacks don't define one's ability to succeed. Practicing self-compassion involves acknowledging difficulties without harsh self-criticism and focusing on what can be learned from the experience.

Additionally, CBT encourages flexibility in goal-setting. If circumstances change or a step in the plan proves too challenging, it's essential to reassess and adjust goals rather than abandoning them. This flexibility ensures that motivation remains sustainable over the long term.

CBT as a Pathway to Goal Achievement

Breaking Down and Achieving Goals Using CBT offers a structured, effective approach to turning ambitions into reality. By integrating the principles of SMART goals, behavioral activation, and cognitive restructuring, CBT provides a comprehensive framework for setting, pursuing, and achieving meaningful goals. It emphasizes not only the importance of clarity and structure but also the need for flexibility, resilience, and self-compassion along the way.

Through this approach, individuals can navigate the challenges that often arise in the pursuit of their ambitions, transforming obstacles into opportunities for growth. With CBT, achieving goals becomes a manageable and fulfilling process, one that aligns with both personal values and the pursuit of a life filled with purpose and ethical living. Turning Ambitions into Achievements, CBT ensures that we remain motivated and empowered every step of the way.

Stoic Strategies for Handling Adversity: Turning Obstacles into Opportunities

Adversity is an inevitable part of life, presenting challenges that test our strength, resilience, and character. In these moments, how we respond determines not only our immediate outcomes but also the development of our inner strength and wisdom. Stoicism, an ancient philosophical tradition founded by thinkers like Epictetus, Marcus Aurelius, and Seneca, offers profound strategies for managing and even thriving amidst adversity. The Stoic approach teaches us to view challenges as opportunities for growth, transformation, and the cultivation of virtues like courage, wisdom, and equanimity.

In this discussion, we will explore the Stoic strategies that provide resilience in the face of difficulty, guiding us to maintain composure and purpose even when confronted with obstacles. From the Dichotomy of Control, which emphasizes focusing on what is within our power, to the practice of Negative Visualization, which prepares the mind for potential hardships, Stoicism offers practical tools for turning adversity into a platform for growth. We will also examine how Stoic thinkers have applied these principles in their own lives, providing insight into how these ancient teachings remain relevant today.

The Stoic Mindset: Embracing Challenges as Opportunities

Reframing Adversity: The Art of Perception

At the core of Stoic philosophy is the belief that it is not the events themselves that disturb us, but our perception of those events. This perspective is crucial when facing adversity. Stoics teach that while we cannot control the external circumstances that befall us, we have full control over how we perceive and respond to these challenges. Marcus Aurelius, the Roman Emperor and Stoic philosopher, emphasized this point, writing in his *Meditations*: "The impediment to action advances action. What stands in the way becomes the way."

This quote encapsulates the Stoic mindset: adversity is not an obstacle, but an opportunity for growth. By reframing challenges as chances to practice and develop virtue, Stoics transform setbacks into powerful tools for personal and moral development. When confronted with an obstacle, the Stoic doesn't see it as a barrier but as a means to exercise courage, patience, or wisdom.

For example, imagine a situation where a project you've been working on for months is suddenly canceled. While the initial reaction may be disappointment or frustration, a Stoic would see this as an opportunity to practice acceptance, detachment, and resilience. Instead of dwelling on the loss, the focus shifts to what can be learned from the experience and how one can move forward with grace and purpose.

The Dichotomy of Control: Distinguishing Between What We Can and Cannot Control

One of the most powerful Stoic strategies for handling adversity is the Dichotomy of Control. This concept, emphasized by Epictetus, divides all aspects of life into two categories: things we can control and things we cannot. According to Stoicism, our peace of mind and resilience depend on focusing only on what lies within our control—our thoughts, attitudes, and actions—while accepting and letting go of everything beyond our control, such as the actions of others, natural events, or outcomes.

In practice, this means when we encounter adversity, we assess the situation through the lens of this dichotomy. If we can influence the situation, we take proactive, virtuous action. If the situation is beyond our control, we accept it as it is, maintaining our composure and adjusting our perspective to see it as an opportunity to practice patience or acceptance.

For instance, in a professional setting where a decision is made that negatively affects you but is beyond your influence, the Stoic response would be to focus on what you can control: your reaction. You might choose to respond with patience, professionalism, and integrity, thereby turning the adversity into a moment that demonstrates your character.

Stoic Techniques for Navigating Adversity

Negative Visualization: Preparing the Mind for Hardship

A central Stoic practice is Negative Visualization (*premeditatio malorum*), which involves mentally rehearsing possible adversities or losses before they happen. This is not meant to induce fear or anxiety, but rather to prepare the mind for potential hardships, cultivating resilience and reducing the shock if and when they occur.

By imagining various worst-case scenarios, such as losing a job, experiencing illness, or facing rejection, Stoics train themselves to remain emotionally stable and calm when confronted with these situations. This practice is rooted in the belief that foreseeing and accepting the inevitability of difficulties makes us less vulnerable when they arise. It also enhances gratitude for what we currently have, as it reminds us that everything is temporary and fragile.

Consider someone who practices negative visualization by imagining the potential loss of a loved one. By confronting this possibility, they cultivate an appreciation for the time they have together, becoming more present and grateful. When challenges arise, such as arguments or misunderstandings, they are better prepared to respond with compassion and patience, knowing that such difficulties are part of the human experience.

Practicing Voluntary Discomfort: Building Resilience

Another Stoic technique for handling adversity is the practice of voluntary discomfort, where individuals deliberately expose themselves to mild hardships or discomforts to build resilience and mental toughness. This practice serves as training for more significant challenges and helps reduce the fear of discomfort or adversity.

For example, a Stoic might choose to occasionally sleep on the floor instead of in their bed or skip a meal to experience hunger. These small acts of discomfort remind them that they can endure more than they think, reducing the fear of future adversity. By voluntarily facing discomfort, they learn to detach from the fear of physical and emotional suffering, enabling them to respond to more significant hardships with equanimity.

Amor Fati: Loving One's Fate

One of the most transformative Stoic strategies is the concept of Amor Fati, or "love of fate." This principle, championed by philosophers like Marcus Aurelius and Friedrich Nietzsche (who was influenced by Stoic thought), encourages embracing everything that happens—both good and bad—as necessary and even desirable. The Stoic believes that everything that occurs is part of a larger, interconnected plan and should be welcomed, not resisted.

Practicing Amor Fati involves cultivating an attitude where one accepts not only the events beyond their control but also learns to appreciate and find value in them. For example, if someone faces a career setback, they would view it as an opportunity to redirect their path, develop new skills, or build resilience. Rather than lamenting the situation, they would strive to find meaning in it, transforming adversity into a catalyst for growth.

Applying Stoic Strategies: Real-Life Examples

Example 1: Facing Rejection with Stoic Resilience

Imagine you apply for a job you are passionate about and believe you are well-qualified for, but you receive a rejection. Initially, you might feel disappointment or self-doubt. However, by applying the Dichotomy of Control, you recognize that while you cannot control the employer's decision, you can control how you respond. You choose to see this as a chance to practice resilience and perseverance, focusing on improving your skills and seeking new opportunities.

If you've practiced Negative Visualization, the rejection feels less devastating because you had mentally prepared for the possibility. You are more likely to maintain your composure and move forward, embodying the Stoic principle of seeing every setback as a step on the path to growth.

Example 2: Embracing Change with Amor Fati

Suppose you experience a sudden life change, such as moving to a new city due to circumstances beyond your control. This change might initially feel overwhelming or unwelcome. By practicing Amor Fati, you shift your perspective, viewing the move as an opportunity to experience new things, meet new people, and grow in ways that wouldn't have been possible otherwise. Instead of resisting the change, you embrace it, finding ways to thrive in the new environment.

Turning Adversity into Strength with Stoic Wisdom

Stoic Strategies for Handling Adversity provide a powerful framework for transforming obstacles into opportunities for growth. By emphasizing practices such as the Dichotomy of Control, Negative Visualization, and Amor Fati, Stoicism teaches us to face life's challenges with courage, wisdom, and grace. These strategies not only help us navigate difficult situations but also cultivate virtues that build character and inner strength.

When we approach adversity with a Stoic mindset, we shift from reacting with fear or avoidance to responding with resilience and purpose. Adversity becomes not just a test of our strength but a valuable opportunity for personal development. Embracing adversity as a pathway to virtue, we can turn every challenge into a meaningful step on the journey of life, building a life that is both resilient and fulfilling.

Reframing Setbacks as Learning Opportunities: Transforming Challenges into Growth

Setbacks and obstacles are inevitable aspects of life that can derail even the most carefully planned goals. How we respond to these setbacks, however, determines their impact on our lives. Do we view them as failures and reasons to give up, or do we see them as valuable lessons that can propel us toward growth and success? The ability to reframe setbacks as learning opportunities is a powerful skill that can transform how we navigate challenges and maintain motivation. By shifting our perspective, we can see setbacks not as dead ends but as detours that offer new insights, skills, and strengths.

We will now explore the process of reframing setbacks through various psychological and philosophical lenses, including insights from Cognitive Behavioral Therapy (CBT), Stoicism, and Buddhism. Each of these disciplines offers strategies for understanding and transforming adversity, helping individuals build resilience and stay motivated even when faced with challenges. By examining real-life examples and applying these frameworks, we will uncover how setbacks can become some of the most valuable opportunities for learning and growth in our lives.

The Power of Perspective: How We Frame Setbacks

Why Reframing Matters: The Mindset Shift

Reframing setbacks is about shifting our mindset—the internal narrative we use to interpret and respond to events. When we encounter a setback, our initial reaction might be disappointment, frustration, or self-doubt. These feelings are natural, but how we interpret the situation determines whether we become stuck or move forward. If we view setbacks as failures or signs of inadequacy, they can become obstacles that erode our confidence and motivation. Conversely, if we view them as learning opportunities, we open ourselves up to growth, resilience, and eventual success.

The concept of growth mindset, developed by psychologist Carol Dweck, aligns with this idea. A growth mindset embraces challenges as chances to develop skills and improve, while a fixed mindset sees challenges as threats to one's abilities or identity. Developing a growth mindset is essential for reframing setbacks. By understanding that difficulties are not reflections of our worth but are instead part of the learning process, we can respond to them constructively and use them to our advantage.

Cognitive Behavioral Therapy (CBT) and the Power of Reframing

CBT provides a practical framework for reframing setbacks. One of the core techniques in CBT is cognitive restructuring, which involves identifying and challenging negative thought patterns that arise in response to adversity. For instance, if a person experiences a setback, such as failing an important exam, their immediate thoughts might include, "I'm not smart enough" or "I'll never succeed." These thoughts contribute to feelings of discouragement and helplessness.

CBT encourages individuals to question these thoughts: Is it true that failing one exam defines intelligence or future success? Are there other explanations for this outcome, such as needing more study time or different strategies? By challenging these negative thoughts and replacing them with more balanced, realistic alternatives—such as, "This is a chance to understand what I need to improve for the next exam"—individuals can transform setbacks into opportunities for growth. This shift in thinking promotes emotional resilience and keeps individuals motivated to try again.

Philosophical Perspectives: Stoicism and Buddhist Wisdom

Stoicism: Adversity as a Path to Virtue

The Stoic approach to reframing setbacks is rooted in the belief that adversity is not only inevitable but also a necessary part of cultivating virtue and wisdom. Stoic philosophers like Epictetus and Marcus Aurelius taught that we do not control external events, but we do have control over how we respond to them. This idea aligns closely with the process of reframing setbacks: instead of resisting or lamenting adversity, we can embrace it as a chance to develop virtues like courage, patience, and perseverance.

For example, Marcus Aurelius wrote, "The impediment to action advances action. What stands in the way becomes the way." This Stoic principle emphasizes that obstacles are not barriers to our goals but are, in fact, essential parts of the journey. When we encounter a setback, such as a failed project or a personal disappointment, the Stoic response is to ask, "What virtue can I cultivate in this moment?" By viewing the setback as a training ground for developing strength or wisdom, we transform the challenge into an opportunity for personal growth.

Buddhism: Embracing Impermanence and Non-Attachment

The Buddhist perspective also offers valuable insights into reframing setbacks. Central to Buddhist philosophy is the concept of impermanence—the understanding that all things, including difficulties, are temporary and ever-changing. By embracing this idea, individuals learn to detach from fixed outcomes and remain open to the flow of life, which includes both success and failure.

In Buddhism, setbacks are seen as opportunities to practice non-attachment and mindfulness. When a setback occurs, rather than becoming attached to feelings of failure or disappointment, practitioners are encouraged to observe their thoughts and emotions without judgment. This practice helps create a sense of distance and clarity, allowing them to respond with compassion and understanding rather than with self-criticism.

For instance, if someone loses a job, the Buddhist approach would involve acknowledging the pain but also recognizing that this is a moment of change rather than a definitive end.

By practicing mindfulness, the individual can explore what new opportunities or paths this setback might open, viewing it as a turning point rather than a failure. This perspective fosters a mindset where every difficulty becomes a moment for growth, learning, and transformation.

Practical Techniques for Reframing Setbacks

Journaling: Reflecting and Learning from Challenges

One effective technique for reframing setbacks is journaling. Reflective journaling allows individuals to process their experiences, identify lessons, and shift their perspectives. When faced with a setback, writing about the event and asking questions like, "What can I learn from this?" or "How can I grow through this experience?" helps reframe the situation as an opportunity for improvement.

For example, someone who has faced rejection in a personal relationship might journal about the experience, exploring questions like, "What patterns led to this outcome?" or "How can I use this to develop better communication skills?" By focusing on what can be learned, the individual shifts from feeling defeated to feeling empowered to grow.

Implementing the "What Went Well" Technique

Another strategy, drawn from Positive Psychology, is the "What Went Well" technique. After experiencing a setback, individuals are encouraged to reflect on the positive aspects of the situation, even if they seem small. This technique helps reframe negative events by highlighting areas where growth or progress occurred.

For instance, if a person fails to meet a professional goal, they might ask themselves, "What did I gain from this experience, despite the setback?" Perhaps they built valuable relationships, developed new skills, or gained insights that will serve them in future endeavors. By focusing on these positives, the individual sees that even setbacks carry elements of progress and opportunity.

Real-Life Example: The Story of Thomas Edison

One of the most famous examples of reframing setbacks is the story of Thomas Edison, who is said to have made over a thousand unsuccessful attempts before inventing the lightbulb. When asked about his "failures," Edison reportedly responded, "I have not failed. I've just found 10,000 ways that won't work." This response reflects the essence of reframing—each setback was not a failure but a step closer to success.

Edison's story illustrates that setbacks often provide essential information that guides us to new, more effective paths. By maintaining a mindset that values learning over immediate success, individuals can sustain motivation and resilience, knowing that each setback brings them closer to their ultimate goal.

Embracing Setbacks as Stepping Stones to Success

Reframing Setbacks as Learning Opportunities is a powerful approach that transforms how we navigate challenges and obstacles. By integrating techniques from CBT, as well as insights from Stoicism and Buddhism, we can develop the skills needed to turn adversity into growth. Whether we face personal, professional, or emotional setbacks, the ability to view these moments as chances for learning and improvement ensures that we remain resilient and motivated.

When setbacks are embraced as stepping stones rather than obstacles, they become essential parts of the journey toward success. Each challenge, rather than pulling us down, lifts us up, offering valuable lessons and insights that guide us forward. In this way, setbacks become not only tolerable but also meaningful and enriching, helping us build a life filled with growth, resilience, and continuous learning. Turning Challenges into Catalysts, we can transform every obstacle into an opportunity for progress and development.

Sustaining Motivation Through Mindfulness and Virtue: A Holistic Approach to Overcoming Setbacks

Staying motivated in the face of challenges and setbacks is a skill that requires more than sheer willpower; it calls for a deep connection to mindfulness and virtue. When adversity strikes, motivation can waver, and the temptation to give up can become overwhelming. However, by cultivating a mindful awareness of our thoughts and emotions and grounding our actions in virtues such as resilience, compassion, and wisdom, we can build a sustainable and lasting source of motivation.

In this discussion, we will explore the integration of mindfulness practices and the cultivation of virtue ethics as strategies for maintaining motivation during difficult times. Mindfulness, drawn from Buddhist traditions, offers a way to stay present and detached from negative thought patterns, while virtue ethics provides a moral and ethical framework for pursuing goals with integrity and strength. By weaving these two powerful approaches together, individuals can develop a resilient mindset that not only sustains motivation but also transforms challenges into opportunities for growth and personal development.

The Foundation of Motivation: Mindfulness and Self-Awareness

Understanding Mindfulness: Staying Present in the Midst of Difficulty

Mindfulness is the practice of bringing one's attention to the present moment, observing thoughts, feelings, and sensations without judgment. Originating from Buddhist traditions, mindfulness encourages individuals to step back from their emotional reactions and observe their experiences with clarity and acceptance. This practice is especially valuable when faced with setbacks, as it allows individuals to detach from automatic negative thought patterns, like self-criticism or defeatism, and instead view their circumstances with a sense of curiosity and openness.

When we experience a setback, such as a professional failure or a personal disappointment, our immediate reaction might be frustration or a loss of motivation. Mindfulness offers a way to pause and observe these reactions without becoming overwhelmed. By practicing mindfulness, we learn to recognize these emotions as transient—acknowledging their presence but not allowing them to dictate our actions or self-perception.

For example, if someone loses their job, the initial reaction might be panic or fear. Through mindfulness, they can take a moment to breathe, observe their thoughts, and recognize that these emotions are natural responses to uncertainty. This awareness creates a space between the event and the reaction, allowing for a more measured and intentional response.

The Role of Self-Compassion in Mindfulness

Mindfulness is also closely tied to self-compassion, the practice of treating oneself with kindness and understanding, especially during times of failure or difficulty. Self-compassion prevents the spiral of self-criticism that often accompanies setbacks, helping individuals maintain motivation by fostering a supportive inner dialogue.

Instead of harshly criticizing oneself for a perceived failure, the practice of self-compassion encourages us to respond as we would to a close friend—with kindness, understanding, and patience. This shift not only softens the emotional impact of setbacks but also nurtures a growth-oriented mindset. When we can recognize that challenges and mistakes are part of the human experience, we become more resilient and motivated to continue our efforts.

For instance, if someone is struggling with a fitness goal and misses a workout, instead of thinking, "I'm so lazy, I'll never succeed," they might reframe their thought to, "It's okay to have an off day. I can start again tomorrow." This kind approach maintains motivation by avoiding the guilt and shame that can lead to giving up.

Virtue Ethics: A Framework for Lasting Motivation

The Role of Virtue in Overcoming Setbacks

While mindfulness provides a means to navigate emotional responses, virtue ethics offers a solid foundation for decision-making and motivation during difficult times. Virtue ethics, as emphasized by philosophers like Aristotle, centers on the cultivation of character traits—virtues—that enable individuals to live a good, meaningful life. These virtues, such as courage, patience, resilience, and wisdom, serve as guiding principles, helping individuals respond to challenges with integrity and strength.

When motivation wanes due to setbacks, leaning on these virtues provides a moral and ethical compass that keeps us aligned with our values. For example, if a person faces a career setback, practicing resilience and patience ensures that they remain steadfast in their pursuit of growth, even if immediate success is not apparent. Similarly, cultivating wisdom allows individuals to assess their situation critically and learn from the experience, rather than viewing it solely as a failure.

Practical Application: Virtue as a Source of Motivation

Virtues are not abstract ideals; they are practical tools that can be applied in everyday life to sustain motivation. For instance, the virtue of courage can be called upon when taking a risk feels daunting, reminding us that true growth often involves stepping outside of our comfort zones. Perseverance helps us maintain our efforts, even when progress seems slow or setbacks occur.

The practice of virtue is also closely linked to purpose. When individuals align their actions with their core values and virtues, they create a sense of purpose that extends beyond immediate results. This purpose becomes a motivating force that sustains effort and engagement, even when outcomes are uncertain.

For example, an artist who feels discouraged because their work isn't gaining recognition can turn to the virtue of resilience and the value of creativity. By focusing on the intrinsic reward of creating art and the process itself, rather than external validation, the artist finds renewed motivation and fulfillment, regardless of external setbacks.

Integrating Mindfulness and Virtue: A Synergistic Approach

Combining Presence and Purpose

Mindfulness and virtue ethics are not separate; they are complementary. While mindfulness helps individuals stay present and observe their emotional responses with clarity, virtue ethics provides the moral grounding that informs their actions and decisions. Together, they form a powerful strategy for overcoming setbacks and maintaining motivation.

When combined, these practices allow for a deeper understanding of both the emotional and ethical dimensions of setbacks. Mindfulness offers the emotional resilience to stay calm and open, while virtues like wisdom and courage guide individuals toward meaningful and constructive responses.

For instance, if someone faces repeated failures in starting a business, mindfulness can help them stay present, manage anxiety, and observe their thoughts without getting caught in cycles of self-doubt. At the same time, the virtues of perseverance and wisdom provide a framework for learning from each failure, adjusting strategies, and remaining committed to their long-term vision.

The Role of Reflection in Integrating Mindfulness and Virtue

A practical way to integrate these two approaches is through reflective practices, such as journaling or evening reviews. By taking time to reflect on setbacks with both a mindful perspective and a focus on virtues, individuals can gain insights into their motivations, challenges, and growth. This reflection process allows them to continually align their actions with their values and adjust their approach as needed.

For example, an evening review might include questions like:

- "What challenges did I face today, and how did I respond to them?"
- "Did I act in accordance with my values and virtues?"
- "How can I use mindfulness to better manage my emotions and remain motivated?"

This combination of mindfulness and virtue-based reflection provides a holistic approach to sustaining motivation and building resilience, ensuring that setbacks become opportunities for growth rather than reasons to give up.

Real-Life Example: A Personal Transformation Through Mindfulness and Virtue

Consider the story of a professional athlete who faced a career-threatening injury. Initially, the setback brought feelings of despair and a loss of motivation. However, by integrating mindfulness and virtue ethics into their recovery process, the athlete transformed their approach to the situation.

Mindfulness allowed them to stay present during painful rehabilitation sessions, managing fear and frustration by focusing on each small improvement rather than the distant goal of full recovery. At the same time, they leaned on virtues like courage and perseverance, reminding themselves that this period was an opportunity to develop mental and physical resilience. Through this combination, they not only sustained their motivation but emerged from the experience stronger and more focused than before.

Motivation as a Practice of Presence and Integrity

Sustaining Motivation Through Mindfulness and Virtue offers a powerful framework for overcoming setbacks and maintaining momentum on the path to personal and professional growth. By staying present and detached from negative thought patterns through mindfulness, and by grounding actions in virtues that align with our values, individuals can cultivate a resilient mindset that sees challenges as opportunities for growth rather than as obstacles.

When mindfulness and virtue ethics are integrated, motivation becomes not a fleeting feeling but a steady, enduring practice rooted in presence and integrity. This approach not only empowers individuals to navigate adversity but also transforms the journey into a fulfilling and meaningful pursuit of personal excellence. Embracing Mindful Virtue, individuals turn every setback into a stepping stone, building a life characterized by resilience, growth, and a deep sense of purpose.

As we transition from the exploration of sustaining motivation through mindfulness and virtue, it's important to recognize that the principles and strategies discussed extend beyond personal growth and resilience; they are equally powerful in shaping our interactions with others. Our motivation, values, and mindset profoundly influence the quality of our relationships and our ability to navigate social dynamics effectively. The next group of topics will focus on **Interpersonal Relationships and Social Well-Being**, diving into how frameworks like **CBT**, **Stoicism**, and **Buddhism** provide practical tools and ethical insights for enhancing communication, managing conflict, and building meaningful, virtuous connections. By understanding how these disciplines guide us in practicing compassion, patience, and detachment, we can develop the skills needed to foster healthier, more resilient relationships while maintaining our own sense of well-being and integrity.

8. Cultivating Meaningful Connections: A Guide to Interpersonal Relationships and Social Well-Being

Human relationships are at the heart of our existence, profoundly influencing our sense of well-being, purpose, and fulfillment. Whether we are navigating friendships, romantic partnerships, family dynamics, or professional connections, the quality of our interactions shapes not only our emotional health but also our personal growth. In this group of topics, we explore the foundations of Interpersonal Relationships and Social Well-Being, using insights from Cognitive Behavioral Therapy (CBT), Stoicism, and Buddhism to enhance communication skills, manage conflicts, and foster deep, meaningful connections. We will delve into how CBT techniques such as cognitive restructuring can improve our ability to communicate and resolve misunderstandings, while Stoic and Buddhist principles help us practice compassion, detachment, and virtue in our relationships. Ethical considerations will also be examined, guiding us through moral dilemmas and highlighting the importance of cultivating patience, forgiveness, and understanding. By integrating these frameworks, we can develop a holistic approach to building and sustaining relationships that enrich our lives and support our overall well-being.

Enhancing Communication and Resolving Conflicts: CBT Techniques for Stronger Relationships

Interpersonal relationships are the cornerstone of our social and emotional well-being. The quality of these connections, whether in friendships, family dynamics, or romantic partnerships, significantly impacts our sense of fulfillment and happiness. However, relationships are not without challenges—misunderstandings, conflicts, and communication breakdowns are common. How we handle these challenges can determine whether a relationship thrives or deteriorates. This is where Cognitive Behavioral Therapy (CBT) offers valuable tools for improving communication and resolving conflicts.

CBT, a well-established approach in psychology, focuses on understanding the connection between thoughts, emotions, and behaviors. Applying CBT techniques to relationships allows us to recognize and restructure negative thinking patterns that might interfere with healthy communication, while also equipping us with skills to manage and resolve conflicts constructively. This discussion explores how CBT can be applied to enhance relationships, focusing on developing effective communication skills through cognitive restructuring and techniques for managing conflict and misunderstandings. By diving into real-life scenarios and practical applications, we can see how CBT not only improves our interpersonal dynamics but also supports a deeper, more fulfilling connection with others.

The Foundation of Effective Communication: CBT and Cognitive Restructuring

Recognizing and Challenging Negative Thought Patterns in Communication

Communication is often influenced by the way we think and interpret the actions or words of others. Our internal dialogue, shaped by past experiences, emotions, and cognitive distortions, can color how we perceive and respond to people around us. In relationships, this can lead to misunderstandings or conflicts if our perceptions are distorted or overly negative. For instance, if someone has experienced rejection in the past, they might interpret a partner's momentary distraction as a sign of disinterest or rejection, even when that's not the case.

Cognitive restructuring, a core component of CBT, is an effective tool for addressing these thought patterns. It involves identifying and challenging negative or distorted beliefs that may be influencing one's interactions. By recognizing cognitive distortions like **mind reading** (assuming we know what others are thinking), **catastrophizing** (assuming the worst outcome), or **personalization** (taking things too personally), individuals can shift their perspectives to more balanced and realistic interpretations.

For example, let's consider a scenario where one partner arrives home late without prior notice. The other partner might think, "They don't care about me or my time," leading to anger or withdrawal. Through cognitive restructuring, this partner can learn to pause and ask, "Is there another reason why they might be late? Could it be unrelated to me?" This shift in perspective opens the door to constructive dialogue rather than escalating conflict, allowing for a conversation that is curious and understanding rather than defensive or accusatory.

Developing Assertive Communication Skills

Effective communication in relationships requires more than just identifying negative thought patterns; it also involves assertive communication. Assertiveness, as opposed to passivity or aggression, allows individuals to express their feelings, needs, and boundaries clearly and respectfully. CBT emphasizes the development of assertive communication skills, helping people learn how to express themselves honestly while respecting the other person's perspective.

An assertive communicator uses "I" statements, such as, "I feel upset when you don't call to let me know you're running late because it makes me worry," rather than "You never call, and you don't care about my feelings." This approach focuses on expressing one's own feelings and needs without blaming or criticizing, making it more likely that the other person will respond positively and be willing to engage in resolving the issue.

By practicing assertiveness, individuals can break patterns of avoidance or confrontation, fostering an environment where both parties feel safe to share their thoughts and emotions. This practice builds trust and openness, which are essential for resolving misunderstandings and preventing conflicts from escalating.

Managing Conflict and Misunderstandings: CBT Techniques for Resolution

Identifying Conflict Triggers and Emotional Responses

Conflicts often arise when specific triggers activate emotional responses that may not align with the present situation. CBT helps individuals become aware of these triggers and understand how their emotional responses are linked to their thoughts. For example, if someone feels anxious or defensive every time their partner asks them about their day, it may be tied to a past experience where similar questions led to criticism or judgment.

Through CBT, individuals learn to recognize these patterns and differentiate between past experiences and present realities. By identifying triggers and the thoughts associated with them, they can develop a more mindful and measured response. Instead of reacting defensively, they might acknowledge the trigger and reframe their thoughts, choosing to see their partner's question as genuine interest rather than a prelude to criticism.

Problem-Solving and Compromise: A CBT Approach

When misunderstandings or disagreements arise, CBT provides a structured approach to problem-solving and finding compromise. Rather than viewing conflicts as confrontations, individuals are encouraged to see them as opportunities for growth and deeper understanding. This involves several steps:

1. **Clarifying the Issue**: Both parties work together to define the problem clearly, ensuring that each person understands the other's perspective. This step requires active listening and a willingness to step into the other person's shoes.
2. **Exploring Solutions**: Once the issue is clarified, both individuals brainstorm potential solutions. CBT encourages creativity and openness during this stage, reminding individuals to avoid rigid thinking.
3. **Evaluating Solutions**: Each potential solution is evaluated based on its feasibility and fairness. This step involves honest dialogue and a commitment to finding a resolution that respects both parties' needs and boundaries.
4. **Reaching a Compromise**: After evaluating options, a compromise is agreed upon. This may involve both individuals making adjustments or meeting halfway, demonstrating flexibility and goodwill.

For instance, if one partner values alone time while the other desires more together time, they might compromise by scheduling specific times each week for solo activities and others for shared moments. This structured approach ensures that both parties feel heard and respected, fostering a sense of collaboration rather than competition.

Practicing Mindfulness to Stay Present During Conflicts

Mindfulness, a technique also integrated within CBT, is valuable in managing conflicts and misunderstandings. When tensions rise, emotions can cloud judgment, leading to reactive or impulsive behavior. Practicing mindfulness helps individuals stay grounded in the present moment, allowing them to observe their emotions without becoming overwhelmed.

In practice, mindfulness during conflict might look like taking a few deep breaths before responding, noticing physical sensations like a racing heart or clenched fists, and consciously choosing to listen rather than react immediately. This pause creates space for a more thoughtful and constructive response, reducing the likelihood of escalation and enhancing the quality of communication.

Real-Life Application: Improving Relationships Through CBT Techniques

Consider a scenario where two colleagues, Alex and Jordan, consistently miscommunicate, leading to friction and resentment. Alex often feels that Jordan's behavior is dismissive, interpreting it as a lack of respect or acknowledgment. On the other hand, Jordan feels misunderstood and undervalued, believing that Alex's frustration is unwarranted. Applying the CBT structured approach to problem-solving and compromise, we will explore how they navigate this issue step-by-step to improve their professional relationship.

Step 1: Clarifying the Issue

The first step in the CBT approach is for both Alex and Jordan to clearly define the problem and understand each other's perspectives.

1. **Setting Up the Conversation**: Alex and Jordan agree to meet in a neutral setting, such as a conference room, where they can talk without interruptions. They establish ground rules for the discussion, agreeing to listen actively without interrupting or making assumptions.
2. **Alex's Perspective**: Alex begins by sharing feelings, saying, "I often feel dismissed when you respond curtly

during meetings or when you don't make eye contact. It makes me feel as if my contributions aren't valued." This allows Jordan to hear Alex's perspective directly, rather than through assumptions or rumors.
3. **Jordan's Perspective**: Jordan then shares, "I didn't realize my behavior came across that way. When I respond quickly, it's usually because I'm trying to get through tasks efficiently, not because I don't value your input. I often feel pressured by deadlines and sometimes overlook how I come across."
4. **Active Listening**: Both parties engage in active listening—repeating back what they've heard to confirm understanding. Alex says, "So, you're saying it's not about my contributions, but rather about the time pressure you feel?" Jordan responds, "Yes, and I understand now that my behavior affects how you perceive my responses."

By clarifying the issue, Alex and Jordan can see that the conflict stems from misunderstandings rather than deliberate actions. This shared understanding forms a foundation for the next step.

Step 2: Exploring Solutions

With the issue clearly defined, Alex and Jordan move on to brainstorming possible solutions, focusing on collaboration and openness.

1. **Brainstorming Together**: Both agree to come up with ideas that could improve their communication. Alex suggests, "What if we set aside a few minutes after meetings to check in with each other? That way, I can clarify any points I'm unsure about, and we can address any misunderstandings immediately."
2. **Jordan's Idea**: Jordan adds, "I could also make an effort to acknowledge your points during meetings by nodding or verbally affirming what you've said, even if

I'm focused on other tasks. This might show that I'm listening, even if I can't engage fully in that moment."
3. **Creating a List of Options**: They jot down other possible solutions, such as scheduling brief weekly check-ins to review progress and ensure they're aligned on priorities. The goal here is to generate multiple solutions without immediately judging them, encouraging creativity and openness to new approaches.

Through this brainstorming process, Alex and Jordan develop a sense of collaboration, moving away from seeing each other as adversaries and toward working as a team to resolve their conflict.

Step 3: Evaluating Solutions

Now, Alex and Jordan evaluate the proposed solutions, assessing their feasibility, fairness, and potential impact on their working relationship.

1. **Assessing Feasibility**: They start with the idea of setting aside time after meetings. Alex notes that while it's a good idea, their schedules are often tight, and they might not always have time immediately after a meeting. They agree that while this could be effective, it might not be realistic to implement every time.
2. **Jordan's Commitment**: Jordan's suggestion of making an effort to acknowledge Alex's points during meetings is seen as practical and feasible. Alex appreciates this idea, saying, "I think even a small gesture like that could make a difference. It would show that you're engaged, even if it's brief."
3. **Compromise on Weekly Check-Ins**: They also revisit the idea of a brief weekly check-in. Both agree that while they can't guarantee time after every meeting, a consistent 15-minute check-in once a week could provide a space to address ongoing concerns. They decide this solution is both feasible and fair, as it

respects their time constraints while addressing their communication needs.

By evaluating each solution together, they choose a practical combination: Jordan will make an effort to show acknowledgment during meetings, and they will commit to weekly check-ins. This evaluation step ensures that both parties' needs are considered, and they collaboratively decide on realistic actions.

Step 4: Reaching a Compromise

After evaluating their options, Alex and Jordan settle on a compromise and develop a plan to implement it. This step involves flexibility and a shared commitment to improving their relationship.

1. **Agreeing on Actions**: Alex and Jordan formalize their agreement:
    - **Immediate Action**: Jordan will consciously work on acknowledging Alex's contributions in meetings through verbal affirmations or gestures.
    - **Ongoing Action**: They schedule a 15-minute check-in every Thursday afternoon to discuss any concerns, review priorities, and ensure they are aligned.
2. **Documenting the Plan**: They write down their plan and set a reminder for their weekly check-ins. This ensures accountability and provides a clear structure for their agreement.
3. **Expressing Appreciation**: Both Alex and Jordan express appreciation for each other's willingness to work on the issue. Alex says, "I appreciate your openness and the effort you're putting in to improve our communication," while Jordan responds, "Thank you for bringing this up in a constructive way. I'm glad we could find a solution together."

4. **Setting a Review Point**: To ensure the compromise is working, they agree to revisit their arrangement in a month. This allows them to assess the effectiveness of their strategies and make adjustments if needed.

By reaching a compromise through this structured CBT approach, Alex and Jordan not only resolve their immediate conflict but also build a system that supports ongoing, open communication. This process demonstrates the power of flexibility and collaboration in creating solutions that respect both individuals' needs.

Throughout their interactions, Alex and Jordan also practice mindfulness to stay present and manage their emotions effectively.

- **Staying Grounded**: During their meetings and discussions, they consciously practice mindfulness by taking a few deep breaths when they notice emotions rising. For instance, when Jordan feels defensive after hearing Alex's concerns, taking a deep breath allows for a pause, preventing a reactive response.
- **Noticing Physical Sensations**: Both colleagues become aware of their physical reactions, such as tension in their bodies, and use this awareness to remind themselves to stay calm. For example, Alex notices a racing heart and reminds themselves to stay open and curious rather than jumping to conclusions.
- **Creating Space for Thoughtful Responses**: By incorporating mindfulness techniques, both Alex and Jordan are able to respond thoughtfully rather than reactively. This practice of taking a pause allows them to choose their words carefully, fostering a respectful and open dialogue.

Building Stronger Relationships Through the CBT Approach

By applying the CBT structured approach, Alex and Jordan demonstrate how real people can effectively navigate misunderstandings and conflicts in a professional setting. The steps of clarifying the issue, exploring solutions, evaluating options, and reaching a compromise provide a practical framework for finding common ground and fostering mutual respect. Additionally, integrating mindfulness allows both parties to manage their emotional responses, ensuring a calm and constructive interaction.

This scenario illustrates how CBT techniques can be used to transform conflicts into opportunities for collaboration and growth, ultimately strengthening relationships and enhancing overall workplace dynamics. Turning Conflict into Collaboration, Alex and Jordan embody how structured problem-solving and open communication lead to more harmonious and productive interactions.

Compassion and Detachment: Stoic and Buddhist Wisdom for Stronger Relationships

Interpersonal relationships, whether they are friendships, romantic partnerships, or professional connections, are vital components of human life. However, they are also inherently complex and challenging. Conflicts, misunderstandings, and unmet expectations can often cause strain, leading to emotional distress or even the dissolution of once-close connections. To navigate these complexities, Stoic and Buddhist philosophies offer profound insights into maintaining healthy, meaningful relationships. Both traditions emphasize the importance of cultivating compassion while practicing detachment, as well as the role that virtues play in building resilient and harmonious connections.

This discussion delves into how the principles of Stoicism and Buddhism can be applied to enhance the quality of our relationships. We will explore how compassion, when combined with detachment, allows for genuine connection without clinging or possessiveness. Furthermore, we will examine the role of virtues, such as **wisdom**, **patience**, and **equanimity**, in strengthening our interpersonal bonds. By integrating these approaches, we can transform how we relate to others, leading to more balanced and fulfilling relationships.

Compassion Without Attachment: A Balanced Approach

Understanding Compassion in Relationships

Compassion, in both Stoic and Buddhist traditions, is a central tenet for cultivating positive relationships. It involves the ability to understand and empathize with others' feelings and experiences, while offering support and kindness. In the Buddhist perspective, compassion (karuṇā) is about recognizing the suffering of others and responding with a sincere wish to alleviate it. This perspective extends beyond empathy; it is an active, intentional practice that seeks to bring relief to those in need.

In practice, compassion might look like being fully present when a friend is going through a difficult time—listening to their concerns, validating their feelings, and offering support without judgment. Compassion in relationships means holding space for others' emotions while offering warmth and kindness, even when we may not fully understand their experience.

The Stoic tradition also values compassion, but it integrates this with a sense of reason and balance. Stoic philosophers like Seneca and Marcus Aurelius believed that showing kindness and empathy was essential, but they cautioned against becoming emotionally overwhelmed or overly attached to others' emotions. For Stoics, compassion involves recognizing the commonality of human struggles while maintaining one's inner tranquility. It's about being there for others without letting their distress pull you into emotional chaos. This concept is closely tied to detachment, which we will explore further.

Practicing Detachment: The Balance Between Involvement and Independence

Detachment, as understood in both Buddhism and Stoicism, does not mean indifference or lack of care; rather, it is about maintaining emotional balance and perspective. In Buddhism, detachment (upekkhā) is about seeing the impermanent and ever-changing nature of life. It teaches that clinging to outcomes or becoming overly attached to people can lead to suffering because everything is subject to change. In relationships, this practice encourages individuals to remain open and caring without becoming overly possessive or dependent on others for their happiness.

For example, a person in a romantic relationship might practice detachment by valuing and cherishing their partner without developing expectations that the relationship must always remain the same or fulfill all their needs. They recognize that people grow and change, and they allow for that growth, understanding that the relationship's dynamic may also shift over time.

In Stoicism, detachment is linked to the concept of the dichotomy of control—the idea that we should focus on what we can control (our own actions and responses) and accept what we cannot control (the actions and emotions of others). A Stoic approach to relationships encourages individuals to care deeply about others but without attachment to specific outcomes. For instance, if a close friend chooses to distance themselves or if a romantic relationship ends, a Stoic would strive to accept this with grace, understanding that they cannot control others' choices. The focus is on maintaining one's integrity and inner peace regardless of external circumstances.

By combining compassion and detachment, individuals can engage fully in their relationships, offering love, support, and empathy without becoming overly reliant on others or overwhelmed by their emotions. This balanced approach fosters healthier and more resilient connections, as it allows for genuine presence and care without the fear of loss or change.

The Role of Virtue in Building Strong Relationships

Stoic Virtues: Cultivating Resilience and Integrity

Stoicism places a strong emphasis on cultivating virtues such as wisdom, justice, courage, and temperance to build strong and meaningful relationships. These virtues serve as guiding principles that inform how individuals interact with others, ensuring that their actions are grounded in reason and integrity.

- **Wisdom**: Wisdom guides us to act with discernment in relationships, helping us understand when to engage and when to step back. It involves recognizing the dynamics at play and choosing responses that align with long-term well-being rather than short-term emotional reactions.
- **Justice**: Justice involves treating others fairly and with respect, regardless of the circumstances. It means valuing the well-being of others and acting in ways that support equity and harmony within relationships.
- **Courage**: Courage is necessary for addressing conflicts and misunderstandings honestly and openly. It allows individuals to express their needs and concerns without fear of confrontation, fostering authentic communication and trust.

- **Temperance**: Temperance is the ability to manage desires and impulses, ensuring that actions are balanced and thoughtful. In relationships, this means avoiding extremes—whether that's being too detached or too dependent.

Buddhist Virtues: Compassion, Patience, and Equanimity

Buddhist teachings also emphasize the cultivation of virtues, particularly those that support harmonious and compassionate relationships.

- **Compassion (Karuṇā)**: As discussed earlier, compassion is fundamental in Buddhism. It involves an active desire to alleviate the suffering of others and is closely tied to empathy and kindness. Practicing compassion means being present for others with an open heart, even in challenging situations.
- **Patience (Khanti)**: Patience is crucial in relationships, especially when misunderstandings or conflicts arise. Practicing patience involves tolerating discomfort and uncertainty without reacting impulsively. It means giving others the space to express themselves and understanding that not everything needs to be resolved immediately.
- **Equanimity (Upekkhā)**: Equanimity, or emotional balance, is essential for maintaining stability in relationships. It is the ability to remain calm and centered regardless of external circumstances. Practicing equanimity allows individuals to navigate the ups and downs of relationships with grace, reducing emotional reactivity and fostering a sense of peace.

These virtues, when applied consistently, strengthen relationships by providing a foundation of mutual respect, understanding, and stability. They encourage individuals to engage with others in a balanced and thoughtful manner, promoting a deeper sense of connection and well-being.

Real-Life Application: Compassion and Detachment in Action

To illustrate how these principles work in real-life relationships, consider the following scenario:

Sarah and Daniel have been close friends for years, but recently, Daniel has been distant and unresponsive. Sarah feels hurt and begins to wonder if she has done something wrong. Instead of reacting immediately, she decides to apply both Stoic and Buddhist principles.

- **Step 1: Practicing Compassion**: Sarah chooses to approach the situation with compassion, considering that Daniel might be going through a difficult time. Instead of assuming the worst or becoming resentful, she sends a message expressing her concern and offering support, without demanding an immediate response.

    Sarah's message is thoughtful, compassionate, and open, demonstrating her concern for Daniel while respecting his space. She writes:

    "Hey Daniel, I just wanted to check in and see how you're doing. I've noticed you've been a bit distant lately, and I want you to know that I'm here for you if you need anything or just want to talk. No pressure to respond right away, but I'm thinking of you and hope everything's okay. Take care."

    This message shows that Sarah is reaching out with genuine care, without making assumptions or demanding a response. It offers support while allowing Daniel the freedom to respond when he feels ready, aligning with her practice of compassion, detachment, and patience.

- **Step 2: Applying Detachment**: While Sarah cares deeply for Daniel, she also practices detachment, recognizing that she cannot control his actions or emotional state. She acknowledges that his behavior may have nothing to do with her, and she refrains from making assumptions or taking his distance personally. This allows her to remain calm and open, avoiding the buildup of resentment.

- **Step 3: Engaging with Virtue**: Sarah applies the virtue of patience, understanding that meaningful conversations take time. She also uses wisdom to decide when and how to follow up, ensuring that her actions are supportive rather than invasive.

By combining compassion, detachment, and virtue, Sarah navigates this challenging situation with grace, maintaining her integrity while offering genuine support. This approach strengthens the foundation of her friendship with Daniel, whether he responds immediately or not.

The Art of Compassionate Detachment

Cultivating compassionate relationships involves a balance of presence, care, and detachment. By integrating Stoic and Buddhist principles, individuals can build strong, resilient connections that are rooted in empathy and understanding without becoming overly attached or dependent on outcomes. Practicing compassion while maintaining detachment allows for a deeper, more authentic connection with others, as it emphasizes giving and receiving love freely without the need for control.

Incorporating virtues such as wisdom, patience, and equanimity further strengthens relationships by ensuring that interactions are thoughtful, balanced, and grounded in ethical principles. By embracing these approaches, individuals can transform their relationships into sources of mutual growth and well-being, creating a network of support that enhances both individual and collective flourishing. Embracing compassionate detachment, we open ourselves to the true depth and richness that relationships offer, while maintaining the emotional balance and clarity needed to navigate life's inevitable changes.

Navigating Moral Dilemmas and Cultivating Virtues in Relationships: An Ethical Approach

Interpersonal relationships are often accompanied by ethical complexities and moral dilemmas that test our character and challenge our principles. Whether in the context of friendships, family, romantic partnerships, or professional connections, we frequently encounter situations where the line between right and wrong is blurred, and the decisions we make can significantly affect both ourselves and others. Navigating these moral dilemmas requires not only a sound ethical framework but also the cultivation of key virtues such as patience, forgiveness, and understanding.

In this discussion, we will explore how to ethically navigate moral dilemmas within relationships using principles drawn from virtue ethics, Stoicism, and Buddhism. We will examine the process of confronting and resolving conflicts that arise when values clash or when we must balance our needs with those of others. Additionally, we will delve into the practice of cultivating patience, forgiveness, and understanding as essential tools for maintaining and deepening relationships. Through life examples and practical applications, we will see how these ethical approaches can transform conflicts and dilemmas into opportunities for growth and connection.

Ethical Considerations: Navigating Moral Dilemmas in Relationships

Understanding Moral Dilemmas: When Values Collide

Moral dilemmas in relationships often arise when two or more values or obligations conflict, requiring individuals to make difficult choices. For instance, a friend may ask for a favor that conflicts with your personal boundaries, or a romantic partner may seek forgiveness for a betrayal. These situations force us to weigh our principles against our emotions and the needs of others, making it crucial to have a clear ethical approach.

Virtue ethics, as developed by philosophers like Aristotle, provides a framework for navigating these dilemmas. This approach suggests that rather than focusing on rigid rules or outcomes, we should consider the virtues we want to embody and how they influence our actions. For example, when faced with a dilemma, one might ask, "What action aligns with patience, integrity, and compassion?" This perspective shifts the focus from finding the 'right' answer to cultivating the right character traits and intentions.

Applying Stoic and Buddhist Perspectives to Moral Conflicts

Both Stoicism and Buddhism offer valuable insights into handling moral dilemmas with clarity and composure.

- **Stoic Approach**: Stoicism emphasizes rationality and the importance of focusing on what is within our control. When encountering a moral dilemma, a Stoic would first pause to assess which aspects of the situation they can influence and which are beyond their control. For example, if a colleague violates one's trust, the Stoic approach would focus on managing one's own response—choosing to communicate calmly and set boundaries—while accepting that they cannot control the colleague's behavior. This detachment helps maintain inner peace, even in challenging ethical situations.

- **Buddhist Approach**: Buddhism, with its emphasis on non-attachment and compassion, encourages individuals to approach moral dilemmas with an open heart and a flexible mind. It teaches that clinging to fixed outcomes or expectations often leads to suffering. Instead, one should focus on intentions and act with compassion, even when facing difficult choices. For instance, if a friend has hurt you but seeks forgiveness, the Buddhist perspective suggests that responding with compassion and understanding, while being honest about one's feelings, can alleviate suffering for both parties. This doesn't mean automatically excusing harmful behavior; rather, it means finding a path that minimizes suffering and promotes healing.

By integrating these Stoic and Buddhist principles, individuals can navigate moral dilemmas in relationships with a balanced and thoughtful approach, ensuring that their actions are guided by wisdom and compassion.

Cultivating Patience, Forgiveness, and Understanding: Essential Virtues for Ethical Relationships

The Power of Patience: Responding, Not Reacting

Patience is a cornerstone virtue in ethical relationships, allowing individuals to respond thoughtfully rather than react impulsively. In conflicts, patience provides the necessary space to process emotions, gather information, and approach the situation with clarity. It helps prevent misunderstandings from escalating and fosters a calm environment where both parties feel heard.

For example, imagine a scenario where a partner cancels plans at the last minute due to work obligations. The immediate reaction might be anger or disappointment, but practicing patience allows one to pause, consider the partner's perspective, and choose a response that maintains respect and understanding. This practice not only diffuses potential conflicts but also strengthens the bond between individuals, as it shows that each person values the other's circumstances and emotions.

From a Buddhist perspective, patience is about accepting the impermanence of life and the uncertainty of outcomes. It teaches individuals to wait without becoming attached to specific results, thereby reducing anxiety and resentment. The Stoics, similarly, view patience as an extension of the dichotomy of control, reminding individuals that while they can control their response, they cannot always control others' actions or circumstances.

Embracing Forgiveness: Letting Go of Resentment

Forgiveness is often one of the most challenging virtues to cultivate, especially when we feel deeply hurt or wronged. However, it is also one of the most powerful tools for healing and moving forward in relationships. Forgiveness doesn't mean condoning harmful behavior or forgetting the past; rather, it involves releasing the emotional hold that resentment and anger have on us.

In relationships, practicing forgiveness allows individuals to acknowledge and process their pain without remaining stuck in a cycle of blame. For instance, if a friend has betrayed trust, the process of forgiveness involves expressing one's hurt honestly while also seeking to understand the friend's actions. It's about finding a balance where one can let go of resentment while still holding the other accountable for their behavior.

Both Buddhism and Stoicism offer guidance on forgiveness. In Buddhism, forgiveness is closely tied to compassion—understanding that everyone is imperfect and that mistakes are part of the human experience. By letting go of anger, individuals free themselves from suffering and create space for healing. The Stoics, on the other hand, encourage viewing others' actions through the lens of understanding and rationality, recognizing that people often act out of ignorance or circumstances beyond their control.

Understanding as a Pathway to Empathy and Connection

Understanding goes beyond merely knowing why someone acts a certain way; it involves an empathetic engagement that seeks to connect with another's emotional experience. When we seek to understand the motivations, fears, and emotions of others, we create a bridge that fosters deeper connection and trust.

Consider a situation where a family member repeatedly cancels planned visits. Without understanding, one might feel rejected or unimportant. However, by seeking to understand—perhaps learning that the family member is dealing with stress or anxiety—one can respond with empathy rather than judgment. This act of understanding can shift the dynamic from conflict to support, allowing for a more authentic and supportive relationship.

In Buddhism, understanding (also known as right understanding) is a core component of ethical living. It requires looking beyond one's own perspective and recognizing the interconnectedness of all beings. In Stoicism, understanding is rooted in the acceptance of human nature. By recognizing that everyone is navigating their own struggles and challenges, Stoics encourage a compassionate and patient response, rather than harsh judgment.

Real-Life Application: Navigating Ethical Dilemmas with Virtue

Let's bring these principles to life with an example:

Emma and Lisa have been best friends for years. Recently, Emma discovers that Lisa shared a personal secret of hers with another friend. Emma feels deeply betrayed and struggles with whether to confront Lisa or end the friendship.

- **Step 1: Applying Patience**: Emma takes time to process her emotions rather than reacting immediately. She allows herself to sit with her feelings and reflect on the situation before making any decisions. This patience prevents an impulsive reaction that could escalate the situation.
- **Step 2: Seeking Understanding**: Emma decides to speak with Lisa, aiming to understand her perspective. She approaches the conversation calmly, saying, "I felt hurt when I learned you shared my secret. I want to understand why you did it." By framing the conversation around understanding rather than blame, Emma opens the door for honest communication.
- **Step 3: Practicing Forgiveness**: After listening to Lisa's explanation—who admits she made a mistake and deeply regrets it—Emma decides to forgive. She acknowledges her hurt but chooses to release her resentment, focusing on rebuilding trust. This doesn't mean forgetting the breach of trust; instead, it's about moving forward with a renewed understanding of boundaries.

By navigating the moral dilemma with patience, understanding, and forgiveness, Emma not only preserves her friendship but also strengthens it. The situation becomes an opportunity for growth and deeper connection, demonstrating how ethical considerations can transform conflicts into moments of compassion and healing.

Virtues as Pillars of Ethical Relationships

It's more than making the 'right' choices; it's about embodying patience, forgiveness, and understanding as guiding principles for meaningful interactions. By navigating moral dilemmas with these virtues, individuals create a solid foundation for their relationships, allowing them to weather conflicts with grace and integrity.

Through a thoughtful and balanced approach, informed by Buddhist compassion and Stoic rationality, ethical living in relationships becomes a practice of growth, connection, and mutual respect. In this way, the inevitable challenges that arise in relationships are no longer threats but opportunities for cultivating deeper bonds and nurturing a life enriched by meaningful connections.

Having explored the ethical dimensions of relationships and the virtues that support meaningful connections, we now shift our focus to the broader perspective of cultivating long-term well-being and life satisfaction. While interpersonal dynamics are crucial, sustaining a fulfilling life requires an ongoing commitment to personal growth and self-reflection. This next section delves into the practices that help maintain and enhance our well-being over time, such as developing a comprehensive self-improvement plan, reflecting on progress, and adjusting practices as needed. We will also examine how to balance the acceptance of life's inherent limitations with the pursuit of personal growth, drawing upon Stoic and Buddhist principles to embrace both contentment and aspiration. Finally, we will explore the ultimate goal of these efforts—achieving eudaimonia, or flourishing—by integrating virtue, purpose, happiness, and fulfillment into daily life. This journey is not a static path but a dynamic, evolving process that seeks to harmonize acceptance and growth, leading to a balanced and meaningful life.

9. Pathways to Flourishing: Sustaining Long-Term Well-Being and Life Satisfaction

Achieving long-term well-being and life satisfaction is a journey that requires sustained effort, thoughtful reflection, and a balance between acceptance and growth. It's not enough to simply set goals or cultivate virtues; maintaining a fulfilling and meaningful life demands an ongoing commitment to evolving practices and embracing life's complexities. In this section, we will explore how to create a long-term self-improvement plan that adapts over time through regular reflection and adjustment. We will also delve into the art of balancing acceptance and growth, integrating insights from Stoic and Buddhist traditions that teach us to accept life's limitations while striving for personal development and fulfillment. Finally, we will discuss the concept of eudaimonia—the state of flourishing through virtuous living—and how to integrate happiness and purpose into everyday life. By understanding these pathways to flourishing, individuals can develop a resilient and adaptable approach to long-term well-being that is both realistic and deeply fulfilling.

Crafting and Sustaining a Path of Growth: The Art of Long-Term Self-Improvement

Achieving long-term well-being and life satisfaction is not about quick fixes or temporary changes; it is a continuous, dynamic process that evolves as we grow and encounter new challenges. The key to long-term flourishing lies in creating a sustainable self-improvement plan that serves as a roadmap for personal and professional development, while allowing the flexibility to adapt and evolve. This plan is not set in stone; rather, it requires regular reflection, assessment, and adjustments to ensure it remains aligned with one's values, aspirations, and circumstances. By committing to a structured yet adaptable approach, individuals can cultivate a life of continuous growth and fulfillment.

This section delves into the components of building an effective long-term self-improvement plan and highlights the importance of ongoing reflection and recalibration. We will explore strategies for setting goals, maintaining consistency, and making necessary adjustments to stay on course. Additionally, we will examine how reflective practices can help evaluate progress, celebrate achievements, and identify areas for further development. By understanding these elements, individuals can create a robust framework that supports their journey toward long-term well-being.

The Blueprint for Lasting Change: Creating a Long-Term Self-Improvement Plan

Establishing a Vision: Knowing Where You Want to Go

Before embarking on any journey, it's crucial to have a clear vision of your destination. In the context of self-improvement, this means defining your goals and aspirations in a way that aligns with your values and sense of purpose. The process begins with introspection: asking yourself what truly matters, what you want to achieve, and what kind of person you aspire to become. For instance, a person might set goals related to professional success, physical health, personal development, or cultivating meaningful relationships. The key is to create a vision that resonates deeply with your inner values and motivates you to take action.

Think of your self-improvement plan as designing a house. You wouldn't start building without blueprints; similarly, in life, you need a well-thought-out plan that includes specific goals and objectives. For example, a professional who values growth and impact may envision themselves as a leader who empowers others. This vision shapes their long-term plan, which might include goals such as obtaining leadership training, building a professional network, and mentoring others.

Setting SMART Goals: The Foundation of Your Plan

With a vision established, the next step is to translate that vision into actionable steps. This is where SMART goals—specific, measurable, achievable, relevant, and time-bound—come into play. SMART goals provide clarity and structure, making it easier to track progress and stay accountable.

- **Specific**: Clearly define what you want to achieve. For example, instead of saying, "I want to be healthier," specify "I want to run a 5k in six months."
- **Measurable**: Establish criteria for measuring progress. In the 5k example, you might measure success by gradually increasing your running distance each week.
- **Achievable**: Ensure the goal is realistic given your current resources and constraints. Setting a goal that is too ambitious can lead to frustration and burnout.
- **Relevant**: The goal should align with your overall vision and values. If physical health is a priority for you, then the running goal aligns well.
- **Time-bound**: Set a timeline for achieving the goal. Having a deadline creates urgency and motivation.

By structuring your self-improvement plan around SMART goals, you transform abstract aspirations into concrete actions that are easier to track and achieve.

Breaking Down Goals into Manageable Steps

Big goals can be overwhelming, but breaking them down into smaller, manageable steps makes them less daunting. This approach not only makes progress more attainable but also provides a sense of accomplishment along the way, which fuels motivation. For example, if someone's goal is to learn a new language within a year, they might break it down into smaller tasks such as:

1. Learning 10 new words a day for the first month.

2. Completing an online course by the end of three months.
3. Practicing conversation with a native speaker weekly.

This step-by-step approach ensures steady progress and keeps the individual focused, preventing the feeling of being overwhelmed by a distant, larger goal.

Reflect, Reassess, and Revise: The Cycle of Sustained Growth

The Power of Reflection: Looking Back to Move Forward

Reflection is a crucial part of maintaining a long-term self-improvement plan. Regularly taking the time to evaluate what's working and what's not helps you stay aligned with your goals and values. This could be a monthly or quarterly practice where you set aside time to reflect on your progress, celebrate your achievements, and identify any challenges or setbacks.

Reflection is not about criticizing oneself for what hasn't been accomplished; rather, it's an opportunity to celebrate milestones and adjust one's approach based on real experiences. For example, if someone aimed to complete a course but found it difficult due to their work schedule, reflection allows them to assess what can be adjusted—perhaps breaking the course into smaller segments or changing the time of day they study.

Imagine a gardener tending to a plant. They must regularly check the plant's health, observe its growth, and adjust their care if it's not thriving—perhaps by watering more or adjusting its sunlight exposure. In the same way, your self-improvement plan needs regular attention and care. Reflection helps you make those necessary adjustments to ensure steady growth and flourishing.

Adjusting Goals: Flexibility as a Strength

Life is unpredictable, and rigidity can hinder progress. When circumstances change, it's essential to remain flexible and adjust your goals accordingly. This doesn't mean abandoning your vision; instead, it's about recalibrating your approach to fit new realities. Flexibility allows you to stay committed to growth even when faced with challenges such as changes in work responsibilities, health issues, or shifts in personal priorities.

For instance, if someone's goal is to run a 5k, but they experience an injury, they may adjust their plan to focus on other forms of physical activity like swimming or yoga until they recover. This flexibility keeps them on the path of growth while respecting the current limitations of their situation.

Building a System of Accountability: Ensuring Consistency

Establishing Accountability Partners

One effective way to maintain consistency in a long-term self-improvement plan is to establish accountability partnerships. Whether it's a mentor, a friend, or a colleague, having someone to check in with and share progress can motivate you to stay on track. These partners provide not only support but also constructive feedback, offering different perspectives and encouragement when challenges arise.

Utilizing Technology and Tools for Accountability

Today, numerous digital tools and apps can assist with tracking goals and habits, providing reminders and visualizing progress. Using these tools can enhance consistency by creating routines and providing regular check-ins, ensuring that goals remain a priority even amidst life's distractions.

The Art of Crafting a Flexible, Long-Term Path

Navigating the journey of self-improvement requires both structure and adaptability. By creating a long-term self-improvement plan grounded in SMART goals and breaking down aspirations into manageable steps, individuals can establish a clear and realistic pathway for growth. However, the true strength of any plan lies in its flexibility—regular reflection and adjustment ensure that the path remains aligned with evolving circumstances and values. Through this thoughtful approach, individuals can sustain their journey toward long-term well-being, maintaining the momentum needed for a life of fulfillment and flourishing.

The Balance of Acceptance and Growth: Navigating Life's Limitations and Aspirations

Long-term well-being and life satisfaction require a delicate balance between accepting life's limitations and striving for growth and flourishing. It's a dance between understanding what is beyond our control and working tirelessly toward meaningful goals. Stoic and Buddhist philosophies offer powerful frameworks for this balance, helping individuals embrace life's inherent uncertainties while cultivating a sense of purpose and fulfillment. These practices teach us that acceptance does not equate to passivity; rather, it creates a solid foundation upon which personal growth can be built.

Now let's explore how the principles of Stoicism and Buddhism guide the acceptance of life's limitations, helping individuals find peace in the face of challenges and uncertainties. We will also examine the concept of eudaimonia—a life of flourishing and fulfillment in alignment with one's values and virtues—and how it ties into the pursuit of personal growth. By integrating these ancient wisdom traditions, we can learn to navigate life's dualities with grace, finding equilibrium between acceptance and aspiration.

The Art of Acceptance: Embracing Life's Limitations

Stoic Wisdom: Understanding the Dichotomy of Control

Central to Stoic philosophy is the dichotomy of control, which emphasizes focusing on what we can control—our actions, thoughts, and reactions—while accepting what lies beyond our influence, such as external events and outcomes. This practice encourages individuals to relinquish anxiety and frustration over circumstances they cannot change, allowing for a sense of peace even amidst chaos.

Imagine a person facing a major career setback, such as losing their job. The immediate reaction might be panic, anger, or despair. Stoicism teaches that while these emotions are natural, they are rooted in the desire to control what is inherently uncontrollable (e.g., economic conditions, company decisions). By shifting the focus to what is within one's power—such as developing new skills, networking, and exploring other job opportunities—individuals can move forward without being weighed down by resentment over circumstances they cannot change.

The Stoic practice of amor fati, or the love of one's fate, further deepens this acceptance. It suggests that individuals should not only accept life's challenges but embrace them as opportunities for growth and resilience. This perspective transforms obstacles into catalysts for personal development, reshaping adversity into a valuable aspect of the journey.

Buddhist Perspective: The Practice of Non-Attachment

Buddhism offers a complementary approach through the practice of non-attachment. In Buddhist philosophy, attachment to desires, outcomes, or material possessions is seen as a root cause of suffering. By letting go of these attachments, individuals can experience a profound sense of freedom and peace, even when life does not unfold according to their expectations.

Consider a person struggling with a personal relationship that is not fulfilling their needs or expectations. While the desire for connection is natural, clinging to a specific outcome or ideal can create suffering when reality doesn't match expectations. Buddhism teaches that by practicing non-attachment, the individual can accept the situation as it is, freeing themselves from the emotional turmoil caused by unmet expectations. This acceptance does not mean indifference; rather, it is about approaching the relationship with openness and compassion while releasing the rigid desire for a particular outcome.

A traveler is caught in a storm while hiking in the mountains. They can either fight the storm, growing frustrated and fearful, or they can accept the reality of the storm, taking shelter and adapting their plans. By accepting the storm, the traveler remains calm and resourceful, navigating the situation with clarity and presence. In life, much like the traveler, accepting circumstances beyond our control allows us to act effectively and wisely without being overwhelmed by frustration or fear.

Finding Peace in Impermanence

Both Stoicism and Buddhism teach the importance of embracing impermanence as a fundamental aspect of life. The Stoic idea that "everything changes" aligns with the Buddhist concept of **anicca** (impermanence), reminding us that all things—relationships, careers, even our physical health—are in constant flux. Accepting this impermanence allows individuals to let go of the fear of change and approach life's transitions with a sense of equanimity.

The Pursuit of Growth: Striving for Eudaimonia

Defining Eudaimonia: A Life of Flourishing

While acceptance is crucial, it does not preclude the pursuit of personal growth and fulfillment. In fact, acceptance lays the foundation for growth by freeing us from the paralysis of fear and anxiety. The ancient Greek concept of eudaimonia, central to Aristotelian virtue ethics, refers to a state of flourishing or living in alignment with one's highest potential. Eudaimonia is not about chasing external success or material wealth but rather cultivating a life of purpose, virtue, and inner satisfaction.

To achieve eudaimonia, individuals must identify their core values and align their actions with these principles. For instance, if one values kindness and integrity, pursuing a career that allows for ethical and compassionate interactions would be more fulfilling than one focused solely on financial gain. The pursuit of eudaimonia is a dynamic process, requiring ongoing self-reflection, learning, and adaptation.

Integrating Stoic and Buddhist Growth Practices

Both Stoicism and Buddhism provide tools for personal growth that complement the pursuit of eudaimonia:

- **Stoic Growth Practices**: Stoicism emphasizes the cultivation of virtues like **wisdom**, **courage**, and **temperance** as essential to flourishing. Through daily practices such as **negative visualization** (imagining potential challenges to strengthen resilience) and **self-reflection**, individuals develop the inner strength to

navigate adversity while staying aligned with their goals and values. This practice of fortifying one's character not only enhances personal growth but also fosters a deep sense of purpose and fulfillment.
- **Buddhist Growth Practices**: Buddhism offers practices like **mindfulness** and **meditation** to cultivate self-awareness and presence. These practices help individuals recognize their habitual patterns and emotions, allowing them to respond consciously rather than react impulsively. For instance, someone striving for professional growth might use mindfulness to manage stress and remain focused, while compassion practices (such as **Metta meditation**) can enhance their relationships and interactions, contributing to their overall flourishing.

By integrating these Stoic and Buddhist practices, individuals can build a balanced approach to growth—one that emphasizes inner development and resilience while maintaining compassion and mindfulness.

Balancing Acceptance and Growth: Finding Harmony

The key to long-term well-being lies in balancing the acceptance of life's limitations with the pursuit of personal growth. Acceptance allows individuals to release the struggle against things they cannot change, freeing up energy to focus on meaningful growth. Meanwhile, the pursuit of growth and eudaimonia ensures that life remains dynamic, purposeful, and aligned with one's highest values.

Think of life as navigating a river. Acceptance is understanding the flow of the river and the presence of obstacles like rocks or currents—things beyond your control. Growth, on the other hand, is learning how to steer your boat, developing the skills and strength to navigate the waters effectively. Together, these practices create a harmonious journey where you move forward with intention while adapting to the inevitable changes of the river.

The Dynamic Balance of a Flourishing Life

Embracing life's dualities for long-term fulfillment requires mastering the art of balancing acceptance with growth. By accepting life's limitations through Stoic and Buddhist principles, individuals can cultivate a peaceful and resilient mindset, allowing them to remain centered even in the face of uncertainty. Simultaneously, the pursuit of eudaimonia guides individuals toward meaningful goals, ensuring that their lives are not only peaceful but also purposeful and fulfilling. This dynamic balance creates a pathway to long-term well-being, where acceptance and aspiration coexist, enriching life with both contentment and growth.

The Pursuit of Eudaimonia: Living a Life of Virtue, Purpose, and Fulfillment

Achieving a state of eudaimonia, or flourishing, is the ultimate goal in the quest for long-term well-being and life satisfaction. Rooted in ancient Greek philosophy, particularly the teachings of Aristotle, eudaimonia transcends simple happiness or pleasure. It is about living in alignment with one's values, cultivating virtues, and engaging in purposeful, fulfilling activities that enrich both the self and the community. This state of flourishing represents the pinnacle of human potential, where one's actions, thoughts, and intentions are harmonized, leading to a deeply meaningful life.

In this section, we explore how to achieve eudaimonia by living a life of virtue and purpose. We will also delve into the ways in which happiness and fulfillment can be integrated into daily life, illustrating how these elements work together to create a sustainable sense of well-being. By understanding and applying these principles, individuals can build a foundation for a flourishing life that is not only personally enriching but also positively impacts those around them.

Virtue as the Foundation of a Flourishing Life

Understanding Virtue: The Pillars of Eudaimonia

Central to the concept of eudaimonia is the cultivation of virtue—the development of qualities and habits that promote moral excellence and align with one's highest values. Aristotle identified several key virtues, such as courage, justice, wisdom, and temperance, which form the foundation of a flourishing life. These virtues are not just abstract ideals; they are practical, lived experiences that guide our actions and decisions. To achieve eudaimonia, one must consciously cultivate these virtues, making them habitual and central to daily behavior.

For example, the virtue of courage involves facing fears and taking risks in pursuit of what is right, even when it is difficult. Whether it's speaking up against an injustice or pursuing a passion despite uncertainty, courage drives action aligned with one's values. Similarly, wisdom involves making thoughtful and informed decisions, applying knowledge and understanding to navigate complex situations in life. These virtues become the compass that directs us toward a fulfilling and purposeful existence.

Living with Purpose: Aligning Actions with Core Values

While cultivating virtue is crucial, it must be paired with a sense of purpose to fully achieve eudaimonia. Living with purpose means identifying what truly matters to you and aligning your actions with these core values. Purpose is the force that motivates individuals to engage with life meaningfully, to contribute positively to the world, and to pursue goals that extend beyond self-interest.

Purpose can manifest in various ways: a commitment to one's family, a dedication to a professional calling, or a passion for social or environmental causes. What unites these diverse paths is the alignment between one's actions and their deeper values, creating a sense of coherence and fulfillment. For instance, an individual who values compassion might find purpose in a healthcare profession, where they can alleviate suffering and support others. Another person who values justice might pursue a career in law or advocacy to defend the rights of marginalized groups.

Purpose does not have to be grand or revolutionary; it is about finding a personally meaningful way to contribute to the world and live in harmony with one's values. This alignment brings a profound sense of satisfaction and motivation, propelling individuals toward a flourishing life.

Imagine a teacher named Alex who feels deeply committed to educating children in underserved communities. For Alex, teaching is not merely a job; it's a calling that aligns with a core value—equity. By dedicating time and energy to making a difference in these children's lives, Alex experiences a sense of fulfillment that goes beyond the challenges and obstacles faced. Each small victory, each child's progress, reinforces the purpose that guides Alex's life, creating a state of flourishing even amid difficulties.

Integrating Happiness and Fulfillment into Daily Life

Happiness Beyond Hedonism: The Concept of Eudaimonic Well-Being

In modern society, happiness is often equated with pleasure or material success. However, in the context of eudaimonia, happiness is not about momentary pleasure; it's about achieving eudaimonic well-being—a state where life's activities are aligned with one's values, and fulfillment is derived from a sense of purpose and virtue. This form of happiness is more sustainable, as it is not dependent on external circumstances or fleeting pleasures. It emerges from living authentically and engaging deeply with life's challenges and opportunities.

To cultivate eudaimonic well-being, individuals must shift their focus from seeking external rewards to developing internal fulfillment. This involves embracing meaningful work, fostering enriching relationships, and pursuing personal growth. For example, rather than focusing solely on financial gain, an individual might seek a career that provides opportunities to learn, grow, and make a difference. Similarly, instead of pursuing superficial connections, they invest in building deep and supportive relationships that nurture their sense of belonging and shared purpose.

Daily Practices for Integrating Happiness and Fulfillment

Achieving a flourishing life is not a distant, abstract goal; it is built through daily habits and practices that reinforce virtue and purpose. Integrating happiness and fulfillment into everyday life requires conscious, intentional actions that align with one's long-term vision of flourishing. Here are some key practices:

- **Mindful Reflection**: Setting aside time each day for reflection helps individuals assess whether their actions align with their values and purpose. This could involve journaling about the day's events, examining decisions made, and evaluating whether they contributed to one's sense of eudaimonia.
- **Gratitude Practice**: Expressing gratitude regularly shifts focus from what is lacking to what is present, fostering a sense of appreciation for life's opportunities and connections. This practice cultivates a positive mindset, reinforcing fulfillment and contentment.

- **Acts of Kindness**: Engaging in small acts of kindness, such as helping a neighbor or volunteering, connects individuals to their communities and strengthens the sense of living a virtuous life. These actions align with values like compassion and generosity, building a foundation for long-term well-being.

These daily practices, rooted in both Stoic and Buddhist philosophies, emphasize the importance of cultivating inner resources and living in harmony with the present moment. They support individuals in maintaining a consistent state of fulfillment that extends beyond external achievements.

The Synergy of Virtue, Purpose, and Fulfillment

The Interdependence of Virtue and Happiness

Aristotle argued that virtue and happiness are interconnected, as the practice of virtue leads to a flourishing life. In other words, one cannot achieve true fulfillment without aligning actions with virtuous principles. This synergy between virtue and happiness ensures that the pursuit of fulfillment does not become a selfish or hedonistic endeavor but remains a balanced approach that benefits both the individual and the community.

For instance, someone committed to the virtue of justice finds fulfillment not by accumulating wealth but by contributing to a fairer society. The happiness derived from this pursuit is rooted in the impact they make, creating a sense of lasting satisfaction. Similarly, an individual who practices the virtue of wisdom finds fulfillment not just in gaining knowledge but in applying it to make wise decisions that benefit themselves and others.

The Pathway to Eudaimonia: An Ongoing Journey

The pursuit of eudaimonia is not a destination but an ongoing journey that evolves over time. As individuals encounter new experiences, challenges, and opportunities, they must continuously adapt and refine their understanding of virtue, purpose, and fulfillment. This dynamic process keeps life meaningful and engaging, as each stage of life presents new avenues for growth and self-discovery.

Flourishing Through Purpose and Virtue

Building a life of fulfillment and happiness is an intentional and evolving process that requires integrating virtue, purpose, and meaningful daily practices. Achieving eudaimonia involves not just pursuing goals but aligning those goals with one's deepest values, ensuring that every action contributes to a state of flourishing. By committing to a life rooted in virtue and purpose, and by finding happiness in the fulfillment of these ideals, individuals create a sustainable and deeply meaningful existence. This pathway to flourishing is a lifelong journey that enriches both the self and the world, embodying the essence of a truly well-lived life.

As we conclude our exploration of long-term well-being and flourishing, it's important to recognize that the journey toward personal growth is deeply individual and ever-evolving. No two people have the same life circumstances, values, or challenges, and as such, a one-size-fits-all approach is rarely effective. The next section focuses on Final Integration and Personalization, where the principles and practices we've explored come together in a tailored, adaptable framework. We will discuss how to personalize these strategies, ensuring they fit individual needs, preferences, and life stages. We'll also explore how to create a comprehensive self-help plan that integrates elements of CBT, Stoicism, Secular Buddhism, and Virtue Ethics, allowing for dynamic growth and adjustment over time. By learning how to monitor progress and make necessary adjustments, you can develop a resilient, sustainable, and effective approach that supports you through life's many changes and challenges.

10. Crafting Your Path: Personalizing and Integrating a Holistic Self-Help Plan

Personal growth is not a one-size-fits-all journey; it is a deeply personal, evolving process that requires a tailored approach to be effective. In this section, Final Integration and Personalization, we bring together the diverse principles and practices from CBT, Stoicism, Secular Buddhism, and Virtue Ethics, offering a comprehensive framework that can be adapted to suit individual needs, preferences, and life stages. The focus is on personalizing these strategies—ensuring they align with your unique circumstances and values. We will explore how to create a holistic self-help plan that integrates these philosophies seamlessly, allowing you to monitor your progress and make adjustments as life's challenges and opportunities arise. By understanding how to adapt and evolve your approach, you can build a resilient and dynamic plan for long-term growth, well-being, and fulfillment.

The Art of Personalization: Tailoring and Adapting Practices for Lasting Growth

Personalizing a self-help approach is essential for achieving meaningful and sustainable growth. While theories and frameworks such as CBT, Stoicism, Secular Buddhism, and Virtue Ethics offer invaluable guidance, their true power emerges when they are tailored to fit the unique needs, preferences, and life circumstances of an individual. Personalization ensures that the tools and practices resonate deeply, fostering a sense of ownership and motivation that is vital for long-term success.

In this discussion, we will explore how to tailor self-help practices to individual needs and preferences, and how to adapt these approaches to the changing demands of different life stages and challenges. Personalization is not just about choosing what works; it's about crafting an approach that evolves with you, allowing for resilience and flexibility in a dynamic, ever-changing life.

Tailoring Practices to Individual Needs and Preferences

Understanding the Importance of Personalization

No two individuals are exactly alike. Each person has a unique set of preferences, values, strengths, and challenges, all of which influence how they respond to different practices. The process of tailoring practices begins with an understanding of these individual differences, ensuring that the approach feels relevant and motivating.

For example, someone with a strong inclination toward mindfulness may find Buddhist meditation techniques most effective, while another individual who values rational thinking might resonate more with Stoic exercises and cognitive restructuring from CBT. Understanding these inclinations allows for a more engaging and effective approach, one that feels authentic rather than forced.

Building Self-Awareness: The Foundation of Tailoring Practices

Before tailoring practices, it's crucial to build self-awareness. Self-awareness involves reflecting on your preferences, strengths, and areas of growth. By taking inventory of what resonates with you—whether it's writing exercises, meditation, physical activities, or engaging in community service—you can create a self-help plan that aligns with your natural inclinations.

Consider Emily, who is navigating a stressful work environment. She finds that sitting meditation doesn't appeal to her, as it makes her feel restless. However, she discovers that walking meditation—a mindfulness practice that combines movement with attention—allows her to connect with the present moment without feeling confined. By understanding her own needs, Emily tailors a mindfulness practice that fits her lifestyle, making it easier to sustain over time.

Matching Practices with Personality and Values

Another key aspect of personalization is matching practices with your personality type and core values. Some individuals may thrive with structured routines and goal-setting, while others might prefer a more fluid and flexible approach. For example, someone who values spontaneity might incorporate mindfulness exercises that fit seamlessly into their daily routines, such as practicing mindful eating or focusing on the breath during a commute.

To personalize effectively, it's essential to align practices with your values. If you value growth and learning, journaling techniques from CBT may be useful for reflecting on thoughts and tracking progress. On the other hand, if you prioritize community and connection, incorporating acts of service and compassion from Buddhist teachings could enhance your sense of purpose and fulfillment.

Adapting the Approach to Different Life Stages and Challenges

Recognizing the Dynamic Nature of Life

Life is not static. As we move through different life stages—whether it's starting a new career, becoming a parent, facing illness, or entering retirement—our needs, priorities, and challenges evolve. An effective self-help plan must be flexible enough to adapt to these changing circumstances.

Recognizing the dynamic nature of life allows us to revisit and adjust our practices, ensuring they remain relevant and effective.

Strategies for Adapting Practices Across Life Stages

To adapt practices effectively, it's crucial to anticipate the changes that come with different life stages and challenges. Below are a few strategies for adapting a self-help approach:

1. **Reassess Priorities and Goals**: At each major life transition, take time to reassess your goals and priorities. For example, someone entering retirement may shift their focus from career success to health and community involvement. By reassessing these priorities, you can realign your practices to support your current goals.
2. **Adjust the Intensity and Focus of Practices**: As life circumstances change, the intensity and focus of your self-help practices may need to be adjusted. A busy professional with a demanding schedule might shorten their meditation practice from thirty minutes to ten, ensuring it remains manageable and sustainable. Conversely, someone experiencing a life crisis may find value in increasing their engagement with supportive community groups or therapeutic practices to bolster resilience.
3. **Incorporate New Tools and Techniques**: As you evolve, so too should the tools you use. Embracing a growth mindset means being open to exploring new practices and techniques that suit your current needs. For example, a parent juggling multiple responsibilities might find that mindfulness techniques focusing on presence and patience are more practical than lengthy meditation sessions.

Adapting Practices Through Different Phases of Life

Let's consider David, who initially uses Stoic practices like negative visualization and journaling to manage stress and build resilience in his demanding job. However, when David becomes a parent, he realizes that his time and energy are more limited. He adapts his self-help plan by integrating quick, practical mindfulness exercises he can do while caring for his child, such as mindful breathing during feeding times. He also shifts his focus from career-centric goals to cultivating patience and balance, ensuring that his practices continue to align with his evolving responsibilities and values.

The Power of Personalization: A Dynamic Approach

Embracing Flexibility and Continuous Growth

Personalization is not a one-time process; it's a dynamic approach that evolves alongside you. This flexibility ensures that your self-help plan remains relevant and effective as you navigate different stages of life. Embracing this dynamic approach requires a commitment to self-reflection and continuous learning, making space for the natural changes that life brings.

The Role of Self-Compassion in Adapting Practices

As you adapt your practices, it's essential to exercise self-compassion. Changes in life stages and challenges often require adjustments that may feel like setbacks or compromises. However, by practicing self-compassion, you can approach these transitions with a sense of acceptance, recognizing that evolving your approach is a sign of resilience and growth, not failure.

Crafting a Personalized Path to Flourishing

The art of personalizing and adapting self-help practices is essential for achieving long-term well-being and fulfillment. By tailoring your approach to suit your individual needs and preferences, and by remaining flexible enough to adapt through life's changes, you create a resilient and dynamic self-help plan that evolves alongside you. This personalized approach not only supports sustainable growth but also ensures that your journey remains meaningful, relevant, and deeply fulfilling.

Integrating Philosophies: Crafting a Comprehensive Self-Help Plan

Building a self-help plan that integrates Cognitive Behavioral Therapy (CBT), Stoicism, Secular Buddhism, and Virtue Ethics is an ambitious and deeply enriching endeavor. Each of these disciplines offers unique tools and insights for personal growth, resilience, and well-being. However, when combined thoughtfully, they provide a holistic framework capable of addressing the complexities of human experience—merging cognitive, emotional, ethical, and philosophical perspectives.

In this discussion, we will explore how to integrate these diverse philosophies into a comprehensive self-help plan that is adaptable, sustainable, and meaningful. We will look at each discipline's contribution and how they collectively reinforce one another, offering a balanced approach to achieving long-term fulfillment and personal growth. By weaving these elements together, we create a powerful strategy that supports a flourishing life, grounded in wisdom, ethical action, and emotional resilience.

The Pillars of Integration: Understanding Each Philosophy's Contribution

1. Cognitive Behavioral Therapy (CBT): Restructuring Thought Patterns

CBT's primary focus is on identifying and changing negative thought patterns that influence behavior and emotions. Its strength lies in its structured, evidence-based techniques that enable individuals to become more aware of their cognitive distortions and gradually replace them with healthier, balanced thoughts. CBT serves as the foundational layer in this self-help plan, providing the cognitive tools necessary to manage stress, anxiety, and depression.

CBT can be seamlessly integrated into the broader self-help framework by using thought records, cognitive restructuring exercises, and behavioral activation strategies. These techniques are practical and effective, empowering individuals to take charge of their mental processes. By combining CBT with other philosophical elements, individuals gain both a practical and theoretical understanding of their thoughts, allowing for deeper introspection and growth.

Sarah, a professional experiencing burnout, begins using CBT techniques to identify her automatic negative thoughts, such as "I'm not competent enough." As she works through these thoughts, she finds that CBT provides immediate relief, helping her challenge and restructure them into more constructive perspectives like "I am capable, and mistakes are opportunities for learning." This cognitive foundation creates a gateway for Sarah to explore Stoic acceptance and Buddhist mindfulness, enhancing her overall resilience.

2. Stoicism: Cultivating Emotional Resilience

Stoicism offers an ancient, time-tested approach to managing emotions and cultivating resilience in the face of adversity. Its central principles, like the dichotomy of control, align well with CBT, teaching individuals to differentiate between what they can and cannot control. Stoicism further complements CBT by adding a philosophical dimension that encourages acceptance of external events while maintaining inner tranquility.

Incorporating Stoic practices like **negative visualization** (imagining potential difficulties to reduce fear) and **amor fati** (embracing one's fate) allows individuals to build emotional strength and maintain equanimity in challenging situations. By linking these practices with CBT's cognitive techniques, one can build a deeper, more philosophically rich approach to managing emotions.

When Sarah faces criticism at work, instead of immediately feeling overwhelmed, she applies Stoic techniques. She practices detachment by reminding herself that others' opinions are outside her control. She combines this Stoic perspective with CBT tools, evaluating her thoughts and reframing them to be more constructive. By integrating these approaches, she cultivates resilience and maintains her well-being, regardless of external feedback.

3. Secular Buddhism: Embracing Mindfulness and Impermanence

Secular Buddhism introduces the essential practice of mindfulness—remaining present, aware, and non-judgmental. It emphasizes the importance of understanding impermanence and accepting the transient nature of emotions, thoughts, and experiences. This perspective aligns closely with both CBT's focus on awareness and Stoicism's emphasis on detachment, offering an additional layer of depth to the self-help plan.

Mindfulness practices from Secular Buddhism, such as breath awareness and body scan meditations, enhance the ability to observe thoughts and feelings without attachment. This mindfulness creates space for reflection and reduces reactivity, making it a vital tool in a comprehensive self-help plan. Combining mindfulness with cognitive restructuring and Stoic acceptance practices leads to a balanced, grounded state of being that enhances emotional and cognitive flexibility.

Sarah incorporates mindfulness into her routine, practicing a short meditation each morning. This allows her to start the day with clarity, setting a foundation for her CBT and Stoic practices. When she encounters stress later in the day, she uses breath awareness to center herself, creating a pause between her emotional reaction and her response. This mindful presence enhances her ability to apply the other techniques she has learned, making her self-help plan more effective and harmonious.

4. Virtue Ethics: Guiding Ethical Action and Purpose

Virtue Ethics, especially as articulated by Aristotle, focuses on cultivating virtues such as courage, wisdom, justice, and temperance. It provides a moral and ethical framework for living a fulfilling and meaningful life. Integrating Virtue Ethics into a self-help plan ensures that cognitive and emotional growth is balanced with ethical development, promoting not just personal success but also positive contributions to others and society.

By aligning personal goals with virtues, individuals can make ethical decisions that are consistent with their values, enhancing their sense of purpose. Practicing virtues also complements Stoic and Buddhist elements, as it encourages living in accordance with one's principles, regardless of external circumstances or emotional states. For instance, practicing compassion aligns well with Buddhist mindfulness, while embracing courage complements Stoic resilience.

Sarah integrates Virtue Ethics by focusing on the virtue of courage. She decides to pursue a challenging project at work that aligns with her values but feels outside her comfort zone. By combining her CBT tools to manage anxiety, her Stoic detachment to handle uncertainty, and her mindfulness practice to stay present, she approaches the project with a clear, ethically guided mindset. The practice of courage not only enriches her professional life but also contributes to her overall sense of eudaimonia, or flourishing.

Creating a Balanced and Comprehensive Plan

Step 1: Assessing Personal Strengths and Needs

The first step in integrating these philosophies into a cohesive plan is to assess personal strengths, needs, and areas for growth. Self-awareness, as explored through CBT and mindfulness practices, helps individuals understand which areas require attention and how best to incorporate the tools each philosophy offers. For instance, someone who struggles with self-doubt may benefit from a combination of CBT's cognitive restructuring, Stoic detachment, and mindfulness practices.

Step 2: Structuring the Plan with Flexibility

An effective self-help plan must be structured yet flexible. It's crucial to establish a daily or weekly routine that incorporates practices from each philosophy—such as CBT journaling, Stoic reflection, mindfulness meditation, and virtue tracking. However, the plan should also allow for adjustments based on changing needs, ensuring it remains adaptable and relevant.

Step 3: Monitoring Progress and Adjusting the Plan

Regular reflection is a key component of a comprehensive self-help plan. By monitoring progress through journaling or mindful observation, individuals can identify what's working and what needs adjustment. This reflective practice, borrowed from both CBT and Stoicism, ensures that the plan evolves as the individual grows, maintaining its effectiveness over time.

The Power of Integration: Crafting a Personalized and Holistic Path

Harmonizing Cognitive, Emotional, and Ethical Growth

Integrating CBT, Stoicism, Secular Buddhism, and Virtue Ethics provides a balanced, holistic approach to self-improvement. Each discipline offers a different lens, and when combined, they create a comprehensive framework that supports cognitive, emotional, and ethical growth. This harmonious integration allows individuals to navigate challenges with resilience, live ethically, and pursue meaningful goals with clarity and intention.

Crafting a Comprehensive Path to Flourishing

A comprehensive self-help plan that integrates CBT, Stoicism, Secular Buddhism, and Virtue Ethics offers a powerful, multi-dimensional approach to personal growth. By harmonizing these disciplines, individuals can build a resilient, adaptive, and ethically grounded life strategy that supports their journey toward eudaimonia—true flourishing.

Monitoring Progress and Making Adjustments: Fine-Tuning Your Self-Help Journey

Creating a comprehensive self-help plan is only the beginning of the journey toward personal growth and well-being. The true power of any self-help approach lies in the continuous process of monitoring progress and making adjustments as needed. No self-improvement path is static; life's unpredictable nature, evolving circumstances, and newfound insights all necessitate regular reflection and modification. This dynamic approach ensures that practices remain effective, aligned with personal goals, and adaptable to new challenges.

Now, we explore the importance of tracking progress in a meaningful way and adjusting the self-help plan when necessary. We will delve into practical methods for assessing the effectiveness of practices, identifying signs that adjustments are needed, and implementing changes that enhance growth. This process is about more than just keeping track of success; it's about cultivating a flexible mindset that embraces change, ensuring that growth remains consistent and sustainable.

The Importance of Monitoring Progress: Keeping Your Growth Aligned

Why Track Progress?

Monitoring progress is crucial because it provides insight into what is working, what is not, and where improvements can be made. Without monitoring, individuals risk becoming complacent, rigid, or disillusioned when results do not align with expectations. Consistent tracking enables individuals to stay connected with their goals and understand how well their chosen practices support those goals.

Progress tracking also serves as a motivational tool. Seeing tangible evidence of growth, whether it's overcoming a specific fear, maintaining a daily meditation habit, or consistently practicing compassion, reinforces the effectiveness of the plan and encourages ongoing engagement.

Methods for Tracking Progress: Practical Tools and Techniques

Tracking progress can take various forms, depending on the individual's preferences and the practices they engage in. Some effective methods include:

1. **Journaling**: Journaling is one of the most versatile tools for monitoring progress. By keeping a daily or weekly log, individuals can record their experiences, thoughts, and emotions, noting patterns and changes over time. Journaling allows for detailed tracking of successes, challenges, and areas for improvement, making it an invaluable method for reflection.
2. **Mindfulness Reflection**: Incorporating mindfulness into the tracking process allows individuals to take a step back and observe their behavior and emotional patterns without judgment. This reflection can occur during a meditation session or as a short pause at the end of each day, where individuals assess their thoughts and behaviors in response to daily events.
3. **Setting Measurable Goals**: Establishing clear, measurable goals aligned with the self-help plan ensures that progress can be objectively assessed. These goals could be related to practicing specific virtues (e.g., showing patience in difficult situations), maintaining mindfulness routines, or applying CBT techniques in stressful situations. By setting and tracking these goals, individuals have a concrete way of monitoring their journey.

Monitoring and Reflecting on Progress

Consider Alex, who has embarked on a self-help journey integrating mindfulness and Stoic practices to manage stress. Alex sets a measurable goal of practicing mindful breathing for 10 minutes each morning and journaling about his emotional responses at the end of each day. After a month, he reviews his journal entries and notices a pattern: he tends to feel overwhelmed on Mondays, leading to inconsistent mindfulness practice at the start of the week. By identifying this pattern, Alex can make specific adjustments—perhaps shifting his Monday meditation time or incorporating a Stoic practice like negative visualization to prepare for the week ahead. This process of reflection and adjustment ensures Alex's practices remain effective and relevant to his evolving needs.

Making Adjustments: Flexibility and Responsiveness in Action

Recognizing When Adjustments Are Needed

The ability to recognize when adjustments are necessary is key to maintaining an effective self-help plan. Sticking rigidly to a plan without considering its effectiveness can lead to stagnation or even frustration. There are several signs that adjustments may be needed:

- **Lack of Progress**: If measurable goals are not being met or if the individual feels that growth has plateaued, it may be time to reevaluate the plan.
- **Emotional Disengagement**: Feeling unmotivated, disengaged, or overwhelmed by the practices can indicate that they are not aligned with the individual's current state of mind or circumstances.
- **Life Changes**: Significant life changes, such as a new job, relationship challenges, or health issues, may require a shift in focus or the introduction of new practices that better suit the current situation.

Strategies for Making Effective Adjustments

Once it's clear that changes are needed, the next step is to implement adjustments thoughtfully. This process involves evaluating which aspects of the plan are no longer effective and finding ways to either modify existing practices or introduce new ones.

1. **Revisiting Goals**: Goals should be revisited and modified as necessary. If a goal feels too ambitious or too easy, it may need to be adjusted to maintain motivation and challenge. For example, if Alex's goal of 10 minutes of mindful breathing becomes overwhelming during a particularly busy period, he might reduce it to 5 minutes or practice a different form of mindfulness, like a body scan.
2. **Incorporating New Techniques**: As individuals grow and gain new insights, they may find that additional practices or techniques can complement their existing routine. For instance, someone using CBT and mindfulness might decide to incorporate Stoic reflection to gain a philosophical perspective on their challenges, enriching their overall self-help plan.
3. **Balancing Consistency with Adaptability**: It is important to strike a balance between maintaining consistency and allowing for flexibility. While sticking to a routine is valuable, individuals should also be willing to experiment and adjust their practices to keep their self-help journey engaging and relevant.

Adapting the Self-Help Plan Over Time

Imagine Maria, who uses a combination of CBT journaling, Stoic reflection, and Buddhist mindfulness to navigate her daily stressors. Initially, these practices help her manage work stress effectively. However, after a few months, Maria begins experiencing stress related to family dynamics, which her existing plan does not fully address. By monitoring her progress and recognizing this shift, she decides to incorporate new mindfulness techniques focused on compassion and acceptance, aligning better with her current needs. This adjustment allows her to remain engaged with her self-help plan, and she continues to experience growth as her circumstances change.

The Dynamic Nature of Growth: Embracing Flexibility

Viewing Adjustments as a Sign of Growth

Adjustments are not an indication of failure but rather an essential aspect of growth. Embracing the need for change demonstrates flexibility and adaptability, key components of long-term well-being. By remaining open to modifying practices and goals, individuals can create a dynamic self-help plan that evolves alongside them.

Practicing Self-Compassion During Adjustments

While making changes is necessary, it's also important to approach the process with self-compassion. Sometimes, goals may need to be adjusted to be more realistic, or practices may need to be simplified during particularly stressful periods. By showing self-compassion and understanding, individuals can view these adjustments as part of their growth rather than setbacks, maintaining motivation and engagement.

Adjusting the Sails: The Power of Flexibility in Personal Growth

Creating a comprehensive self-help plan is a powerful step, but monitoring and making adjustments are what keep the journey dynamic and effective. By regularly assessing progress, recognizing when adjustments are needed, and implementing changes with flexibility and self-compassion, individuals can sustain meaningful growth over time. This adaptive approach ensures that the self-help plan remains relevant, empowering individuals to navigate life's challenges while continuously striving toward fulfillment and well-being.

With a comprehensive self-help plan in place and a clear understanding of how to monitor progress and make adjustments, the next crucial step is to gather the resources and support needed to sustain this journey. While self-improvement is deeply personal, it is also enriched by accessing the right tools and connecting with others who share similar goals. The final section of this guide focuses on resources and tools that enhance your path toward growth. We'll explore recommended books, courses, and apps that provide valuable insights and techniques across various disciplines, from CBT to mindfulness practices. Additionally, we will discuss the importance of building a personal support system and how to effectively engage with online communities and support groups. By equipping yourself with these resources, you can create a strong foundation that reinforces your self-help journey and offers support, motivation, and new perspectives along the way.

11. Empowering Your Journey: Essential Resources and Support Systems for Personal Growth

No self-help journey is complete without the right resources and support systems to guide and sustain progress. While personal growth often begins with introspection and self-directed practices, accessing external tools and connecting with a supportive community can enhance the process significantly. In this section, we explore essential resources and tools that empower your journey, including recommended books, courses, and apps tailored to various aspects of cognitive, philosophical, and mindfulness practices. Additionally, we delve into the importance of building a personal support system, offering strategies for finding and maintaining relationships that uplift and motivate. Finally, we examine the role of online communities and support groups, highlighting how they provide a platform for shared experiences, encouragement, and learning. By integrating these resources and support systems, you create a holistic framework that not only enhances your knowledge and skills but also builds a resilient network that supports long-term well-being and fulfillment.

Empowering Your Journey: A Comprehensive Guide to Resources and Support Systems

In the pursuit of personal growth and self-improvement, knowledge and introspection form the foundation, but they are greatly enriched by access to external resources and support systems. Whether you are exploring cognitive behavioral techniques, mindfulness practices, or philosophical principles, the right tools and connections can transform your journey from a solitary effort into a deeply engaging and supported endeavor. This section offers a detailed guide to recommended books, courses, and apps that provide valuable insights and techniques across various disciplines. We also delve into creating a personal support system and utilizing online communities and support groups—each an integral part of sustaining motivation and growth. These resources, when thoughtfully integrated, serve not only as sources of information but also as pillars of support that guide you through challenges and reinforce your progress.

Recommended Books, Courses, and Apps: Building Your Knowledge Arsenal

Books: Timeless Wisdom and Modern Insights

Books are a powerful resource for deepening your understanding of various practices, from cognitive behavioral therapy (CBT) to Stoicism and mindfulness. They provide structured knowledge, case studies, and practical exercises that can be revisited and applied in your daily life. Some books, like Aaron Beck's *Cognitive Therapy and the Emotional Disorders*, offer a foundation in CBT, while others, like Marcus Aurelius's *Meditations*, provide Stoic wisdom that has stood the test of time. By combining classic and contemporary works, you can create a balanced reading list that supports both theoretical understanding and practical application.

Books such as *The Daily Stoic* by Ryan Holiday and Stephen Hanselman offer daily reflections that make Stoicism accessible, blending ancient philosophy with modern relevance. Meanwhile, Thich Nhat Hanh's *The Miracle of Mindfulness* provides readers with practical steps for integrating mindfulness into daily life, drawing on centuries of Buddhist practice. Engaging with these works not only expands your knowledge but also allows you to draw from the lived experiences and wisdom of others.

Courses: Structured Learning for In-Depth Exploration

Online courses are an excellent way to engage with expert instructors and explore topics in a structured, interactive environment. Platforms like Coursera, Udemy, and Insight Timer offer courses that range from introductory to advanced levels, covering subjects such as mindfulness meditation, Stoicism in modern life, and cognitive-behavioral strategies for managing anxiety and depression.

For example, a course on mindfulness meditation might guide you through daily practices, helping you to build a consistent routine while understanding the science behind mindfulness. A Stoicism course might explore key texts like *Epictetus's Discourses* while providing exercises to integrate Stoic principles into daily decision-making.

The benefit of these courses is that they combine theoretical learning with practical application, often including exercises, peer discussions, and feedback loops to deepen your understanding. Engaging with such courses ensures that you not only absorb information but also practice and integrate the principles into your own life.

Apps: Practical Tools for Daily Use

Apps like *Headspace, Calm,* and *Mindfulness Coach* offer guided meditations and mindfulness exercises, making it easy to incorporate these practices into your daily routine. For those interested in CBT, apps such as *Moodfit* and *CBT Thought Diary* provide a platform for tracking thoughts, managing emotions, and practicing cognitive restructuring.

By using apps, you have the convenience of accessing tools anytime and anywhere, allowing you to practice mindfulness during a lunch break or record thoughts and emotions as they arise. These digital tools act as both reminders and guides, helping to maintain consistency and engagement in your self-improvement practices.

Creating a Personal Support System: Building a Network of Encouragement

Why a Support System Matters

While personal growth is an individual journey, having a network of supportive people enhances and sustains that growth. A personal support system offers encouragement, accountability, and a space to share progress and challenges. Whether this network is composed of close friends, mentors, or like-minded individuals, the presence of others creates a sense of belonging and motivation that reinforces your efforts.

Building Your Support System: Identifying Key Relationships

Creating an effective support system begins with identifying individuals who share similar values, goals, or interests. These could include friends who practice mindfulness, colleagues who engage in philosophical discussions, or mentors who guide your CBT journey. Cultivating relationships with people who inspire and challenge you ensures that your network remains dynamic and growth-oriented.

When seeking support, consider the balance between giving and receiving; a healthy support system involves mutual growth, where you not only gain insights and encouragement but also offer the same to others. This reciprocal dynamic strengthens connections and creates a supportive environment where everyone benefits.

Nurturing and Maintaining Supportive Relationships

Once you've identified the people in your support system, it's important to nurture these connections. Regular check-ins, whether through scheduled calls or meet-ups, help maintain strong bonds. Sharing your progress, discussing new insights from books or courses, or practicing mindfulness together can deepen your relationship and provide mutual motivation.

For instance, you might decide to read a book on Stoicism with a friend and discuss each chapter weekly, exploring how the ideas can be applied to your lives. Alternatively, you might attend a mindfulness class with a group of friends, allowing shared experiences to reinforce your commitment.

Utilizing Online Communities and Support Groups: Expanding Your Circle

The Power of Online Communities

In today's digital age, online communities offer an opportunity to connect with individuals across the globe who share similar interests and goals. Platforms like Reddit, Facebook Groups, and specialized forums for Stoicism, mindfulness, or CBT provide spaces where people exchange knowledge, support, and encouragement. These communities can be particularly valuable when in-person connections are limited or when seeking a diverse range of perspectives.

Engaging in online discussions, participating in group challenges, and sharing experiences allow you to feel part of a larger network, adding depth and richness to your self-help journey.

Finding and Joining the Right Groups

The key to utilizing online communities effectively is to find groups that align with your interests and values. It's essential to join spaces that are supportive, respectful, and oriented toward growth. Look for groups that encourage open, non-judgmental discussions and offer resources like book recommendations, guided meditations, or group challenges. Engaging with these communities not only provides a sense of belonging but also introduces you to new perspectives and techniques that enrich your practice.

For instance, joining a Stoicism group might provide daily quotes for reflection and group discussions on applying Stoic principles to modern challenges, while a mindfulness community might offer live meditation sessions, creating an opportunity for shared practice and feedback.

Balancing Online and Offline Interactions

While online communities are valuable, balancing them with offline support ensures that your network remains robust and diverse. The combination of face-to-face interactions and digital connections allows you to draw from multiple sources of support and insight, enhancing your overall experience. This balance prevents isolation and reinforces the practical application of knowledge gained through books, courses, and online discussions.

Connecting the Dots—Creating a Comprehensive Support Network

Accessing the right resources and building a support system are pivotal steps in sustaining and enriching your self-help journey. By leveraging books, courses, and apps, you can deepen your knowledge and engage with practical tools that make self-improvement accessible and engaging. Simultaneously, creating a personal support system and engaging with online communities foster a sense of belonging and accountability, making the journey less solitary and more dynamic. Together, these elements create a comprehensive framework that empowers you to navigate challenges, remain motivated, and continually grow, ensuring that your path toward well-being and fulfillment is both supported and sustained.

Integrating Wisdom, Practice, and Growth—A Path to Fulfillment

As we come to the close of this comprehensive exploration into self-improvement, it becomes evident that the path to well-being and fulfillment is not a one-size-fits-all journey but a dynamic and ever-evolving process. The integration of Cognitive Behavioral Therapy (CBT), Stoicism, Secular Buddhism, and Virtue Ethics creates a multi-dimensional framework that supports growth, emotional resilience, ethical decision-making, and sustained motivation. By weaving these philosophies and practices together, you can develop a personalized approach that not only aligns with your values and goals but also adapts to the inevitable changes and challenges that life brings.

Lessons Learned: The Power of Holistic Integration

1. **Thought, Emotion, and Behavior: The CBT Foundation.** One of the most fundamental insights we have explored is the relationship between thoughts, emotions, and behaviors—a core tenet of CBT. Recognizing and challenging cognitive distortions, setting realistic goals, and breaking down overwhelming tasks into manageable steps allow for greater control over one's mindset and actions. These tools empower you to identify negative patterns and replace them with healthier, more constructive responses.
2. **Mindfulness and Detachment: The Practices of Stoicism and Buddhism.** The Stoic and Buddhist practices of mindfulness, detachment, and acceptance offer powerful techniques for managing emotions and navigating life's unpredictability. Stoicism teaches us to focus on what is within our control, fostering resilience through practices like negative visualization

and the cultivation of equanimity. Meanwhile, mindfulness from Buddhist teachings encourages us to remain present, observe our thoughts without judgment, and detach from the outcomes that often cause distress. Together, these approaches provide a roadmap for living with balance and clarity, even amidst adversity.

3. **Virtue Ethics: Living with Integrity and Purpose.** Virtue Ethics adds a moral dimension to our journey, guiding us in making ethical choices that align with our values and contribute to a life of purpose. By identifying and cultivating core virtues such as wisdom, courage, justice, and temperance, we not only improve our relationships but also build a foundation for personal growth and well-being. Aristotle's concept of *eudaimonia*, or flourishing, reminds us that true happiness comes from living virtuously, finding fulfillment in the journey itself rather than in external achievements.
4. **Practical Tools for Daily Application.** Integrating these philosophies into daily life requires practical tools and consistent effort. Whether it's journaling to track thoughts and behaviors, practicing meditation to cultivate mindfulness, or engaging in virtue tracking to reflect on ethical behavior, these habits anchor the abstract concepts into actionable, daily practices. They help create a routine that sustains growth, allowing progress to become measurable and rewarding.

The Journey Ahead: A Call to Continued Growth and Exploration

As you move forward, it's important to remember that the journey of self-improvement is continuous and non-linear. Challenges, setbacks, and moments of doubt are natural; they are opportunities for growth rather than signs of failure. The practices and principles outlined provide a sturdy foundation, but it is your commitment, curiosity, and openness to learning that will propel you forward.

1. **Stay Adaptable and Open to Change.** Life is fluid, and circumstances often evolve in unexpected ways. The ability to adapt your approach—whether through adjusting goals, embracing new practices, or seeking additional support—ensures that you remain aligned with your values while navigating life's transitions. The flexibility built into this multi-framework approach empowers you to respond to these changes with resilience and wisdom.
2. **Nurture Support Systems and Community Engagement.** Building and sustaining motivation also require external support. Nurturing your relationships, seeking out mentors, and engaging with online or local communities dedicated to similar practices will enrich your journey. These connections not only provide a sense of belonging but also offer a space for learning, sharing experiences, and finding encouragement.
3. **Celebrate Small Wins and Practice Self-Compassion.** Recognizing and celebrating progress, no matter how small, builds momentum and reinforces positive habits. Similarly, practicing self-compassion when things do not go as planned is essential for maintaining motivation and avoiding burnout. This balance of striving for growth while accepting imperfections allows for a sustainable approach to self-improvement.

Embrace the Journey

Remember, the journey toward well-being and fulfillment is not about perfection; it is about progress. It is about taking each day as an opportunity to grow, learn, and refine your approach. The integration of these frameworks—CBT's structured techniques, Stoicism's resilience, Buddhism's mindfulness, and Virtue Ethics' moral grounding—offers a rich and versatile toolbox to draw from.

Allow yourself the freedom to explore, to make mistakes, and to evolve. Each step forward, even the smallest one, contributes to a life that is more mindful, resilient, and purpose-driven. As you continue on your path, may you find the strength to navigate challenges with grace, the wisdom to seek balance between acceptance and growth, and the fulfillment that comes from living a life aligned with your highest values.

Embrace the Journey—The Best Is Yet to Come.

APPENDIX

A list of identifiable emotions:

1. **Happiness** – A feeling of joy, pleasure, or contentment, often arising from positive experiences or achievements.
2. **Sadness** – A state of feeling sorrowful, disappointed, or mournful, usually in response to loss or difficult experiences.
3. **Anger** – A strong feeling of displeasure or hostility triggered by perceived wrongs, frustration, or injustice.
4. **Fear** – A feeling of anxiety or dread in response to perceived threats or danger, either real or imagined.
5. **Disgust** – A strong aversion or repulsion, often triggered by something perceived as offensive, unhealthy, or unpleasant.
6. **Surprise** – A brief emotional response to an unexpected event, which can be positive, negative, or neutral.
7. **Anxiety** – A state of worry or unease, often in anticipation of future events or uncertain outcomes.
8. **Guilt** – A feeling of remorse or responsibility for having done something wrong, whether real or perceived.
9. **Shame** – A painful feeling of humiliation or distress caused by the awareness of having done something dishonorable or embarrassing.
10. **Envy** – A feeling of discontent or resentment aroused by someone else's possessions, qualities, or achievements.
11. **Jealousy** – A feeling of insecurity or fear that something valued (such as a relationship) might be taken away by someone else.
12. **Pride** – A sense of satisfaction or accomplishment in one's own or others' achievements, abilities, or qualities.
13. **Love** – A deep feeling of affection, care, and connection toward someone or something.
14. **Gratitude** – A sense of appreciation and thankfulness for something received, whether tangible or intangible.

15. **Hope** – A feeling of optimism or desire for a positive outcome in the future.
16. **Relief** – A feeling of relaxation or reassurance after anxiety, fear, or tension has been resolved or lessened.
17. **Contentment** – A peaceful state of satisfaction and ease, often associated with being at peace with one's current situation.
18. **Frustration** – A feeling of annoyance or helplessness that arises from obstacles or difficulties preventing a goal from being achieved.
19. **Embarrassment** – A feeling of self-conscious discomfort or awkwardness, typically in social situations where one feels exposed or judged.
20. **Compassion** – A deep awareness of the suffering of others, coupled with the desire to alleviate that suffering.
21. **Loneliness** – A sense of isolation or disconnection from others, often accompanied by a longing for companionship.
22. **Boredom** – A feeling of restlessness or dissatisfaction caused by a lack of engagement or stimulation.
23. **Awe** – A feeling of wonder, amazement, or admiration, often in response to something vast or extraordinary.
24. **Confusion** – A state of uncertainty or lack of clarity, often caused by complex or unclear situations.
25. **Empathy** – The ability to understand and share the feelings of another person, often leading to a supportive response.
26. **Resentment** – A feeling of anger or bitterness about a perceived unfairness or insult, often lingering over time.
27. **Disappointment** – A feeling of sadness or dissatisfaction when expectations or hopes are not fulfilled.
28. **Elation** – A heightened state of joy or exhilaration, often resulting from success or a significant positive event.

29.   **Curiosity** – A strong desire to learn or know more about something, often accompanied by a sense of wonder or intrigue.
30.   **Regret** – A feeling of sorrow or remorse for something that has been done, often tied to missed opportunities or mistakes.

This list offers a wide emotional vocabulary, providing deeper insight into the range of emotions we experience in everyday life. Each emotion, when recognized and named, becomes easier to understand and manage.

SOURCES

1. Introduction to the Self-Help Approach

- **CBT, Secular Buddhism, Stoicism, and Virtue Ethics Overview:**
    - *Burns, David D.* **Feeling Good: The New Mood Therapy.** Avon Books, 1999.
    - *Batchelor, Stephen.* **Buddhism without Beliefs: A Contemporary Guide to Awakening.** Riverhead Books, 1998.
    - *Ryan, Holiday.* **The Daily Stoic: 366 Meditations on Wisdom, Perseverance, and the Art of Living.** Portfolio, 2016.

- Hursthouse, Rosalind. **On Virtue Ethics.** Oxford University Press, 1999.

2. Foundational Concepts of Each Framework

- **Cognitive Behavioral Therapy (CBT):**
  - Beck, Aaron T. **Cognitive Therapy and the Emotional Disorders.** Penguin Books, 1979.
  - Clark, David A., and Aaron T. Beck. **Cognitive Therapy of Anxiety Disorders: Science and Practice.** Guilford Press, 2010.
- **Secular Buddhism:**
  - Batchelor, Stephen. **After Buddhism: Rethinking the Dharma for a Secular Age.** Yale University Press, 2015.
  - Goldstein, Joseph. **Mindfulness: A Practical Guide to Awakening.** Sounds True, 2013.
- **Stoicism:**
  - Epictetus. **Discourses and Selected Writings.** Translated by Robert Dobbin, Penguin Classics, 2008.
  - Aurelius, Marcus. **Meditations.** Translated by Gregory Hays, Modern Library, 2002.
- **Virtue Ethics:**
  - Aristotle. **Nicomachean Ethics.** Translated by Terence Irwin, Hackett Publishing, 1999.
  - MacIntyre, Alasdair. **After Virtue: A Study in Moral Theory.** University of Notre Dame Press, 1981.

3. Daily Practices and Habits

- **Mindfulness and Meditation:**
  - Kabat-Zinn, Jon. **Wherever You Go, There You Are: Mindfulness Meditation in Everyday Life.** Hachette Books, 1994.
  - Williams, Mark, and Danny Penman. **Mindfulness: An Eight-Week Plan for Finding Peace in a Frantic World.** Rodale Books, 2011.

- **Journaling Techniques:**
  - *Burns, David D.* **The Feeling Good Handbook.** Plume, 1999.
  - *Holiday, Ryan, and Stephen Hanselman.* **The Daily Stoic Journal: 366 Days of Writing and Reflection on the Art of Living.** Portfolio, 2017.
- **Habit Formation:**
  - *Clear, James.* **Atomic Habits: An Easy & Proven Way to Build Good Habits & Break Bad Ones.** Avery, 2018.
  - *Duhigg, Charles.* **The Power of Habit: Why We Do What We Do in Life and Business.** Random House, 2012.

4. Self-Reflection and Cognitive Restructuring

- **Identifying Negative Thought Patterns:**
  - *Beck, Judith S.* **Cognitive Behavior Therapy: Basics and Beyond.** 2nd ed., Guilford Press, 2011.
  - *Leahy, Robert L., Stephen J. Holland, and Lata K. McGinn.* **Treatment Plans and Interventions for Depression and Anxiety Disorders.** 2nd ed., Guilford Press, 2012.
- **Cognitive Restructuring Techniques:**
  - *Padesky, Christine A., and Dennis Greenberger.* **Mind Over Mood: Change How You Feel by Changing the Way You Think.** 2nd ed., Guilford Press, 2015.
  - *Beck, Aaron T., and Brad A. Alford.* **Depression: Causes and Treatment.** 2nd ed., University of Pennsylvania Press, 2009.

5. Emotional Regulation and Resilience

- **CBT Techniques for Emotional Management:**
  - *Ellis, Albert, and Raymond Chip Tafrate.* **How to Control Your Anger Before It Controls You.** Citadel, 1997.

- *Bourne, Edmund J.* **The Anxiety and Phobia Workbook.** 7th ed., New Harbinger Publications, 2020.
- **Stoic Practices for Emotional Resilience:**
  - *Pigliucci, Massimo.* **How to Be a Stoic: Using Ancient Philosophy to Live a Modern Life.** Basic Books, 2017.
  - *Robertson, Donald.* **The Philosophy of Cognitive-Behavioral Therapy (CBT): Stoic Philosophy as Rational and Cognitive Psychotherapy.** Routledge, 2010.
- **Buddhist Approaches to Suffering and Impermanence:**
  - *Nhat Hanh, Thich.* **No Mud, No Lotus: The Art of Transforming Suffering.** Parallax Press, 2014.
  - *Dalai Lama, and Howard C. Cutler.* **The Art of Happiness: A Handbook for Living.** Riverhead Books, 1998.

6. Ethical Living and Decision-Making

- **Applying Virtue Ethics in Daily Life:**
  - *Annas, Julia.* **Intelligent Virtue.** Oxford University Press, 2011.
  - *Swanton, Christine.* **Virtue Ethics: A Pluralistic View.** Oxford University Press, 2003.
- **Integrating Stoic and Buddhist Ethics:**
  - *Sellars, John.* **Stoicism.** University of California Press, 2006.
  - *Rahula, Walpola.* **What the Buddha Taught.** Grove Press, 1974.
- **Case Studies and Real-Life Applications:**
  - *Johnson, Robert.* **Ethical Theory: Classical and Contemporary Readings.** 7th ed., Wadsworth Publishing, 2014.
  - *Little, Margaret Olivia.* **Moral Particularism.** Oxford University Press, 2000.

7. Building and Sustaining Motivation

- **Identifying Personal Values and Goals:**
    - *Kasser, Tim.* **The High Price of Materialism.** MIT Press, 2002.
    - *Ryan, Richard M., and Edward L. Deci.* **Self-Determination Theory: Basic Psychological Needs in Motivation, Development, and Wellness.** Guilford Press, 2017.
- **Overcoming Obstacles and Setbacks:**
    - *Carson, Ben, and Cecil Murphey.* **Take the Risk: Learning to Identify, Choose, and Live with Acceptable Risk.** Zondervan, 2008.
    - *Duckworth, Angela.* **Grit: The Power of Passion and Perseverance.** Scribner, 2016.

8. Interpersonal Relationships and Social Well-Being

- **Applying CBT to Improve Relationships:**
    - *Gottman, John M., and Nan Silver.* **The Seven Principles for Making Marriage Work.** Harmony, 1999.
    - *Gilbert, Paul.* **Compassionate Mind: A New Approach to Life's Challenges.** New Harbinger Publications, 2010.
- **Stoic and Buddhist Approaches to Relationships:**
    - *Hanh, Thich Nhat.* **True Love: A Practice for Awakening the Heart.** Shambhala, 2006.
    - *Robertson, Donald.* **How to Think Like a Roman Emperor: The Stoic Philosophy of Marcus Aurelius.** St. Martin's Press, 2019.
- **Ethical Considerations in Relationships:**
    - *Gilligan, Carol.* **In a Different Voice: Psychological Theory and Women's Development.** Harvard University Press, 1982.
    - *Held, Virginia.* **The Ethics of Care: Personal, Political, and Global.** Oxford University Press, 2006.

9. Long-Term Well-Being and Life Satisfaction

- **Sustaining Practices Over Time:**
    - *Schwartz, Barry, and Kenneth Sharpe.* **Practical Wisdom: The Right Way to Do the Right Thing.** Riverhead Books, 2010.
    - *Csikszentmihalyi, Mihaly.* **Flow: The Psychology of Optimal Experience.** Harper Perennial, 1990.
- **Balancing Acceptance and Growth:**
    - *Hayes, Steven C., and Spencer Smith.* **Get Out of Your Mind and Into Your Life: The New Acceptance and Commitment Therapy.** New Harbinger Publications, 2005.
    - *Davidson, Richard J., and Sharon Begley.* **The Emotional Life of Your Brain: How Its Unique Patterns Affect the Way You Think, Feel, and Live—and How You Can Change Them.** Plume, 2013.
- **Achieving Eudaimonia (Flourishing):**
    - *Seligman, Martin E. P.* **Flourish: A Visionary New Understanding of Happiness and Well-Being.** Free Press, 2011.
    - *Aristotle.* **The Nicomachean Ethics.** Translated by W. D. Ross, Oxford University Press, 2009.

10. Resources and Tools

- **Books and Online Courses:**
    - *Harris, Russ.* **The Happiness Trap: How to Stop Struggling and Start Living.** Trumpeter, 2008.
    - *Kabat-Zinn, Jon.* **Full Catastrophe Living: Using the Wisdom of Your Body and Mind to Face Stress, Pain, and Illness.** Bantam Books, 1990.
- **Creating a Personal Support System:**
    - *Cloud, Henry, and John Townsend.* **Boundaries: When to Say Yes, How to Say No to Take Control of Your Life.** Zondervan, 1992.
    - *Snyder, C. R., and Shane J. Lopez.* **Positive Psychology: The Scientific and Practical**

Explorations of Human Strengths. 2nd ed., Sage Publications, 2009.

11. Final Integration and Personalization

- **Personalizing the Approach:**
    - *Miller, William R., and Stephen Rollnick.* **Motivational Interviewing: Helping People Change.** 3rd ed., Guilford Press, 2012.
    - *Prochaska, James O., John C. Norcross, and Carlo C. DiClemente.* **Changing for Good: A Revolutionary Six-Stage Program for Overcoming Bad Habits and Moving Your Life Positively Forward.** William Morrow Paperbacks, 1994.
- **Creating a Comprehensive Self-Help Plan:**
    - *Young, Jeffrey E., Janet S. Klosko, and Marjorie E. Weishaar.* **Schema Therapy: A Practitioner's Guide.** Guilford Press, 2003.
    - *Dweck, Carol S.* **Mindset: The New Psychology of Success.** Ballantine Books, 2006.

www.ingramcontent.com/pod-product-compliance
Lightning Source LLC
Chambersburg PA
CBHW050159240426
43671CB00013B/2177